EVALUATION RESEARCH AND PRACTICE

EVALUATION RESEARCH and PRACTICE

Comparative and International Perspectives

Robert A. Levine
Marian A. Solomon
Gerd-Michael Hellstern
Hellmut Wollmann

Editors

 SAGE PUBLICATIONS   Beverly Hills   London

For information address:

SAGE Publications, Inc.
275 South Beverly Drive
Beverly Hills, California 90212

SAGE Publications Ltd
28 Banner Street
London ECIY 8QE, England

Printed in the United States of America

Library of Congress Cataloging in Publication Data

American-German Workshop on Evaluation Research,
   Free University of Berlin, 1979.
   Evaluation research and practice.

   Papers drawn from the American-German Workshop on
Evaluation Research held at the Free University of
Berlin, June 1979.
   Bibliography: p.
   Includes index.
   1. Evaluation—Congresses.   I. Levine, Robert A.
II. Title.
AZ191.A43   1979   001.4   80-26531
ISBN 0-8039-1561-6

FIRST PRINTING

CONTENTS

Introduction

The emergence of evaluation research as an international activity provides a potential for knowledge production and transfer which has been largely underexplored. The international scenery of evaluation research may provide the opportunities and the potential for future growth and will shape the direction evaluation research will take in the future. The movement of evaluation research into the international community may prove the most important contribution social science has to offer for the eighties:

—The diffusion of evaluation research across borders may not only open new markets for evaluation but will shed some light on the convergence and divergence of our interdependent societies and illustrate the varied factors which hinder and favor the distribution of evaluation and its use in the political and administrative process.

—The comparative dimension in evaluation may serve to aid understanding of the process and evolution of evaluation, to isolate the common international factors, and to stimulate its growth. By drawing on the structural similarities among societies, it may encourage more situational variety and heterogeneity to fit national, regional, and local problems that have been examined too narrowly.

—The international development of evaluation research may speed knowledge production and use. Comparative evaluation may be regarded as a tool for exchanging ideas and transferring and translating evaluation research technology into different societal contexts. Future evaluations may develop from a mutual learning process, which will help to eliminate the trial and error process so common in the beginning of evaluation research.

—As a result, the international dimension in evaluation research can both increase the process of learning and theoretical understanding and open future directions for evaluation research.

As evaluation research has evolved as an international exercise, many evaluators have become aware of the growing potential for international exchange of ideas and "technology transfer." Multiple attempts have already been made by UNESCO, WHO, World Bank, OECD, INTOSAI, private foundations like the German Marshall Fund and national development banks like the Inter-American Development Bank, the Asian Development Bank, the German Foundation for International Development to stimulate the exchange and promote the development of evaluation research ideas and techniques. The American Evaluation Research Society has established an international branch, and European evaluation researchers are beginning to form their own society.

Very often, evaluations are hidden behind different names, rooted in everyday administrative practice, and less sophisticated in style than glamorous designs of large-scale experimental research. But the small-scale evaluations may provide the bases for the growth of evaluation research. It is therefore not surprising that even in the smaller countries interest in evaluation research is growing, although this is often limited to policy areas such as education, health, or social affairs. The form and role of evaluation within a country are largely dependent on national institutions. A systematic comparison is still lacking. In some cases, attempts at those comparisons have come too early.

This collection of papers was initially inspired by the American-German Workshop on Evaluation Research held in Berlin, West Germany and sponsored by Stiftung Volkswagenwerk. The purpose of this conference was to stimulate concern for international and comparative dimensions of evaluation research—opening the American and German evaluations to a wider audience, questioning the future prospects of evaluation research, and shedding light on the past metamorphosis of evaluation from an experimental science technique to a management tool for a responsive government and administration (see Freeman and Solomon, Ferné, and Levine in this volume). Suggestions to improve the usefulness of evaluation research included reform of the user system by providing incentives for change in our growing bureaucracies (Hellstern and Wollman, Wholey, Rein). The conference brought out some reasons for the lack of utilization of evaluation in the policy area and suggested techniques for improvement in the utilization and diffusion of evaluation research results (Rich, Kiresuk, Larsen, Lund, Fitzsimmons). It addressed the question of blending theory and method by reflecting on the use of sophisticated American research techniques and European tradition (Kaufmann, Strohmeier, Küchler, Nacken). And it asked whether the growth of variability will continue in evaluation research, and whether it will still serve as a crossfertilization process drawing on different sources and disciplines (Rossi).

The workshop combined participants from different organizational communities from the United States and Germany:

—researchers from universities,
—researchers from private research institutions,
—administrators from federal offices and agencies, and
—members of independent organizations and agencies.

The workshop included some of the most active researchers and administrators in the field of evaluation from different universities with major interests in program evaluation research: from the Free University of Berlin, the Bielefeld University, the Bundeswehrhochschule Hamburg, University of Frankfurt, University of Konstanz; from such commercial research institutions as Abt Associates, Infas Bonn-Bad Godesberg, Infratest Muenchen; as well as representatives from those agencies and federal ministries with major interests and work commissioned in evaluation research, including representatives from the Chancellor's Office, the Federal Ministries of Labor and Social Affairs, of Food, Agriculture and Forestry, of Research and Technology, of Regional Policies, Housing and Construction, of Economics, of Foreign Aid, of Transportation, and the Federal Audit Court. In addition, a representative from the Centre de Sociologie de l'Innovation in France attended. Some of the best-known evaluation researchers in the United States also attended. They represented a number of institutions and organizations which have provided leadership in the evaluation field, such as UCLA, University of Massachusetts, the Massachusetts Institute of Technology, Princeton University, the American Sociological Association, the System Development Corporation, Abt Associates, the U.S. Department of Health, Education and Welfare, the National Science Foundation, and the Program Evaluation Resource Center.

This book may not serve as a systematic handbook on international evaluation research—such a guide has yet to be written—but for those interested in the evolution of research, these chapters may be stimulating reading, to be used as sources for ideas and techniques, to aid understanding of the factors which shape evaluation research and form its future. For all readers it may reflect some of the interest and challenge that the workshop provided.

We wish to acknowledge the assistance of Stiftung Volkswagenwerk (the Volkswagen Foundation) in funding the American-German Workshop on Evaluation Research, from which these chapters were drawn. The conference was held in June 1979 at the Free University of Berlin, which served as a gracious institutional host. The editors are appreciative of the environment provided by System Development Corporation and the Free University of Berlin, which encouraged the scholarly efforts of this volume. Howard Freeman's continuous commentary throughout the preparation of this manuscript was both instructive and helpful. Special thanks go to Heidrun Veith, Cornelia Eichenhoeffer, and Inge Siegel, who assisted in preparing the conference and the volume. We also thank our secretary Dagmar Castiglione, who was not only patient with the numerous retyping of sections of this book but whose bilingual abilities bridged many a transatlantic communications gap.

Robert A. Levine
Marian A. Solomon
Gerd-Michael Hellstern
Hellmut Wollmann

PART 1

THE SPREAD OF EVALUATION
RESEARCH

Evaluation has crossed national boundaries and spread into the daily routine of policy makers, managers, and administrators in many countries. In this process of diffusion, evaluation researchers take on different faces and don dazzling robes, hiding their common origin by promoting the common interest in rationalization of policy by empirical social science research. In a provocative chapter, Howard Freeman and Marian Solomon show the changing faces of evaluation research, which has grown from a tool to shape and test innovations to a flexible management technique to increase program effectiveness, to handle public accountability demands, and to foster administrative responsibility. They speculate on the forces at work which shape evaluations, illustrate the emergence and evolution of evaluation research, and predict the future direction evaluation research will take in the 1980s. Georges Ferné illustrates the conflict between the scientific orientation and the political factors fostering and constraining the spread of evaluation into the daily routine of policy makers in the OECD countries. Robert Levine, associated with evaluation research from the perspective of both the government policy maker and outsider evaluator, provides an overview on the spread of evaluation and policy research and illustrates the structural conditions for evaluation in different European countries which give rise to divergent forms of evaluation research.

1

The Next Decade in Evaluation Research

Howard E. Freeman

University of California, Los Angeles

Marian A. Solomon

System Development Corporation

In terms of world culture, perhaps the two most distinctive U.S. contributions of the 1970s are the movie *Star Wars* and evaluation research. There are many similarities between them: Both are a mixture of reality and fantasy, both have proved lucrative, both have been critically examined and acclaimed by other nations, and both will be refined and expanded in concept during the next decade. Neither, of course, is really a new invention. Buck Rogers was the 1930 United States science fiction counterpart of Luke Skywalker, and Kurt Lewin the depression twin of Donald Campbell in advocating and conducting social experiments, (Freeman, 1977; Rossi et al., 1979). But the 1970s were very special times politically, socially, and economically—in the U.S. and elsewhere—and it is another case of the Mertonian dictum (Merton, 1965) that readiness to adopt and encourage utilization of inventions, including social inventions, depends upon their compatibility with social structure.

This theme of the fit between the times and the concept of program evaluation has been expanded upon elsewhere (Freeman, 1977), and rehashing the discussion here is unnecessary. Thinking about the development of evaluation research in life cycle terms, it is a fair description that after an extended and deprived infancy and childhood of perhaps one-half a century (for example, Stephan, 1935), the field enjoyed a comparatively brief adolescence encompassing the decade of the 1970s. Like most adolescent periods, it was characterized by conflict, feelings of worthlessness, anxiety, rejection, and forays into settings and environments that were previously foreign. Out of it has emerged a still somewhat gawky and floundering adult; but one destined to have a long, successful and influential life, unless, of course, either the temptation for power and riches becomes too overwhelming or the consortium of governmental and foundation support vanishes.

The description in terms of adolescence is reasonably accurate, for the decade now ending saw a remarkable spurt of growth and development in the field in the United States, including:

1. The establishment of what may be described as a new industry of considerable proportions. U.S. Federal expenditures for evaluation efforts were over 243 million dollars in 1977 (OMB, 1977), and probably have risen to around 300 million dollars in 1979 (Shapley and Phillips, 1978). This trend was accelerated in the early '70s by the availability of set-aside funds to evaluate some HEW programs (U.S. Senate, 1977).
2. The emergence of a new profession, evidenced by the founding of several journals and two professional associations, the publication of texts, handbooks, and readers, and the offering of graduate courses and post doctoral fellowships in the field (Morell and Flaherty, 1978).
3. Recognition of the role of evaluations in Federal decision-making by the establishment of key executive positions to manage evaluation policy within the senior staff offices of federal executive departments such as the U.S. Departments of Health, Education, and Welfare, and of Housing and Urban Development.
4. Efforts at quality control and improvement of procedures by government watchdog groups, such as the General Accounting Office (1979), government and foundation evaluation funders, firms within the industry, and persons within academia.
5. Recognition of the need to codify the contextual and practical problems that impede evaluations, and to devise means to maximize the utility of studies (Wholey, 1979).

The list could be expanded, of course. The central point, however, is what is important. The field of evaluation research, to use the jargon of the sociologist, rapidly has become "institutionalized" (Morell and Flaherty, 1978). What has emerged is a very special coalition in which power is shared by government and foundation executives and administrators, principals in profit-making corporations, and individuals located in academic and non-profit centers. The work being undertaken varies from the occasional glamorous, important "policy" evaluations to numerous run-of-the-mill administrative and managerial efforts. Although some of the work is very costly and long in duration, most is moderate in cost and brief in time. Finally, the procedures undertaken and the products produced may compare favorably with the very best in social research, or may be highly incompetent and amateurish. These observations are by nature of background to our task of speculating about the field during the next decade.

THE CHANGING CONDITIONS
FOR EVALUATION RESEARCH

Adults never quite turn out like one may predict during their teenage years. This will be true of evaluation during the 1980s. The field will blossom during this period, but neither the trees that grow now nor the fruit they yield will correspond to those found in the forest of saplings during the 1970s. There are three major reasons that taken together probably explain the shifts in outlook.

Decline in Innovative Programs

The 1970s started with a spillover, or at least a residue, of optimism about the potential for social programs that would markedly change the life chances and human conditions of the poor, the disenfranchised, and the physically and emotionally deficient. Evaluations of innovative programs were the name of the game; they were to demonstrate clearly that creative ideas, resources and enthusiasm could change the face of the land. Alas, what results:

1. Manpower programs showed little impact, and hardly any compared with costs (Nay et al., 1971).
2. Crime control efforts may have put somewhat of a lid on the crime rate, but the incidence of crime rose so rapidly from the 1960s to make any impact of programs imperceptible.
3. Head Start does not seem to effect educational skills, or even if it does, the magnitude of impact is miniscule (Barnow and Cain, 1977).
4. Medicare and Medicaid have provided access to care for many persons in the U.S., but have also been major stimuli for inflation and have resulted in unchecked expenditures by hospitals and unreasonable fees by our doctors (Aiken and Freeman, in press).
5. Sesame Street may work, but its impact on educational skills is a difference of about one-half a letter in the alphabet, and middle-class children watch more than poor kids and benefit the most (Cook et al., 1975).

Thus, there are few new, bold ventures today, either at the comprehensive level of OEO (Office of Economic Opportunity) or the less stratospheric and programmatic ones of either neighborhood health centers or neighborhood schools. What did exist has either been abandoned or conventionalized. The cynic may tell us there really was not much new during the 1950s and 1960s, but it was simply better packaged then. In any event, there is little to evaluate that is bold in concept either now or in the short-term future.

Human Service Expenditures

Alongside the disenchantment with innovation, there are strong forces pressing for cost containment across the human services sector. In part, this pressure is governmentally inspired as a means to contain inflation; in part, it is a manifestation of our "Proposition 13" mentality—the revolt of middle-income America to their taxation (Mushkin et al., 1979), to their assuming responsibility for the plight of less fortunate community members, and to their support of even bigger governments. The slogan of the times is zero-based budgeting (Salasin, 1977).

Increasingly, the concepts of "accountability," "performance monitoring," and "program efficiency" will dominate the contracted evaluations as well as the cocktail hour discussions of planners and evaluators. Evaluation research is gaining acceptance as a managerial tool. Indeed, almost all federal human services legislation now includes mandatory evaluation requirements (Salasin, 1977). The ultimate is the press for "sunset" legislation, which provides for the automatic termination of programs after a given number of years, unless efficacy has been demonstrated (Price, 1978).

Programs do not remain static, of course. There are constant modifications to existing programs and initiatives. For example, the Department of HEW, in collaboration with the Robert Wood Johnson Foundation, is supporting the testing of whether or not neighborhood health centers affiliated with teaching hospitals are a better investment than "free-standing" ones. The Law Enforcement Assistance Administration of the Department of Justice is concerned with the comparative costs and outcomes on juvenile offenders of various types of community alternatives to institutionalization, and so on.

Admittedly, there is a thin line between policy and administration and procedural decisions. Much of what is taking place is more in the nature of "fine-tuning," however, than bold innovation, and more in the nature of accountability and managerial evaluations of ongoing programs than of true experiments to test newly created ventures.

Conduct of Evaluation

There is a relative decline in the number and dollar expenditures for evaluations undertaken by researchers in universities. The profit-making firms and a few aggressive non-profit groups more and more dominate the field from the standpoint of the actual conduct of studies. In part, this is related to contract procedures and the short turn-around times required from when requests for proposals are advertised, and when bids from prospective

contractors must be submitted. Also, the time allowed for contract performance makes it impossible, oftentimes, for academic groups to compete.
Then, too, the commercial sector organizations and the "non-profits" may
do a job at less cost, sometimes because they cut corners, but more often
probably because they have smaller bureaucracies and more incentives to be
efficient than universities.

Perhaps more to the point, the shift from academic to entrepreneurial
settings has an impact on what and how work is done. In a now dated study
(Bernstein and Freeman, 1975), the evidence indicated that the general
research quality of the profit-making firms was inferior to work carried on in
universities—whether this is still the case is an open question. Certainly,
now, individual firms can be found whose staff, by credentials and performance, are more technically astute and operationally sophisticated than their
peers in the academy.

The shift in the conduct of evaluations to the "firm" will influence the
way the field develops methodologically. "Discoveries" in method will be
more practical than basic. The work of the firm, not the admiration of the
scholar, often will be the dominant concern. There is some justification,
anyway, to the position that it is a lack of knowledge about *how* to successfully undertake evaluations, not a lack of technical procedures, that stymies
work in the field.

These remarks, we believe, have validity for the U.S. scene. It is clear
that the political structure, levels of technological development, and the
outlook of a country's people are related to the extent to which these remarks
pertain to other nations. The same is true about the specific directions of
change to be discussed subsequently. But for other nations, there are lessons
to be learned from the past and predicted trajectories of development of the
field of evaluation research in the U.S.

DIRECTIONS OF CHANGE
IN EVALUATION RESEARCH

It is easier to discuss specific ways in which the evaluation enterprise is
changing than to convey the different gestalt that is emerging. The perspectives of governmental and foundation sponsors on the support of social
research in general has shifted, and funding for evaluation is part of the
change in outlook.

Support in early post-World War II decades, the age of plenty for social
researchers (Freeman et al., 1975), was predicated on investigators initiating
proposals, and having them reviewed by peers for scientific significance and
methodological sophistication. Once funded, the investigator is virtually
never bothered again. But the last three to five years has seen reductions, in

TABLE 1.1   Contracts Offered in 1977

Dept. or Agency	Total RFPs
Action	16
Dept. of Agriculture	21
Dept. of Commerce	28
Consumer Product Safety Commission	14
Dept. of Denfense	106
Environmental Protection Agency	60
Energy R&D Administration	48
Federal Energy Administration	63
Gen'l Services Admin/Gen'l Acctg. Office	22
Dept. of Health, Education, and Welfare	499
Dept. of Housing and Urban Development	28
Dept. of Interior	41
Dept. of Justice	22
Dept. of Labor	72
Miscellaneous	64
NASA	10
Nuclear Regulatory Commission	19
National Science Foundation	16
Dept. of State	22
Dept. of Transportation	144
Total	1,315

SOURCE: The Washington Researchers Information Report (September-October 1978:4).

real dollars, of almost all social research grant programs, the funding source for investigator-inspired studies.

From various vantage points the same question is voiced: What is the utility and practical significance of the work? One vocal senator, Proxmire, has had a major impact on the program of basic social research by beating upon the National Science Foundation. To meet the criticisms and threats to their organizations, traditional grant-oriented agencies have turned to what are referred to now as "targeted grant programs"—a euphemism for saying to the investigator: "Do what we say, not what you want."

Many social researchers, even most of us whose applied interest makes us the beneficiaries of the changed viewpoint, are seriously concerned about the situation and fearful it could result in a lost generation of investigators and students, particularly since more and more applied work will be done outside the academy. Notwithstanding personal views, it is a fact that today virtually all major and most minor evaluation studies, at least at a national level, are initiated by government and foundation staff, either at the direction of legislative bodies, policy level persons, or to meet their own administrative and managerial purposes. Fewer and fewer studies are investigator-inspired.

The shift is not simply in how the money is given out, although how it is given out is related to who gets it, as we have already noted. It has resulted in marked changes in control of activities—from planning of projects to their reporting and dissemination. It has resulted, in response to claims of wasted evaluation research efforts, to closer monitoring and more stringent contracting requirements. Moreover, it has led to increased in-house staff by funding and sponsoring groups, and more participation in design and implementation aspects of contracts. Finally, it has culminated in increased intramural evaluations, particularly in planning and monitoring evaluation activities.

The debate of an earlier era was whether or not evaluation groups should be independent of program staff, i.e., separately funded and independently organized. The debate now, and increasingly in the future, is on how to maximize the participation of policy-makers, planners and program managers in the conduct of evaluations. The party-line is that their maximum participation will result in evaluations of most relevance and utility.

The evaluator of the 1980s will no longer receive a research award, and go about the work at his or her pace. Rather, there are PERT chart (planning schedule) tight deadlines to conform to GAO scrutiny of data collection (GAO, 1979), an evaluation library to provide access to reports (HEW, 1977), a bibliographic service (Human Services, monthly) waiting to catalog and disseminate results, and a Freedom of Information Act that critics fall back on when threatening public organizations for data and reports (Chelimsky, 1978).

The point should be clear. Evaluation research is not an activity likely to be undertaken between classes by a professor in a university with a graduate assistant at a pace they set. Rather, it has become a high pressure, often economically lucrative, and politically sensitive activity—a high stakes game.

In fiscal year 1977, thirty-nine executive departments and agencies not only spent, as earlier noted, 243 million dollars on evaluation of social programs, but one-quarter—61 million dollars—were spent to support almost 2,200 full-time federal staff, whose major assignment was to develop, coordinate, monitor, and stimulate the utilization of evaluations, and to conduct in-house evaluations on their own. These funds supported in-house staff, grants, and over 1,300 contracts (see Table 1.1).

A narrower definition of program evaluation, which only includes evaluations which "seek to systematically analyze federal programs to determine the extent to which they have achieved their objectives" would reduce markedly the amount spent to 63.6 million dollars. While still a healthy sum, it is only 3.4% of federal funds spent on knowledge production activities by executive departments and agencies (Abramson, 1978).

The U.S. Congress has strengthened the capabilities of the General Accounting Office, the Congressional Research Service, the Congressional Budget Office, the Office of Technology Assessment, and the Congressional committee staffs to stimulate what are deemed relevant evaluations, and to oversee the conduct of extramural and intramural efforts in the federal government (Rivlin, 1979). Less is known and more variations certain at state and local levels. But the general thrust of control by evaluation funding and sponsoring groups is evident at all levels of government and in the foundation sector as well.

We can increasingly expect that legislation will specifically allocate a proportion of funds for evaluation and establish requirements for monitoring program performance, and assessing program impact and efficiency (i.e., cost to benefits). The "ideal legislation" will specify the scope of the evaluation activity, the questions to be addressed, and the procedure for reporting these results to Congress, and to the responsible program and oversight groups. There are many such acts even now. An example of a comparatively early one is Title III, the Runaway Youth Act of the Juvenile Justice and Delinquency Act of 1974 (P.L. 93–415). It requires an annual report evaluating "runaway houses" funded under it, identifies the criteria of effectiveness, and pins future funding on the results of the effort. Currently, almost all new human service legislation includes performance criteria and enforcement requirements are increasing.

Departments and agencies responsible for programs, in response to these tightened requirements, have increased size and status of their evaluation staffs. In HEW, although there were evaluation groups much earlier at bureau and agency levels, it was not until fall of 1978 that a strong office emerged at the policy level (i.e., in the Office of the Assistant Secretary for Planning and Evaluation). In 1969–70, a similar office was established but underwent significant changes in size and scope during the 1970s and exercised only limited control over HEW's evaluation efforts. Now, central staff are concerned with quality of work, overlapping evaluations, competence of federal staff to monitor evaluations, the contract award process, and so on. Its long term direct influence on the evaluation effort is still unclear. But it is like replacing a captain with a general in the military—everyone below becomes concerned and recognizes the importance of the mission.

Choice of Methods for Impact Measurement

The debate of the past few years has focused on the pitfalls of the quasi-experiment and the implementation problems of the "true experiment." There is little to be gained by continuing it. First, it is clear, as Boruch's bibliography (Boruch et al., 1978) informs us, there are many more true experiments undertaken than most imagine. Second, there are many situations, however, in which the only choice is a quasi-experimental design. Third, problems of implementation, including non-participation and drop-out from treatment, often require converting true to quasi-experiments. While the matter of drawing firm conclusions from quasi-experiments will continue, the fervor of the debate will diminish.

One reason the debate is cooling off is that much of it is interesting, but academic. Small differences, albeit statistically significant, are difficult to sell as the basis for program support in the times of tight money. It is conceivable that applications of statistical controls can either conceal large differences or create them, but probably not unless the study is flawed in other ways (e.g., in measurement reliability).

The second, and major reason, is that neither the true nor quasi-experiment is applicable, in many cases, to the evaluation of ongoing programs. The inclusive and national character of many programs saturates targets so that any "quasi-control" group selected necessarily would be markedly different in every sense with the exposed population. Increasingly, with all of the cautions of using "indicators" to study impact, it is necessary to turn to time-series analyses with appropriate disaggregation to examine programs. This is certainly the case with those programs that result in huge federal expenditures. There needs to be both increased methodological development, including computer software, and increased training of persons in time-series procedures. Experiments and quasi-experiments will continue to be methods of choice for the study of innovations, initiatives, and procedural and administrative changes. But the press, consistent with the sunset law movement and the new "Proposition 13" mentality, is to use evaluations to assess the impact of ongoing programs (Kirlin, 1979).

Efficiency Evaluations

The difficulties of designing "successful" human services programs, and the moral imperative to help the unfortunate resulted in a stress on impact or efficacy, rather than on efficiency or costs to either benefits or effectiveness. But this is not the case any longer. The health field illustrates the point well. The 1960s and 1970s saw a major press to improve access to care and equality in services provided. Presumably because of the programs of these years, only scattered pockets exist in the U.S. where services are really sparse. White, non-white, and middle-lower-income differences in use of services have virtually disappeared.

But at what costs, and to what ends? Procedures, such as annual physicals for middle-aged, healthy adults at $100 to $500 per person can hardly be justified in cost-effectiveness terms; likewise access of women to specialists in female diseases has little benefits compared with costs, for a significant part of their practices consist of the treatment of ordinary acute illness (Aiken et al., 1979). Preventive programs of medical and dental care for children in their costs may be far in excess of their benefits (i.e., it costs more to prevent cavities than to fill the decayed teeth). In the extreme, there is talk of "health care rationing" because of the high costs of care. Such a policy may never come to pass fully, but there clearly is major concern in health care and across the board in program efficiency. Again, this is an important area for further methodological development. Cost-benefit and cost-effectiveness analyses have their roots in efforts of economists to explicate the national and international consequences of major inputs (Rossi et al., 1979); conceptual and technical developments are necessary in order to make the approach and methodology amenable to the human services area (Abt, 1979).

Evaluation to Improve Managerial Effectiveness

As the press for efficiency increases, there is pressure for accountability of programs on their managers. This results in the use of evaluation procedures on a periodic basis to gauge performance in achieving explicit and specific goals. These periodic assessments provide program managers with information that permits them to make internal adjustments in their efforts, and at the same time allows their superordinates to have a basis for intervening, or to use the polite phrase, "provide technical assistance." In many large-scale established efforts, such evaluations represent extremely small expenditures compared with program costs, and an appreciation of the potential of these efforts to provide timely decision-making inputs is expected to increase enthusiasm and further support for them (Windle and Woy, 1977). Advocates maintain "managerial evaluations" will become an integral administrative tool at every level of program organization (Attkisson et al., 1978).

The idea of performance evaluations for accountability purposes does not presuppose any new methods; it is simply the way the procedures are conceptualized and undertaken. During the planning phase of programs, the emphasis is on operationalization and refinement of indicators along which managers agree to be held responsible for achieving. It provides the impetus for programs having specific objectives and measurable outcomes, rather than the traditional vague goals and sloppy outcome criteria. It presses for objective, not subjective, outcome measures, and permits a clear basis on which program managers may negotiate with their directors.

Currently at the U.S. Department of Health, Education, and Welfare, one way in which the management-accountability perspective is manifest is in the installed MITS (Management Initiative Tracking System). Selected

HEW programs are required to specify performance indicators and magnitudes of gain to be expected of them. Both the indicators and the magnitudes of change specified are negotiated at periodic intervals, and agreements reached with the upper echelons in the Office of the Secretary. For example, all community delivery systems sponsored by the Federal government are expected to deliver a specific set of services to a designated proportion of persons in a specified catchment area after two years in operation. Additional resources accrue to sites meeting objectives; technical assistance, and more severe sanctions are meted out to those who fail to meet the specified levels of performance.

Program performance information also helps managers and "headquarters" deal with the increasing requirements of various oversight groups for information (Barnes et al., 1977). Without such an accountability system in place, requests for performance information often disrupt special evaluation efforts, and general managerial activities. Thus, there is increased pressure for performance and accountability data. Accountability evaluations, as an integral part of managerial efforts, is a response to the right to know internally and externally (Anderson, 1978).

Evaluability Assessments

The emphasis on evaluation of established programs, the press for management-relevant evaluations, and the recognized under-utilization of "outside" evaluations have led to the development of procedures for evaluation planning activities, or as they sometimes are called, "snapshot evaluations." In intent, if not always in practice, they are intended to be more than either quick and dirty or process evaluations. Rather, "evaluability assessments" or "exploratory evaluations" are seen as the beginning of ongoing monitoring and impact evaluation efforts, including the establishment of accountability criteria for program managers.

Evaluability assessments have at their core the view that the utility of evaluations requires negotiating with policy makers and program managers to identify standards of program performance, and that full-fledged evaluations should take place only of programs "ready" for such efforts (Schmidt, 1978). Such a procedure requires identifying the expectations of "stakeholders," including policy staff, program managers and staff and practitioners at the client delivery level.

The process is an attempt to codify pre-evaluation activities. It involves a review of the following:

1. The description of management's program objectives in measurable terms.
2. The degree to which the conceptualized program is actually implemented.
3. The extent to which appropriate evaluation criteria have been explicated.
4. The opportunities available to collect relevant information.

5. The intended and likely use of program performance information.
6. The identification of management's authority and responsibilities to implement evaluation activities.
7. The extent to which changes in program activities, objectives, and available
   information could enhance program performance.

Evaluability assessment activities include extensive interviews with managers and staff, and feedback and negotiation sessions to share information
uncovered, to refine objectives, program procedures and evaluation perspectives. These assessments are also impossible to undertake exclusively
by outsiders. Rather, they represent the engagement of persons with a strong
stake in the organization, knowledge of program, and an ability to engage in
a political negotiating process with program managers who often control
much in the way of resources and thus power. It is an effort to meet the need
for an amenable climate, both for the successful implementation of monitoring and impact studies, and for maximizing utilization of results. Similar
efforts are undertaken in order to establish ongoing performance information systems.

    These notions raise different levels of concern than the former arguments
about whether evaluators must be entirely independent of program staff.
Rather, the tables are turned and evaluability assessment is an opening
wedge into the redefinition of responsibilities and roles. Evaluators under
the new scheme of things are most likely to be perceived like company
auditors, who simultaneously have an obligation to protect the stockholders,
and the best interests of the managers of the organization for whom they
work.

Increased Emphasis on Monitoring

    The directions outlined above suggest increased concern with the key
monitoring questions of appropriateness of the target population, and of the
extent programs are conducted as planned. Monitoring or "process" evaluations were formerly conceived as essential parts of comprehensive evaluations of innovative programs in which impact studies were done as well.

    Now, with the managerial orientation that is emerging, monitoring evalu-
ations are seen as an ongoing part of the daily activities of human service
organizations. Of all evaluation tasks, program monitoring activities require
the most methodological development and codification (Fincher, 1978).
Record systems, client interviews, practitioner reports, and so on, it is
commonly observed, are of variable quality, reliability, and utility (Windle
and Sharfstein, 1978).

    If there is one area of urgent study to be pressed in the forthcoming
decade, it is the design, testing, and implementation of uniform procedures
in various fields to obtain process data, and to have the means to analyze it

rapidly so that feedback to program managers is feasible while the information is still relevant. There is little point in contemplating the implications of
the increased oversight and control of evaluations by sponsors, and the
utility of evaluability assessments, unless we can devise, specify and obtain
acceptance of rigorous procedures for monitoring evaluations.

Continued Institutionalization of Evaluation Research

A theme of this paper is the institutionalization of evaluation, with increased emphasis on professional action, credentials, trade and scholarly
association membership, and the like. Then too, as noted earlier, there is
increased scrutiny of evaluation activities, by sponsors, oversight groups to
whom they are responsible, and persons in academia. All of these efforts,
most of us believe, are inevitable, and some are useful.

At the same time, some of us can only express anxiety at some of the
directions the field has taken. It is becoming less identified with the general
social research community, and the "professionalization" of evaluation specialists may separate them from "true" social scientists. As noted, it probably
is the posture of the academic community more than anything else that
accounts for the development. But the consequences, as we have noted,
need serious consideration. The issue has relevance for graduate training,
the direction of all social research activities, and perhaps the very life of
academic social science.

CONCLUSION

Predicting the future is always hazardous; indeed, not everyone will
agree completely with our analysis of the past and the present. We began by
placing evaluation research alongside *Star Wars*. In both, it is still not
entirely clear who are the heroes and the villains, whether future products
will be better, exactly how long a life the enterprises will lead, whether or
not there is a lasting social good from either of them, and how well they do
when exported out of the United States. Only careful observation of the
future allows answers.

REFERENCES

ABRAMSON, M A. (1978) The Funding of Social Knowledge Production and Application: A
    Survey of Federal Agencies. Washington, DC: National Academy of Science.
ABT, C.C. [ed.] (1979) Perspectives on the Costs and Benefits of Applied Social Research.
    Cambridge, MA: Council for Applied Social Research.

AIKEN, L. H. et al. (1979) "Contributions of specialists to the delivery of primary care: a new perspective." New England Journal of Medicine 300: 1363–1387.

————and H. E. FREEMAN (in press) "A sociological perspective on science and technology in medicine." In P. T. Durkin (ed.) A Guide to the Culture of Science, Technology and Medicine. New York: Free Press.

ANDERSON, S. B. (1978) "Editor's notes: the expanding role of program evaluation." In New Directions for Program Evaluation: Exploring Purposes and Dimensions Fall, 2: vii–xii.

ATTKISSON, C. C. et al. [eds.] (1978) Evaluation of Human Service Programs. New York: Academic Press.

BARNES, R. T., J. N. NAY, and J. S. WHOLEY (1977) "Purchasing evaluation and research in a federal block grant program: LEAA's national and evaluation program." Evaluation 4: 197–200.

BARNOW, B. S. and G. G. CAIN (1977) "A re-analysis of the effect of Headstart on cognitive development: methodology and empirical findings." Journal of Human Resources 12: 177–197.

BERNSTEIN, I. and H. F. FREEMAN (1975) Academic and Entrepreneurial Research. New York: Russell Sage.

BORUCH, R. E., A. J. McSWEENEY, and E. J. SODERSTROM (1978) "Randomized field experiments for program planning development and evaluation." Evaluation Quarterly 2: 655–696.

CHELIMSKY, E. (1978) "Differing perspectives of evaluation." In New Directions for Program Evaluation: Monitoring Ongoing Programs Fall, 2: 1–18.

COOK, T. et al. (1975) Sesame Street Revisited. New York: Russell Sage.

FINCHER, C. (1978) "Program monitoring on higher education." In New Directions for Program Evaluation: Monitoring Ongoing Programs Fall, 3: 63–74.

FREEMAN, H. E. (1977) "The present status of evaluation research." In Evaluation Studies Review Annual, Vol. 2. Beverly Hills, CA: Sage.

————E. F. BORGATTA, and N. H. SIEGEL (1975) "Remarks on the changing relationship between government support and graduate training." In Social Policy and Sociology. New York: Academic Press.

KIRLIN, J. J. (1979) "Proposition 13 and the financing of public services." In S. J. Mushkin (ed.) Proposition 13 and Its Consequences for Public Management. Cambridge, MA: Council for Applied Social Research.

MERTON, R. K. (1965) On the Shoulders of Giants. New York: Harcourt Brace Jovanovich.

MORELL, J. A. and E. W. FLAHERTY (1978) "The development of evaluation as a profession: current status and some predictions." Journal of Evaluation and Program Planning 1: 11–17.

MUSHKIN, S. J., F. H. SANDIFER, C. L. VEHORN, and C. G. TURNER (1979) "The taxpayer revolt: An opportunity to make positive changes in local government." In S. J. Mushkin (ed.) Proposition 13 and Its Consequences for Public Management. Cambridge, MA: Council for Applied Social Research.

NAY, J. N., J. W. SCANLON, and J. S. WHOLEY (1971) Benefits and Costs of Manpower Training Programs: A Synthesis of Previous Studies with Reservations and Recommendations. Washington, DC: The Urban Institute.

PRICE, D. R. (1978) "Sunset legislation in the United States." Baylor Law Review 3: 401–462.

RIVLIN, A. (1979) "Congress, the budget, and policy analysis." In C. C. Abt (ed.) Perspectives on the Costs and Benefits of Applied Social Research. Cambridge, MA: Council for Applied Social Research.

ROSSI, P. H., H. E. FREEMAN, and S. R. WRIGHT (1979) Evaluation: A Systematic Approach. Beverly Hills, CA: Sage.

SALASIN, S. (1977) "Technology transfer—from the private to the public" (An interview with Peter A. Pybrr). Evaluation 4: 35–37.

SCANLON, J. and J. WALLER (1979) "Program evaluation and federal programs." GAO Review 14: 32–35.

SCHMIDT, R. et al. (1978) Evaluation Assessment: Making Public Programs Work Better. Washington, DC: The Urban Institute.

SHAPLEY, W. H. and D. I. PHILLIPS (1978) Research and Development in Federal Budget: FY 1979, R&D, Industry, and the Economy. Washington, DC: American Association for the Advancement of Science.

STEPHAN, A. S. (1935) "Prospects and possibilities: The new deal and the new social research." Social Forces 13: 515–521.

United States Department of Health, Education and Welfare (1977) Compendium of HEW Evaluation Studies, Office of Assistant Secretary for Planning and Evaluation. Washington, D.C.

United States General Accounting Office (1979) A Framework for Balancing Privacy and Accountability Needs in Evaluations of Social Research. Washington, D.C.

United States Office of Management and Budget, Executive Office of the President (1977) Resources for Program Evaluation: Fiscal Year 1977. Washington, D.C.

United States Senate (1977) "Cost, management and utilization of human resources program evaluation." Hearings before the Committee on Human Resources, 95th Congress, 1st Session (October 6 and 27; John Evans, testimony). Washington, D.C.

WHOLEY, J. S. (1979) Evaluation: Promise and Performance. Washington, DC: The Urban Institute.

WINDLE, C. and S. S. SHARFSTEIN (1978) "Three approaches to monitoring mental health services." In New Directions for Program Evaluation: Monitoring Ongoing Programs Fall, 3: 63–74.

WINDLE, C. and J. R. WOY (1977) "When to apply various program evaluation approaches." Evaluation 4: 35–37.

AUTHORS' NOTE: The material in this paper was originally prepared for the American-German Workshop on Evaluation Research, held in Berlin, June 29–30, 1979.

2

Program Evaluation and Policy Analysis in Western Nations
An Overview

Robert A. Levine

System Development Corporation

This is the report of a pilot project sponsored by the German Marshall Fund of the United States, to examine the evaluation of public programs in western nations. The analytical purpose of the project has been to provide an initial frame of reference for understanding the different ways in which public authorities may use program evaluation and related forms of policy analysis. The normative objective is to draw on the experience in various countries to suggest to authorities in other countries means by which public policy can be improved through the use of evaluation and other analysis. It should be stressed that this objective is to improve policy-making, not to improve analysis; a less effective piece of analysis more readily usable by policy makers may be preferable to a better piece provided too late, written too obscurely, or focused on issues not relevant to the needs of the policy makers. Thus, the overview concentrates on the uses of analysis, not on its creation.

This report consists of an introduction; a framework of issues; a discussion of the role played by evaluation and analysis in each of the nine countries visited (United States, Canada, France, United Kingdom, Federal Republic of Germany, Belgium, Sweden, Norway, and Netherlands, in the order they were visited) and the European Economic Communities; and some general conclusions. Because it is a pilot, however, neither the framework nor the conclusions is definitive; rather, they suggest hypotheses for confirmation (or rejection) by further investigation. The material for the report was gathered primarily by interviews with middle- to high-level officials in the various countries, and by documents they supplied.

INTRODUCTION

The initial focus of the project was on "evaluation," defined as "the *ex post* examination of the effects (outputs) of a public program, and the comparison of these effects to the intended objectives of the program (stated or implicit) or perhaps to other public purposes." It was later broadened to the more general field of planning for public policy. Although the entire policy-planning process is not included, this chapter does cover the systematic use of analyses, studies, and organized data in the planning and making of public policy. This includes, but is not limited to, program evaluation. It also includes, for example, statistical and qualitative studies of the special needs of national subpopulations, even though these needs are not yet covered by national programs. The change deliberately leaves the borderline between evaluation and other kinds of policy analysis quite fuzzy. This may distress some program evaluators, but it is consistent with the focus on the use of analysis for policy-making, rather than the process of analysis itself. Indeed, some experience with evaluation strictly separated from other policy analysis—such as in Sweden, where independent evaluative organizations tend to fade out—indicates that such separation does not work very well.

The report focuses on domestic policy decision-making and analysis, using the processes of foreign and military policy mainly for historical and comparative context. Domestic policy includes the range of social policies, relating to the uses of national income and resources and their distribution among population groups. It also covers public policy having to do with resource production—energy policy, industrial policy, and the like.

At the edge of this focus, however, are two approaches to domestic policy analysis which might be integrated but which in recent years have usually been held separate from "general" policy analysis. One of these is macroeconomic policy analysis which, from the time of Keynes and the monetary theorists before him, has tended to be an esoteric field of its own, whose practitioners have analyzed movements of the economy as a whole but have made only partial contributions to partial fields such as health, education, poverty, or energy policy. The other approach is that of "science policy," which has concentrated on public policy relating to scientific and technological change. The subject matter of "general" and "science" policy analysis converges over issues such as energy, but the approaches remain very different. The third approach investigated in this report is that taken by budgeteers, economists other than macroeconomists, political scientists, public administrators, and those who are difficult to characterize more narrowly than as policy analysts. The boundaries between this approach and the others may be logically very unclear, but historically and traditionally they are distinct enough.

The quest of the project has been for common aspects in the use of policy analysis in the different countries, with a view toward transnational transfers. One conclusion of this report is that such transfers are possible if they are carried out carefully, in light of the major differences that still exist among the various countries. Lacking such attention to differences, casual attempts to take a process that seems to have worked in one country and apply it to another is likely to fail—and this has happened in recent years. The common thread among all the democratic nations is that political institutions and political decision-making form the basic mode of policy determination—and properly so. The implication, however, is that simple applications across political systems are unlikely to succeed.

That government *is* politics is a basic premise of this report. The primary mode of public decision-making in complex democracies will remain political bargaining and mutual adjustment of interests. But it does not follow that no place remains in political decision-making for "rational discourse," including evaluation and other forms of policy analysis. Politics concerns different views of the common interest, as well as adjustment of self-interests, and policy analysis can illuminate the meaning of the common interest and sometimes even self-interest. (A story is told in Washington of a congressman who habitually voted for high tariffs because of a particular small manufacturer in his district who wanted the protection, until it was pointed out to the legislator that his district formed part of a harbor and that international trade was the engine that ran the district's economy.) Policy analysis can thus help. What it sometimes attempts to do, however—and cannot do—is to override basic political and power relationships.

The major policy conclusion of the report depends on the premise of the value of rational discourse within a political process. The conclusion is that a relatively new British institution—the Central Policy Review Staff (CPRS), an analytical group reporting and responsible directly to the cabinet—may, if carefully adapted to different surrounding environments, provide an important model for improving top-level policy-making in a number of other nations, most notably the United States. This stress, however, is on adaptation rather than simple adoption.

Less adjustment may be needed for transnational transfers at lower than top levels of decision-making—in ministries and operating agencies. The problems of democratic industrial societies are similar. Health systems, for example, are administered very differently in different European countries; however, problems of health care, hospital costs, and the like are similar, and health evaluation is a vigorous activity in most of the relevant countries. It seems likely that many aspects are transferable.

Nonetheless, the caveat remains: Careless transnational transfers can work very badly indeed. A major example can be taken from one striking commonality among the countries discussed here. Each one has had an unsuccessful experiment in Planning, Programming, and Budgeting (PPB) in the last fifteen years. PPB was a system designed largely in the United States and first applied in the Department of Defense by Secretary Robert McNamara in 1961, where in many ways it worked well and still does. In 1965, President Lyndon Johnson mandated its application to the different culture of the domestic agencies of the federal government where, with important exceptions, it worked rather badly. The failures of American PPB were not as immediately obvious as the problems it was intended to solve, however, and these problems were common to the western industrial democracies. Based largely on the American model, the various nations tried PPB and in each one it failed for peculiarly national reasons.

The common thread, then, is that political institutions and political decision-making properly form the basic mode of policy determination in a democracy, and that simple applications across political systems (even from defense to domestic systems) are unlikely to succeed.

FRAMEWORK OF ISSUES

Different Concepts of Evaluation
and Policy Analysis

The simplest model of the application of evaluation and other policy analysis to the making of public policy is that the analyst, having received a set of policy objectives from the decision maker, does his analysis and informs the decision maker as to the most cost-effective means of reaching these objectives. The next simplest model is that the analyst, receiving a less well-specified set of objectives, constructs a number of options from which the decision maker can choose. Ex post evaluation enters into these processes because it provides data on cost-effectiveness under actual operating conditions. Sometimes such evaluation even provides cost-benefit data, with the benefits measured in the same money terms as the costs, so that a cost-benefit ratio equal to or greater than unity indicates that the project is worth doing.

None of these models has much to do with decision-making reality, although they have, in fact, been the implicit models behind the introduction of much policy analysis (including PPB) into government. Rather, the policy process has been one in which the analyst (assuming he has any influence at all) interacts with the decision maker and provides him with pieces of analyzed information which help him choose among courses of action according to some poorly specified set of personal, political, and national criteria (not necessarily in that order).

The uses of analysis are different in different countries and in parts of the same country depending on the ways in which policy processes explicitly or implicitly solve certain conceptual and operating issues about these uses. Some of these processes are described below.

Truth versus advocacy. How near can policy analysis, including evaluation, come to providing objective and value-free information; how much should it be understood in light of the views and interests of the analyst or the organization providing the analytical information? In the United States, with a political system based on advocacy by adversaries, for example, the ordinary assumption is that an evaluation provided by an organization will serve the interest of that organization. In Scandinavia, by contrast, evaluation is understood to be relatively objective and disinterested.

Outside versus inside. Analysis can come into the policy-making process through one or both of two different channels. Analytical information can be provided to decision makers by people or organizations responsible to these decision makers, with the analysis to be used directly by the decision makers; or it can be provided to those to whom the decision makers themselves are responsible, particularly parliaments and electorates. In the second case, the analysis is likely to affect the decisions through political pressures. Within political and bureaucratic decision-making systems the most common belief is that the most effective kind of analysis is that which is intended for use within the system only, and thus can be quite frank. However, in many countries, notably Scandinavia and more recently the United States, the freedom of information laws make this virtually impossible.

Open versus closed. Closely related to the previous issue is the question of whether analytical results should be held closely within governmental structures, or whether they should be published and made generally available.

Analysis versus analysts. One way to introduce policy analysis into decision-making is by supplying analytical reports for decision makers to read; another way is for policy analysts to work closely with decision makers. In fact, the pressures on decision makers are such that few will have the time to read more than thoroughly summarized analytical reports, and thus analysts somewhere will have to write or brief the summaries and help choose which ones should reach the decision makers. But the issue remains whether the analyst should produce studies, bringing analyses directly into the process; or whether he should act simply as another kind of decision

maker with a mode of thought somewhat different from the ordinary politician or bureaucrat and with some knowledge of the kinds of relevant analysis
being carried out in the rest of the world.

There are those who contend that the analyst in a decision-making position is the crucial element in bringing this form of rational discourse to
decision-making, and that analyses as such count for less. Analysts operating outside of their analytical role, however, can run into certain dangers. In
the United States, President Carter's original cabinet had four holders of
Ph.D.s in economics who can be presumed to have been trained in one
variety of policy analysis. About a year into the Carter administration, a
national newsmagazine rating of cabinet effectiveness listed all four at the
bottom of the scale, with lawyers at the top. Three of the four have subsequently been replaced by businessmen.

Assistance versus performance measurement. Another issue is whether
the evaluation is intended to measure the performance of a program, an
organization, or an individual; or whether it is intended to assist those being
evaluated in doing their jobs. The two objectives might overlap, but in
practice an individual or organization feeling that an evaluation will lead to
reward or punishment will work very differently with an evaluator than will
someone who is convinced that the evaluator is there only to help. And an
evaluation will have to be designed very differently to convey one or the
other message.

Programs versus governmental activities. Finally, an issue frequently
raised by Europeans in comparing their evaluation efforts with those in the
United States is that the United States has "programs" in a sense that many
European nations, notably Germany, do not, and that such programs can be
evaluated in ways that ordinary governmental activities cannot.

In the United States, the typical mode of federal operations is for the
Congress to legislate a program and appropriate money for it. Even with a
decentralized program to be administered by states and localities, the executive branch ordinarily sets up a new organization (most likely in an existing
department or agency) to administer the program and distribute the federal
monies *to* the states and localities.

In Germany, at the other extreme, new directions are taken typically by
"marginal changes to existing organizations," as one German put it, and the
organizations are ones that have existed in much their current form at least
since the organization of the Federal Republic and frequently since Bismarck. One reason for this difference between the United States and Europe
is that the United States has a greater tendency (and more reason) to identify
specific population subgroups (for example, the poor, minorities, inhabi-
tants of depressed areas) than Germany and the rest of Europe and to direct

programs at them. In Germany it is assumed that governmental activities apply to the entire population.

Differences in Social and Political Structure

Social Structure

Consensus and nonconsensus nations. Probably the most important difference among the nations, as it affects the making of policy and the uses of analysis in policy-making, is between those nations in which a relatively homogeneous society leads to a broad area of consensus on government policy and those without such a consensus. By "consensus" is meant a general agreement on the objectives of government, particularly on the role of government in dividing income and power into shares and in balancing interests. This does not imply a consensus on what the shares should be, only on the ways in which government should affect these shares. This type of consensus appears to exist in Sweden, Norway, and the Netherlands. It does not exist in the larger nations, where size itself seems to lead to a degree of complexity which precludes consensus, and where elections can lead to real changes of direction.

The relevance to evaluation and policy analysis is that in consensus nations the agreement on the objectives of government leads to a focus on efficiency in achieving these objectives—what in the United States is termed "good government" focus—and to the use of evaluation and analysis very much in the "truth" as compared with the "advocacy" mode. Such nations approach the abstract ideal of objective evaluation; those with less consensus find it more difficult to do so.

Capital-city concentration. It was pointed out by a British MP that "London is a village," in which virtually all of the individuals—governmental and nongovernmental—who are significant for policy-making reside', because London is not only the governmental center of Great Britain, but also the business and the cultural center. Much the same is true of Paris. For different reasons, the same "village" atmosphere is likely to be true for the Netherlands, which is small enough that the Amsterdam/Rotterdam/Hague complex might be considered to have the same attributes. It is not true elsewhere, (except perhaps Denmark, which is not covered by this report). The most relevant implication of the "village" is that "everybody knows everybody." When this is true of the elite of the interest groups as well as the elite of the government, it encourages governance by "insiders," which in turn encourages the holding close of information and the inside use of policy analysis as compared with its outside use through public opinion, parliament, and the electorate. The "village" discourages the questioning of assumptions, a fact which bold analysis may try to counteract.

Political Structure

Federalism. The United States, Canada, and Germany are federal countries, with a good deal of significant power residing in the separately elected governments of the states/provinces/Laender. Even though some tendency toward decentralization exists in all of the other countries, nowhere does it approach these. Diffusion of power through federalism makes "insider" governance difficult; it also leads to the use of analysis to affect decision-making through public opinion, and its use in a bargaining and advocacy mode, as contrasted to a search for the objective truth.

Constitutional structure. Probably the most important difference in political structure among the nations is one which is so obvious that it is sometimes forgotten. Only in the United States are the executive and the legislative powers separate and largely equal—and therefore inherently adversary. This is the central reason why the entire form of government in the United States is based upon adversary relationships, even beyond the adversary roles of political parties that characterize the United States as well as other democratic systems. The "separation of powers" means that evaluations and other analyses will almost always be of an adversary nature, and frequently duplicated, for the executive branch and the Congress. It also throws particular doubt for the United States on the viability of the "helping" evaluation, since evaluatees will always feel that they are being judged by someone. This difference also is likely to mean that the quest of other parliaments for analytical and other staff facilities similar to those of Congress (demonstrated by a number of serious exploratory visits from other capitals to Washington) is doomed to failure, because no other constitution gives a parliament independent power anywhere approaching that of the Congress. Some European parliaments have some independent power based on constitutional or political factors, and as a result use analysis as a means to strengthen parliamentary ability to affect public opinion.

Parliamentary structure. In fact, all parliaments are not the same. In Germany, Norway, and Belgium, the parliament is a factor to be contended with even after it has chosen the government. The government has to bargain with parliamentary leadership on *specific* points of policy. In Germany this is currently the case in part because the government is a coalition. On the other hand, in Sweden and the Netherlands, coalition government does not seem to lead to parliamentary strength. In any case, where parliament has this kind of power, it can be enhanced by access to analysis.

Party structure. A government consisting of a single, disciplined majority party is less frequently forced to bargain than one which is less solid. It can use analysis more objectively and less for advocacy, and will be tempted to keep evaluation and other analysis inside rather than making it public. Such a strong single-party government is traditional and current in the United Kingdom, although the last Labour government was an exception. In effect, France has been governed this way for fifteen years. Every other European country, however, is governed by a coalition or a minority party; and in the United States the single party that dominates both the executive and legislative branches is so undisciplined that the concept of singleness loses definition.

Cabinet structure. Although the cabinets in each of the countries aside from the United States are similar in form, the relationships among the ministers are quite different. In Britain, the prime minister is truly prime, with a de facto ability to dismiss other ministers. Together with the strength of the cabinet vis-à-vis the parliament and the strength of party government, this means that Britain has a very strong central government indeed. With this strength comes an ability to use closely held inside analysis to strengthen even further. At the other pole, the German chancellor has only limited power to dismiss ministers, who can and do thus act very independently; in the early 1970s, the ministers defeated an attempt to increase the relative strength of the chancellor's office by building in a major analytical capability. In Belgium, the premier is similarly weak.

Structure of administration. If the German ministers are strong relative to the chancellor, they are exceptionally weak relative to the administration of governmental operations. The Laender carry out most of the operations of government programs. Beyond that, however, when the federal government does operate programs, these are typically administered by agencies that are autonomous from the ministers. The ministerial function is more to legislate the new than to run the old. This means that to be effective in monitoring operations, the evaluation of public activities in Germany must be very decentralized, which it is. Public activities are similarly run by autonomous agencies in Sweden. Elsewhere, they are much more centralized into ministries, and so is operational evaluation and analysis.

Civil service. In the United States and in Belgium, several so-called "policy" jobs change hands when the government changes. In the United Kingdom practically none change; the fabled permanent Civil Service holds sway. In France it is probable that the civil service and its elite groups, the Inspectorate of Finances and the Court of Accounts (which date back to Napoleon), would continue in effective power under any conceivable change of government. The political government has been so stable in recent years that it has become a relatively permanent political/civil service complex that maintains control. The German civil service is strong on a personal basis—no one loses a job when the government changes—but the expectation is that a shift of political power to the CDU would lead to a shift of top civil servants to positions of less power. The other nations are in between, although weighted heavily on the side of a permanent and nonpolitical civil service. Again, the more permanent and nonpolitical the civil service, the greater the chances for relatively objective nonadvocacy policy analysis, with such analysis perhaps strengthening the civil service as such, at least in some countries.

NINE COUNTRIES AND
AN INTERNATIONAL ORGANIZATION

The Four Big Countries

The United States

The United States is very different from any of the other nations, not only in size but also in complexity. The most important distinguishing feature—for the uses of evaluation and other analysis in policy-making—is the constitutional structure of the United States. The president and the Congress are elected in separate votes, are absolutely independent of one another, and their coordinate powers mean that each has the power to negate almost anything done by the other. Some of the relevant results of this unique system are that

- action is ordinarily based on compromises, and compromises cannot always stand the searching light of policy analysis;
- neither side fully trusts the other, and analyses and analytical organizations must thus be duplicated (which may lead to waste, but may also lead to better analysis through competition);
- the spirit of the entire system is pervaded with advocacy, and analysis is frequently intended and used as part of an adversary process; and
- Congress holds the executive branch responsible for the implementation of policies as intended by the Congress, even for some policies whose direct administration has been decentralized to the states and the localities. This is a major reason why Congress tends to create identifiable programs, the executive tends to set up identifiable agencies to administer these programs, and evaluation tends to examine such identifiable programs.

Although, in the United States, public policy has never really been unplanned, the best date on which to pinpoint the beginning of conscious policy planning and evaluation is 1961, when Secretary Robert McNamara introduced into the Defense Department a Planning, Programming, and Budgeting (PPB) system. PPB was constructed both from ideas he had brought with him from the Ford Motor Company and concepts of defense planning developed largely at the Rand Corporation. The basis of the system was the division of the defense budget into program packages defined by the military purposes of various capabilities, such as Strategic Forces and General Purpose Forces, rather than the conventional division of forces and budgets among Army, Navy, and Air Force, each of which was multipurpose. Individual decisions were to be justified by their contributions to these program package purposes; and, to some degree, evaluation of existing forces was to be made on the same basis.

In retrospect, the introduction of PPB into defense, although by no means perfect, should be considered a major success. In the short run the system, assisted by the strength of purpose of McNamara and his staff, forced defense decisions onto a far more rational basis than before. True, errors were made, including some big ones—the building of the TFX fighter-bomber was an excellent example of both the success and failure of the system. But in general, the military forces of the United States, particularly the strategic forces, were made far more cost-effective through McNamara's ministrations. Further, PPB had the lasting effect of forcing the military services, in their own self-defense, to promote a much more analytical group of officers than had gone into top positions before.

What worked for defense, however, did not work as well elsewhere. As has been mentioned, in 1965, President Johnson decreed that all the good things that had been done in PPB in defense should be spread through the civilian departments of the government. The system was to be managed by the Bureau of the Budget (BoB), the predecessor of the current Office of Management and Budget (OMB), and BoB took the curious step of making a major effort to introduce PPB into the departments but denying it a major role in its own budgetary decision-making. In most departments, PPB introduced a multiyear process of designing program packages which had little to do with the real decisions being made or the way they were made.

The real triumph of civil PPB, however, is that, as in the case of the Defense Department, it left behind a residue of good policy analysis in strong analytical groups which have had an effect on the making of policy in the executive branch. Such groups, typically headed by assistant secretaries for planning who report directly to the Cabinet secretaries, now exist in the Departments of Health, Education and Welfare (HEW); Housing and Urban Development (HUD); Labor; Agriculture; and Interior; as well as a number of independent or subordinate agencies. Within their departments or agencies the groups provide objective analysis, supplying top management with the best information and advice available; outside the departments they are advocates of the departmental interests in other organs of the executive branch and with the Congress. They are prototypical analysts in government, who function well insofar as they translate analysis into assistance with the perceived policy and political needs of their bosses. They also form a government-wide analytical community.

What exists in substantial measure in the executive departments of the United States federal government, however, does not exist at the center, for domestic policies (other than macroeconomic policy, which, as has been noted, is a special case). It does exist for defense and foreign policy in the staff of the National Security Council (NSC), but defense and nondefense cultures are very different. The determination of science policy, as has also been noted, is another special case with a different culture.

The failure to introduce meaningful policy analysis into the Bureau of the Budget during the heyday of PPB was not remedied under the Nixon administration when the bureau was converted to the Office of Management and Budget, with a corresponding shift of focus toward management and a softening of the strong role the earlier bureau had played in helping the president make budgetary choices. By the end of the Ford administration, the staff and powers of OMB were both much weaker than they had been eight years earlier; and President Carter's focus on the management issues he had dealt with as governor of Georgia, rather than the issues of choice and priorities that are the stuff of federal governance, weakened it further.

One potential alternative locus in the federal government for this kind of policy analytical capability was created in 1969 under the aegis of President Nixon's first domestic advisor, Daniel Patrick Moynihan. Moynihan set up the Domestic Council within the White House, but it did not develop an analytical capability, in spite of some initial intentions to use it in this direction. When John Ehrlichman succeeded Moynihan, the chance was lost. In 1977, the Domestic Council was reconstituted for the Carter administration, under Stuart Eizenstat, but it turned in the direction of being a coordinating and trouble-shooting organ for Eizenstat and the president, with little in the way of either analysts or analytical capabilities.

Since some departments continue in the post-PPB tradition of effective analysis, however, this lack of such analytical capability at the center leads to an imbalance which can have unfortunate results. A department with a superior capability to present an analytical case may win a battle for the wrong reasons, lacking a central capability to weigh conflicting analyses according to central (presidential) criteria. Examples of such a phenomenon exist.

Even where effective policy analysis is carried out in the United States, however, it deals largely with the ex ante choice of options rather than the ex post evaluation of programs. This is true even though probably a larger part of the public budget is devoted to evaluation in the United States than anywhere else. Evaluations are carried on within government, and government sponsors evaluations carried on by universities, companies, and nonprofit institutions. But, in contrast to the ex ante options analysis within the departments, it is difficult to establish a clear connection between evaluation studies and policy-making. Examples do exist—the effect of some early evaluations on the growth of the Headstart program for preschool poor children, for example—but they are infrequent.

One result of this tenuous connection between evaluation and policy-making has been a recent movement, particularly in HEW, to change from impact evaluations designed to provide a potential basis for major allocation decisions to smaller-scale efforts to work with program managers to identify the key changes needed to improve their programs. This is a move from performance measurement toward assistance evaluations. One difficulty with a full movement to assistance, however, is that Congress has been increasingly mandating large-scale impact evaluations, intending to use them when considering whether to renew programs, kill them, or change them. Indeed, the Congress is currently giving serious consideration to "Sunset Legislation" which would dictate periodic review of most programs.

A congressional mandate for performance measurement evaluation, however, is not necessarily followed by congressional use of the evaluative information. One reason has been alluded to: The adversary relations built into the U.S. Constitution make the Congress inherently distrustful of information received from the administration, even though the Congress has dictated that an administrative agency provide this information. One might then ask why the Congress does not set up an evaluative organization on its own side of the fence separating legislative from executive power. The congressionally established General Accounting Office (GAO) has, under congressional prodding in recent years, been moving from strict fiscal auditing and management evaluation toward ex post impact evaluation of federal programs. The newer ex ante policy option analyses of the Congressional Budget Office (CBO) have had more impact on various pieces of legislation (perhaps because ex ante studies are easier to carry out than ex post), and CBO analyses have increasingly been in demand by Congress in the four years of that organization's existence—against the predictions of many knowledgeable people who felt that such analyses could only upset the subtle bargaining processes by which Congress functions. One reason for the CBO's success is that, since the onset of PPB in 1965, Congress has been inundated by studies from the executive branch, many of which seemed to be of high quality but none of which were completely trusted. When congressional committees discovered they could get a high quality of analysis from an organization directly responsible to Congress, they gobbled it up.

In any case, to summarize the current evaluation and analysis needs of the federal government of the United States:

- The mismatch between the high level of activity and the low level of utilization of ex post evaluation in the executive branch indicates a need for some

changes, perhaps in the direction of the "helping" evaluations now being promoted in HEW.
- Congress increasingly needs and wants good ex post evaluation as an aid to legislative program review and decision.
- The lack of analytical capabilities for the central decision-making apparatus—the White House and environs—should be remedied.

The United Kingdom

Despite the common language, the United Kingdom is very different from the United States and indeed is quite different in real governmental form from other European countries with ostensibly similar structures. Like all European countries and Canada, the British government is unitary in form, without the executive/legislative split of the United States. But the British government is more unitary than most of the others. As in all complex countries, policy is subject to a multiplicity of constituency, interest group, and other pressures; as in all democratic countries, decision-making takes these pressures into account. Nonetheless, the decision-making process in Britain is far less divided than in the United States and substantially less than in a number of other European countries.

- Parliament chooses the prime minister, who chooses the cabinet. The cabinet—the government—makes policy and Parliament ratifies it, with any consistent failure to ratify ordinarily meaning the fall of the government. Since party discipline is strong enough to keep the majority party in line behind the government, this means that the government backed by a majority party normally need not fear parliamentary changes of any important policies. A prudent government will consult key Members of Parliament in advance, but it need not. The House of Commons is the world's premier debating society, and as such it affects policy through public opinion, but that is the major way it affects policy. This is quite different from some other European countries where the government must refer back to parliament on many issues.
- The prime minister substantially controls the cabinet and has the power to replace any other minister; the prime minister is thus literally "prime," which is different from some other European countries where ministers have independent power.
- The tradition of government is secrecy, more so than in any other western democracy. The papers of an outgoing government, for example, are sealed by civil servants from the incoming government. Although leaks do occur, the basic secrecy tradition leads to quiet government by insiders and, again, unitary power.
- Not only is the cabinet ruled by the prime minister, but cabinet ministers are victims of extreme overload. A minister must attend cabinet meetings and join in cabinet decisions; defend his policies and the government on the floor of the Parliament; give the ordinary speeches expected of high-level politicians in all democracies; attend to the needs of his parliamentary constituency; and run an

    operating department. The British cabinet minister does all this with virtually no staff other than the civil servants in his department. The most relevant result for this report is that he does not run his department very much.

- The traditionally very strong and politically neutral British Civil Service holds almost all operating posts except that of the minister, in all departments, and thus effectively run the departments.

- As has been noted, "London is a village." A small group of leading politicians, senior civil servants, and influential outsiders runs the village and the surrounding kingdom. This is not to imply that Britain is not democratic—the top village leadership is chosen democratically, and the civil service remains as strong as it is in large measure because its own strongest tradition is to follow the policies of the democratically chosen leadership. But it does mean that the day-to-day decisions and many of the major directions of public affairs are closely held, largely by civil servants.

Examples of analysis and evaluation should be sought, then, in the operating departments whose evaluation can be used as an aid to the efficient running of those departments. Such evaluation is done mostly by civil servants within the departments—excellent and effective policy analysis and real ex post evaluation is carried out and connected with policy making in health, housing (which is part of the Ministry of Environment), the Home Office, and elsewhere. It is not universal, because it requires the top civil servants of the department to be interested in such things, and not all are— but when they are it works well. Such evaluation and other analysis is carried out in the "truth" or governmental efficiency mode, as compared with the "advocacy" mode, although sometimes it is brought to the cabinet and considered in the light of political needs and ideologies. The story is told by some civil servants, for example (and denied by others), that a housing study which indicated that Britons are housed better than other Europeans was suppressed by the Labour government which wanted to continue heavy public housing programs, but has recently been picked up by the new Conservative government as indicating one area for the budgetary cutbacks desired by that government.

    The British have also had their tries at top-level PPB. In the 1960s, the Public Expenditure Survey (PES) was initiated, but this was primarily an effort to gather data to forecast expenditures for some years ahead, rather than an attempt to evaluate them, either ex ante or ex post. PES was followed in the early 1970s by Program Analysis Review (PAR), an attempt to begin a strong series of ex post evaluations of programs, under the aegis of the Treasury (which does the budgeting for the government). The civil servants in the ministries were reluctant to cooperate, and PAR has not worked very well.

    Treasury demands on departments for options on spending proposals have engendered more and better policy analysis in the departments. As with the United States Budget Bureau/Office of Management and Budget, how-ever, Treasury has not built its own analytical staff to weigh these options. More recently, an attempt has been made to strengthen and restructure some major parliamentary committees, particularly the Committee on Expenditure. Such a strengthening might carry with it the possibility for a searching review of governmental activities, with such review including evaluation. It is difficult, however, to find many people willing to take this possibility very seriously; a striking fact is that while parliament does substantially affect public opinion through Question Time and the like, parliamentary examination of public programs is deliberately made difficult. The key British tradition of separating political matters from those of the civil service leaves program operation on the nonpolitical side of the fence. Civil servants resent parliamentary interference with the efficiency of the way departments are run—and "efficiency" is interpreted very broadly. The other side of this coin is that civil servants are not supposed to utter public opinions on many matters.

One other British device that is sometimes used for evaluation is the commission—departmental, extradepartmental, and, for the most important issues, Royal. The commissions do in fact carry out evaluations when appropriate, and these do affect policy; but, unlike Swedish Royal Commissions, to mention another example, they are occasional rather than standard devices.

More significant, however, is an additional piece of machinery, recommended in a 1970 White Paper titled *Reorganisation of Central Government*. This is the Central Policy Review Staff (CPRS). CPRS is a group of 15 to 20 professionals, drawn both from within and outside of the civil service, for terms of about two years. It is nonpartisan in the tradition of the civil service, in fact as well as in concept. It reports to the cabinet as a whole. (Prime Ministers Wilson and Callaghan had, in addition, small staffs of their own, which carried out effective policy analysis, particularly in economic fields. However, that form did not become institutionalized and has not been recreated by Prime Minister Thatcher.)

In function, CPRS is halfway between the Eizenstat Domestic Council staff in the United States, which coordinates but does not analyze, and the offices of the Assistant Secretaries for Planning in the U.S. cabinet departments, which analyze and translate analysis for policy makers but tend to stay out of day-to-day management and political jockeying. CPRS is a coordinating and trouble-shooting staff, but is also analytical. Some of its analyses—notably one on the foreign service and another on the British motor car industry—are published, which is out of the ordinary for analyses done within the British public services. The more effective work of CPRS is inside, however, in the form of pieces containing or summarizing analysis, succinct enough to be read and understood by top civil service decision makers and ministers.

CPRS is not without flaws or fears. One fear mentioned by several observers, for example, is that the ratio of civil servants to outsiders is increasing and that the staff might be captured by the traditional Civil Service. A more overarching criticism was expressed in a recent, unsigned article in a British journal (*New Society*, 1979):

> The founding father of the CPRS, Lord Rothschild, listed seven main aims for the CPRS. On all of them it has fallen short. . . . it has lacked not brains, but clout—the clout to transform bright ideas into practice. . . . Should this half-cock CPRS . . . be wound up? That would be a pity. How could it be made to work better? One change, above all, could achieve this. The myth that CPRS serves ministers collectively could be abandoned, and the CPRS converted into a Prime Minister's Department—her (or his) ears and arms in the Whitehall jungle.

The disappointment expressed in this critique is echoed by some British observers, but from other well-informed Britons the praise is stronger. The difference may be one of half-full/half-empty; more concretely, it may depend on the expectations one had for such policy analysis. An American who has had his expectations for the effectiveness of policy analysis suitably modified by the failure of PPBS and subsequent events can give CPRS, even as it exists, high marks relative to the possible if not to the ideal.

More important than abstract grade-giving for the applicability of the CPRS concept elsewhere, however, is the suggestion that CPRS become "a Prime Minister's Department." A parallel institution in the United States would constitutionally have to be "a President's Department"; and if the major flaw in Britain's CPRS has been its responsibility to the cabinet as a collective, then this would automatically be avoided in the United States.

Were CPRS to be paralleled in the United States, however, one of its key attributes could not be reproduced, nor would it be replicable in other western countries. CPRS was set up initially under Prime Minister Heath's Conservative government, survived the transition to Labour government without any extraordinary personnel changes, and has now apparently survived the transition back to Prime Minister Thatcher's Tory government. This is in the British nonpartisan Civil Service tradition, but in the United States and other nations where this tradition is weaker, a staff that highly placed would undoubtedly have to turn over almost completely in personnel with a change of administrations. Nonetheless, CPRS represents, at least potentially, the highest and best use of policy analysis—including evaluation—in western governments, and as such may form an important western model.

On the other hand, the needs of Great Britain itself may require a move toward some other western forms—more openness in particular, but connected with this is an advocacy role and increased flexibility of and around the civil service. In addition, ministers need time and/or staff to become effective administrators of their departments. Given all this, policy, and analysis as an aid to policy, may become much more effective.

France

Britain has a civil service tradition going back at least to the time of Queen Victoria which has been strong enough to survive and in many ways to dominate major changes of government in a nonconsensus society which has been and remains riven by real class hostilities. France has a civil service which, while in many ways different, is at least as strong and goes back at least as far as Napoleon (and in some ways much further). Furthermore, in France this civil service has been working in tandem with a political government which has in effect remained unchanged for almost two decades under the Fifth Republic.

The implied stability underlies public processes and the application of analysis to these processes in France. The stability is not always obvious, but at the level of real day-to-day governance it is always there. It is true that the French government has changed in form more frequently than have those of the United States or the United Kingdom, but it is also true that the basic institutions of government have survived at least eight successful revolutions since 1789, and a number of unsuccessful ones, including those of the Algerian *colons* and the students, in the last 25 years. When one naive foreigner, hearing French officials talk about the strength of the establishment, mentioned that he had always thought of France as being very much a divided society, he was informed that the divisions are philosophical, abstract, and ideological and that real government goes on unchanged.

Various waves of reform, including a French version of PPB, have crashed on this rock of governmental stability and eroded it only a little, if at all. The governmental establishment itself, however, contains traditional instruments that are to some extent applied to evaluation and other policy analysis. Two of these are the Court of Accounts (Cour des Comptes) and the Inspectorate of Finances. The Court, as its name indicates, is a judicial (or perhaps quasi-judicial) body. Its major function is fiscal audit, but in recent years it has been extending at least as far as management analysis of French administration. It publishes an annual review of its audits and carries out a good deal of behind-the-scenes activity to improve administrative management; but it does not undertake impact evaluation. The Inspectorate of Finance is the traditional elite corps, taking in the top graduates of the Ecole National d'Administration. The Corps of inspectors divides itself between two segments. One, the Inspectorate itself, is another audit body—within the administrative structure. The other consists of individual inspectors within the administrative agencies who carry out ad hoc audits of major expenditures, at the request of the Minister of the Budget, but also advise decision makers. It is not clear to what extent the inspectors are evaluators or analysts, but they probably are not. Nonetheless, the Inspectorate, because it is very much a part of the establishment, may have a potential for carrying out effective evaluation within the system—if the establishment sees the need for such evaluation.

Somewhat less traditional, but still very much within the system, is the Commissariat du Plan, ordinarily known as Le Plan, which carries out the five-year (largely economic) planning for the government. Le Plan does not receive very high marks within France for effectiveness in changing long-run directions or outcomes. The 1976–80 national plan was generally considered a wish list and was not followed in detail or in the large; however, the 1981–86 plan, now being debated, does stress specific priorities and may have more effect. In any case, Le Plan carries out policy analysis, but this is mainly of a traditional economic type; it does not extend with any regularity to particular program operations and directions. An occasional program memorandum is written for and used by the Premier or the Council of Ministers, thus providing France with some central policy analysis.

Outside this traditional structure, France, too, has made its try at PPB—known as Rationalisation des Choix Budgetaires (RCB). RCB has largely faded out, leaving behind two residuals. It still exists in the Ministry of the Budget, which was always the central organization. Within the ministry it is run by the short-range economic forecasting group. Most officials outside the ministry contend that, aside from standard forecasting, the group and RCB have very little effect. What is clear, however, is that the Budget Ministry RCB group is not the nerve center of a vital agency-crossing policy analysis group as it was supposed to have been. The cause to which this is attributed in France is its nontraditional nature, which is related to the causes for PPB failure in the other countries.

RCB still exists in small groups in some ministries, where one may get an argument about whether or not it is isolated and ineffective—although the evidence seems heavier that it is isolated. One individual in a subministerial position approximating an American Assistant Secretary for Planning indignantly denied that he had anything to do with RCB. He thought the ministry still had an RCB group, but he wasn't sure.

To sum up, at the central level of France there seems to be little real analytical or evaluative activity *a la* CPRS, or even a central staff like that of the U.S. Domestic Council, with any significant and regular effect on cabinet or presidential decision-making. Nor does there seem much immediate hope for any regularized central analytical capability, although it is possible that Le Plan or the Inspectorate of Finances will move that way. The very centralization of the French establishment and institutions, however (Paris, too, is a village), creates an environment in which such a central group could be very effective, if the establishment felt the need for such assistance.

Nonetheless, France does seem to have a substantial amount of effective evaluation and analysis affecting policy decisions in some of its ministries, including at least health, labor, industry, agriculture, higher education, and energy. In addition, an occasional special committee, frequently headed by a counsellor of state, may sponsor or carry out and use analysis effectively.

When a foreigner commented that France seems to have a lot of active evaluation and other analysis at detailed and functional levels, one perceptive (if dour) French observer conceded that this activity does have substantial influence on the periphery, but contended that it does not touch the central institutions of France. This leaves the outsider somewhat puzzled. The specific case of effective evaluation which had been brought up had to do with the creation by the Ministry of Higher Education of new university-level technical institutes, which seemed to be well designed for their purpose, and further, seemed to have well-conceived evaluations feeding back into continuing design of the institutes. The French observer, however, noted that the traditional and very strong university structure of France remained unaffected by the new institutes, by the Ministry, or by evaluation.

This leads, however, to a philosophical question (as do so many issues in France): Does one effect change better by changing institutions or by adding to them? Given the strength of French institutions, it is clear that policy analysis at the ministry and functional level is much more likely to add than to change. New forms of educational institutions, health institutions, industrial institutions, and so forth, will keep France abreast or ahead of the rest of the modern world, but they will not substitute for the old institutions which not only remain in existence but remain very powerful. For the governmental center, however, the attempted addition of RCB has not worked; adaptation can, but only when the central institutions see a clear need for adaptation.

The Federal Republic of Germany

Germany is as decentralized as the United Kingdom and France are centralized.

- In some ways Germany is even more federal than the United States. The 11 German Laender vary less in their policies than the 50 American states. Virtually all tax policy is made in Bonn, for example, although a much larger portion of tax revenues is sent down to the Laender than to the American states under revenue-sharing. However, the German Laender administer practically all governmental activities—with federal funds and under general federal guidelines, but without federal control. This is particularly important because most of the Laender are governed by the CDU/CSU coalition, which is the minority opposition in the Federal Bundestag.

- The Bundestag is much more powerful than the British House of Commons or the French Assembly. The formal system of parliamentary government is similar to that of Great Britain, but in Germany the parliament must be reckoned with by the cabinet on specific policy issues as well as the major issues of state. This is true at least under coalition rule, which has governed Germany for more than a decade. It was probably less true under Adenauer, but Germans consider the current situation to be the norm. In addition, the coalition parties themselves must be consulted over policy issues.

- Unlike British or French ministers, the German ministers themselves are strong and independent. Also partly an effect of coalition government, Helmut Schmidt is considered a strong chancellor, and, like the British Prime Minister, he has the de jure power to dismiss ministers. Politically, however, this power is more difficult to use than in Britain. Presumably, ministers can be dropped or would leave if they fell out of line with governmental policy, but the relative weakness at the center means that ministers can and do act independently in wide areas of policy.

- On the other hand, the ministers do not administer directly even many of those governmental activities which are not delegated to the Laender. Federal operations are ordinarily managed by autonomous agencies not fully responsible to the ministries. Federal manpower programs, for example, are not administered by the Labor Ministry but by an autonomous institution, located in Nuremberg, 400 kilometers from Bonn. The Nuremberg organization has its own research and analysis institute. Autonomous federally funded policy research institutions abound throughout Germany. Although many of these are concerned more with various aspects of economic policy than with program operations and evaluation, they set a very different scene than that, for example, in France.

This degree of decentralization leads to a strong likelihood that opportunities for policy analysis and evaluation will be diffuse. They *are* diffuse, although Germany has had its fling at central PPB, which failed. Although the reasons for the failure are somewhat different from those in other countries, they all fit under the general heading of failure to meet political realities.

In Germany in 1970, an attempt was made to establish a central planning office in the office of the chancellor. This was part of a conscious effort to strengthen the chancellor relative to the other ministers. It was killed by the ministers and ministries. A useful facility still exists and provides analysis, including political analysis, to the chancellor, but it is much less effective than had been the hope. This weakening is attributed to several causes, some of which are idiosyncratic: First, both the leader of the attempt and other observers agree that he did it rather clumsily. Second, Chancellor Willy

Brandt did not fully appreciate the uses of an analytical capability, being more of an ad hoc operator; Helmut Schmidt, who was a powerful finance minister at the time, led the attempt to kill it—now, it is said, he wishes he had it. Nonetheless, the underlying reality seems to be that it is difficult to change a political power structure that does not care to be changed by tinkering with institutions. As noted, the same is true in France; the one place where centralized policy analysis has worked relatively well is Britain, with an already strong centralism.

As with other PPB failures, a number of analysts remain in various ministries, as well as a small informal analytical community. As in the United States, these analysts are in positions of influence in many areas. The departmental analytical organizations in both countries are effective insofar as they translate analysis to fit the perceived needs of ministers and other top decision makers, and they are both political—at least compared with the British model of nonpartisanship. The German analytical groups, however, are substantially more political than the American in at least one way. Those analysts who are party-affiliated tend to be members of the SPD, the larger government party, while the more conservative regular civil servants tend to belong to various parties or none at all. The analytical groups thus function informally to ensure that government policy is carried out in the ministries. Indeed, even in ministries whose ministers are members of the FDP, the other coalition party, the analysts are sometimes the SPD chancellor's people in the ministry.

In any case, these analytical groups do carry out analysis, including ex post evaluation in some agencies—foreign aid, regional development, some aspects of health and manpower—but their potentialities are limited by the decentralized administrative structure and by a limited view of the needs of evaluation. Possibilities are also limited by political needs such as that expressed by one high-level civil service policy analyst—that analysis can upset the delicate structures created by political bargaining: "The German government must run to consensus, and evaluation is helpful precisely insofar as it helps establish and maintain that consensus," a view similar to that expressed in regard to the U.S. Congress.

Germany combines the homogeneity and much of the consensus of such smaller countries as Sweden. The consensus itself is an interesting one. As put by one official, the basic German political/economical beliefs are in independent ministries, a free economy (a belief frequently violated in practice), the social programs established by Bismarck, and program administration by the Laender. Another person added to this list a belief in the perfection of German officials—which makes evaluation difficult.

Given all this, a remarkable quantity of evaluative and other study is carried out in Germany in contexts where it can and frequently does have an effect on policy. The diffusion of German public administration means that evaluation becomes a game everyone can play. Perhaps most interesting are advocacy evaluations carried out by or on behalf of interest groups. For example, the health care field in Germany is at least as decentralized as any other. National health insurance is administered by independent organizations at the Laender level. In recent years, different interest groups involved in health care—the organization of Laender health-care groups, hospitals, physicians working in offices, industrial physicians—have set up their own research facilities which carry out serious evaluation studies as an input to the bargaining of their parent groups.

Indeed, evaluation research in Germany is still mainly a tool of defending or attacking positions. Not all German evaluation is advocacy, but one gets the feeling that such evaluation is as useful and may be more effective than more objective evaluations carried out elsewhere.

In any case, Germany conducts diverse but active evaluation and other analytical efforts in a vigorous but atomized overall system. The prospects for any kind of central policy-analytical aid to decision-making in German are dimmer than those in the United States or France. Even France could effectively build such a facility, if it were desired, but in Germany political and administrative centralization would have to come first, however unlikely. As things now stand, an attempt to centralize administration by using central planning would be likely to fail, as it has before.

Three Small Consensus Nations

Sweden, Norway, and the Netherlands are all small nations: slightly more than 10 million people in the Netherlands, 8 million in Sweden, and about 4 million in Norway. They are all governed by coalitions of more than one party. The key point for this report, however, is that all three nations are governed largely by consensus. (That this is true is in itself a consensus view.) The range from left to right among groups with any meaningful constituencies is not great; and although there is no consensus about relative shares of income and power, there is consensus about the role of government in determining those shares.

As a result, the main role of public administration is to improve itself—to search for efficiency and "good government." Within this context, the function of evaluation and other policy analysis is not advocacy and not clarifying positions on great issues, but truth-finding. Analysis brings nonpartisan expertise to this good government search, just as in the similar American movement which began in municipalities and western states at the turn of the century and which still continues.

Sweden

Sweden is almost a nonpartisan state. After years of majority Social Democratic rule were ended by electoral erosion in the early 1970s, this party ruled as a minority for a few years and then was upset again by a coalition of what are called the "bourgeois parties" (although to an outsider, Sweden appears a bourgeois nation, from left to right). The upset was based not on a social issue but rather on the largely symbolic issue of the uses of nuclear power for energy generation. The bourgeois coalition was out of power for a time, and Sweden was ruled by the Liberal Party with about one-tenth of the seats in the Riksdag; however, elections in September 1979 made possible the reestablishment of the coalition under the leadership of the Center Party.

It makes little difference which party governs, however, since most policies change little. One of the chief characteristics of Swedish public affairs is that most activities are run by independent agencies not really responsible to the ministries. The structure is similar to that of Germany, where change in activities occurs more through marginal changes to a permanent structure than through programs in the American sense. In Sweden, the independence of administration from politics is much stronger than in Germany. Swedish public agencies (as well as other concerned Swedes), for example, have a right *(remissinstitut)* to be heard before new legislation is passed. (One Swedish observer did suggest, however, that agency independence had been weaker under the Social Democratic government, when the civil servants and the politicians were much closer to one another.)

The independent operating agencies carry out much self-evaluation designed to improve the efficiency of their operations. In addition, in Sweden, the Royal Commission is a way of life. It is an unwritten rule that no major public changes shall take place without first being examined by a Royal Commission, which also carries out evaluation.

Evaluation is thus endemic throughout the Swedish system; further, it is all carried out and published openly. The trouble with this, however, is that, as one political official said, the evaluation is evaluation of problems and always comes out with a recommendation for increased expenditures to solve the problems. Sweden, however, is now in an era of relatively declining resources available for public purposes, and evaluations that suggest ways to spend more money do not help. As a result, a need felt at the political level is for a CPRS-like group responsible to the prime minister or the cabinet to use analysis and evaluation in ways that are responsive to the government's perceived problems, including tight budgetary requirements.

This is the basic picture: independent agencies independently evaluating themselves, but with a feeling at the governmental center that more is needed. Left out of this picture are the parts of the Swedish system of evaluation and analysis one hears about most frequently. They are left out because their significance is ordinarily substantially exaggerated by non-Swedes. Three separate organizations have been the subjects of major attention:

- The National Audit Board (Riksrevisionverket) is an independent commission similar to those running governmental activities. It represents one more example of a failed PPB experiment. The Audit Board was begun about 12 years ago to do large studies—effectiveness auditing on a cycle that would cover all public activities over a number of years. For a while it did with a flair. The difficulty has been, however, that flamboyance brought with it political liabilities. In addition, effectiveness auditing is difficult and prone to produce generalities which are of little operational assistance to anyone, which is a potentially important lesson for anyone who contemplates a strict separation of evaluation from other forms of policy analysis. Finally, the Audit Board's effort to cover every public activity on a cycle became overwhelming, substituting a fetish for a necessity. This also carries with it a possible warning for devices such as "Sunset Legislation," designed to let nothing slip through the net, or nothing but specified exceptions. In any case, the Audit Board is now rethinking its overall strategy, retreating, in the meantime, from effectiveness evaluation back to management audit, although not all the way back to purely fiscal audit.
- The Management Agency (Statskontoret) is intended in some general way to carry out management rationalization projects. It is not now doing policy analysis, but is notable mainly for being a 300-year-old body whose main current function is supervising Swedish computer capabilities.
- The Secretariat for Future Studies began, under Social Democratic Prime Minister Palme, as something close to the British CPRS. As it became more analytical ("academic," in the word of a former member), it moved further away from policy, both in subject matter and organizational location within the government. It is now generally viewed as irrelevant. Without any specific evidence on this point, it seems possible that it became too rigid—too unwilling to translate its analysis into forms relating to the concerns of the decision makers.

These formal organizations of Swedish evaluation are thus not relevant to the real course of evaluation and other analysis in the nation. The real course is that much is going on at operational levels—as in every other country. In Sweden, however, the new resource stringency leads to a demand for even more, and consensus makes it possible that the demand will be filled.

Norway

In Norway, unlike Sweden, the ministries run government activities. Otherwise, similarities dominate. Norway is governed by a stable minority government—slightly less than a majority, with sufficient outside support. Further, despite North Sea oil, Norway, too, feels constrained economically, although these constraints arrived perhaps two years later than in other western countries. Norway is less concerned with evaluation than elsewhere (it is less concerned with most things, perhaps because it is a very small country).

Nonetheless, the Norwegians manifest the standard pattern of a variety of management-oriented evaluation studies in the ministries. Since these affect programs for which the ministries have responsibility, the evaluations have influence. In addition, Norway has two central organizations in the Ministry of Finance which carry out analysis and evaluation.

The long-range planning section of the Finance Ministry is separate from the budgetary section. Like Le Plan in France, it produces a regular plan, but this is a four-year plan deliberately tied to the four-year election cycle. The plan is produced in election years, with the staff analysis done by the planning group, and it becomes the platform of the incumbent government. Like all multiyear plans, it has a certain abstract quality, but in the course of working on the plan the long-range planning group produces or sponsors a number of studies which feed into annual budget choices.

Within the budget section of the Finance Ministry is a short-range planning group. Rather than carrying out any comprehensive program of analyses, this group devotes itself largely to promoting and assisting with studies in the various ministries. It carries out exemplary analyses, but the preferred mode is to work with the ministerial departments in designing and executing policy studies.

In addition to these two in-government organizations, Norway has its parallel to the Royal Commissions in Sweden and the United Kingdom— 400–500 ad hoc committees delving into a variety of subjects, frequently carrying out or promoting analytical approaches.

Some Norwegians caution that the overall picture of policy analysis feeding into decision-making should not be overplayed—the decisions are still political, and, as in the case of the four-year plan, the analyses are used politically. Nonetheless, if one begins with the premise that public decisions are always political, the low-key contribution of analyses to these political decisions seems at least as high in Norway as in any other nation.

The Netherlands

The Netherlands is a consensus country similar in many ways to the Scandinavian nations. It is typically ruled by a coalition—at the moment a center-right coalition, but frequently a center-left one. The ministers are not staffed to run the operating departments of the government, and the agencies thus tend to run themselves and do routine management evaluations as in Norway and Sweden. As one Dutchman in a high but nonofficial position put it: "Democracy in Holland, in fact, means that government officials run the country, advised by committees they appoint, and they allow the ministers to sign their documents."

The Netherlands has neither a strong central government nor an effective central evaluation facility, but it does have three organizations which carry out analysis at higher or more general levels than the individual ministries. Two of these are within the public administration:

- The Netherlands Scientific Council is a long-range planning organization. It originally tried to coordinate the analyses of others, but it now does its own studies of a long-range type, either on its own initiative or on government request. These are automatically included on the agenda of the cabinet, and the cabinet must react to their recommendations within three months. The reports are published and may thus also affect public decisions through their effects on public opinion. In a larger nonconsensus nation, this degree of openness would raise questions concerning the abilities of a group that concentrates on published work to affect the inner operations of government, but the council denies that this is a problem in the Netherlands.
- The Commission for the Development of Policy Analysis (the Dutch acronym is COBA) is a group with a much shorter time focus. It is part of the Ministry of Finance, and, like the short-run planning group in Norway, it sees its job more as stimulating and improving analyses within the various operating ministries than in carrying out studies on its own. COBA works with the ministries and allows them the publication rights on various joint analyses. It is being pushed toward becoming more of a central analytical group, but seems to be resisting.
- The Netherlands Organization for Applied Scientific Research (TNO) is a quasi-governmental, nonprofit organization. It is very large; with 4500 employees, it would, if scaled to the size of the United States, employ about 90,000, or 20–25,000 in Britain, France, or Germany. Such comparisons, of course, are not meaningful, because governmental complexity does not increase proportionally with size, but they do make the point that TNO is very large for Holland. At this size, TNO studies are mostly outside of policy analysis, stressing in particular engineering and other aspects of hard science. But it does carry out some policy analyses, and even a small portion of so large an organization is relevant in the Netherlands.

As noted, all the current activities in the Netherlands add up to a great deal of analysis mainly at departmental levels. The Dutch, however, have devoted some effort and discussion and some interorganizational political controversy to the possibility of a central policy analysis "think tank." At one point, one governmental organization asked an American group to set up such a think tank for them, but this request was declined. Although a question exists why one more organization is needed in a country of this size, one way or another the Netherlands does seem to be moving toward a central analytical capability.

Canada: An In-Between Country

Canada is in-between in many ways. Its population is less than half that of France, and only slightly less than twice that of the Netherlands. It is British in traditions and governmental form, but American in many habits and in geographical spread. Its federalism is more diffuse than that of the United States, but less than that of Germany. It is Scandinavian in location and climate; it resembles Belgium in divided ethnicity.

Canada is thus something of a contradiction in terms of the issues discussed here. The government of Canada must grapple with very large issues and divisions—English versus French and West versus East—which prevent it from becoming a consensus state and may lead to its demise as a single country. Nonetheless, in the focus of governmental administration on improving the efficiency and effectiveness of ongoing programs, it bears some resemblance to a consensus state, with an intent to use policy analysis and evaluation for purposes of objective improvement rather than as an input to partisan positions for bargaining.

Canada seems to resemble Britain more than any of the other countries so far discussed. Even though in recent years Canada has been governed by minority governments with all of the potential need for parliamentary bargaining that implies in other countries, the Canadian parliament is quite weak. While preserving the British form of a parliament which appoints the government and then is rarely consulted on policy matters, Canadian parliamentarians are divided among three parties and four regions, which means that important committees and other groups must be composed of multiples of 12. This, in turn, leads to a lack of stability and a failure of individuals to build up expertise which in Britain helps make parliamentary debate a meaningful procedure. Nor is Ottawa a village in the sense that London is; with the exception of government, the most important Canadian activities are carried out in other cities, some of them very distant. This weakens parliament even further by inhibiting the development of strong "in-groups."

As in Britain, however, the Canadian prime minister has the power to appoint and dismiss the other ministers; as in Britain, ministers run their departments de jure, with the senior civil service occupying virtually all of the department posts except that of the minister, so that the de facto situation is in somewhat more doubt. The Canadian civil service is perceptibly more partisan than the British, with some movement by defeated or other politicians into the senior civil service in Canada.

Overall, then, Canada has a strong central government, capable of creating and administering a variety of programs. The main constraint on this is federalism, with the political issues over the federal structure paralleling the social issues that divide the country. The divisions, however, have thus far not had a major effect on the administration of welfare programs or, to a somewhat lesser extent, resource programs.

Like all the other countries, Canada has had a PPB experiment which failed. Like Germany, it has also failed in its attempt to create a central analytical facility similar to CPRS in Britain. In Canada, the reasons for failure were more fortuitous than in Germany; indeed, some Canadians want to try again. In the meantime, as in all of the countries, policy analysis is going on in the departments, in areas as diverse as manpower and mineral resources.

The PPB and CPRS attempts took place, beginning in the late 1960s, in the Treasury Board, which carries out the central budgetary function. From 1969–1970 through 1975–1976, a Planning Branch in the Secretariat to the Treasury Board began turning out an increasing number of apparently policy-relevant studies, blending ex ante policy options analysis with ex post program impact evaluation. These were intended both as important studies in their own right and as evaluation examples for the departments of government. From 1976 to 1978, these activities were tuned down and moved toward management analyses under a new structure. The reason for this change is the subject of disagreement. The studies were either too irrelevant or they were too relevant and they hurt. What may well have been the case is that they were relevant to policy but paid too little attention to the political concerns that change policy. They were too relevant from the standpoint of a "truth" model of the uses of policy analysis; irrelevant from the standpoint of an advocacy model. In any case, they were ended.

In 1977, however, the auditor-general of Canada, an independent watchdog official, wrote a report decrying the lack of effective evaluation of public programs. As a result, a new post was created, again under the Treasury Board. The comptroller-general of Canada reports to the Treasury Board in a channel separate from the budgeting function. The comptroller-general inherited part of the staff of the old Planning Branch, but their primary current function is not to do policy analysis, but rather sponsor ex post evaluation within the departments.

After the election of May 1979, the new Progressive Conservative government began making major changes in the structure of government, and these seemed likely to portend changes in these functions. The short tenure of the Clark government, however, and the return of the first Canadian government in many years with a full parliamentary majority reopened the situation. At this writing it is not clear where the Liberals will move in regard to policy analysis and evaluation.

Belgium: A Special Case

Belgium is, by the admission of many of its own officials, a somewhat artificial country, created a century and a half ago and still trying to find itself. The dominant fact is biculturalism, the division between French-speaking Walloons in the south and the larger number of Dutch-speaking Flemings in the north. In addition, Brussels, although heavily French, is a separate entity. A plurality of French speakers in Wallonia and Brussels are Socialists, a plurality of Flemings are Christian Democrats. Given other divisions as well, Belgium is governed under an eight-party system (plus minor linguistic parties), which requires a difficult balancing act. Add to this the existence of both a clerical-anticlerical conflict and very strong pressure groups—trade unions and others—and both government and society in Belgium become exercises in political bargaining.

Biculturalism is, of course, a central fact in Canada also, but differences between the two countries lead to completely different styles of governance. Belgium seems to have substantially less potential of actually splitting apart than sometimes seems to be the case in Canada; but keeping the country unified dominates every other political and social issue in Belgium, whereas in Canada many public issues have very little to do with the French/English division. As a result, the Canadian potential for using evaluation and policy analysis to assist in bringing about better public policy seems—both to Canadians and to foreigners—to be substantial; the Belgian potential seems—again, to both Belgians and foreigners—to be virtually nonexistent.

The Belgian system of compromise has led to a government structure with:

- relatively independent ministers, with ministries distributed to balance the structure of the governing coalition;
- minsterial cabinet—25 or so political appointees in each ministry, changing with the minister, drawn in substantial measure from the pressure groups, and working more as political operatives than as analysts;
- a low-status civil service, making few decisions; and
- a poor statistical system, not equipped, among other things, to produce regional statistics which might provide a basis for analysis to support the compromise (among other reasons, there is a suspicion that statistical analysis might instead undermine the compromise).

Belgium tried PPB and failed because of the fear that it might upset the balance. It has also tried to use Le Plan—similar to the French organization of the same name—to affect policy; and although this has had some marginal effect on capital budgeting (Belgium is one of the few countries to have a capital budget at the national level), it marks the upper limit of the use of policy analysis in Belgium. Unlike the other countries, little significant or effective work seems to take place even in the departments.

If, to an American, the consensus nations of Sweden, Norway, and the Netherlands bear some resemblance to middle-size American states, Belgium seems similar to New York City—with the analogy providing the following insights:

- In both Belgium and New York, government is based on a set of ethnic/political compromises.
- In both Belgium and New York, financial auditing is important and tends to divert what impulses exist toward policy evaluation. Belgium has a Cour des Comptes similar to the French version, except that the Belgian court has no

pretenses toward evaluation. New York has long put major importance on the function of the comptroller and, since that city's fiscal crisis, on a parallel set of other auditing institutions.

- Both governments separate their current and capital budgets, with only the latter, in principle, financed by borrowing. To an economist, this makes sense for a city which, unlike a nation, must limit its borrowing power because it cannot print money to pay back the loans. It makes less sense for a large country, but may also be reasonable for a smaller country very dependent upon international trade and finance.
- Capital budgeting, however, is a useful device only if it is used as intended. New York, before its fiscal crisis, loaded more and more current items into the capital budget so that it could finance them by borrowing. Belgium is doing the same.
- Both Belgium and New York have the feeling of heading toward fiscal disaster, with commitments exceeding any possible resources, but with the delicate nature of the basic compromise making it politically impossible to do anything about it until it happens. New York said, "The federal government won't let us go down the drain," and turned out to be right. The most optimistic statement heard in Belgium (the likelihood of disaster is a Belgian, not a foreigner's, observation) is that "things will change because they cannot be managed on the current basis."

In any case, the implication for this report is that policy analysis has very little to do with it at this stage. The paradox is that such analysis—were it allowed by the political situation—could be extremely useful in Belgium, as it could have been in New York. Policy analysis works at its best when it can dive into a bad situation, point out a lot of obvious and some not-so-obvious errors, and create some options out of what remains; it is less effective when dealing with subtleties which may depend upon necessary analytical simplifications. In Belgium, the problems susceptible to analysis are gross ones, but they do not yet transcend the problems that would be brought about by breaking the political compromise.

The European Communities: A Very Special Case

The European Communities is an entity with three heads and a thin, but not illusory body. It has an administrative apparatus in Brussels, a parliament in Strasbourg, and a judiciary—including a Court of Auditors—in Luxembourg. The policy reality of the Communities contains one major program, agriculture, which is a true multinational effort controlled by the government-appointed Council of the Communities rather than the popularly elected parliament. This is a uniquely international program; it is said in Bonn that most German programs are operated by the Laender, defense is national, but to find out about German agriculture one must go to Brussels.

In addition, the Communities run one minor but hopeful set of programs in regional development and allied fields. These small discretionary efforts are at least nominally responsible to the elected parliament.

Both the administrative apparatus and the Court of Auditors have, separately, become interested in evaluation centered initially on the discretionary programs. In both cases, the interest is only beginning and thus can show no effects. Ultimately, it is hoped that evaluation will go beyond the discretionary programs to the larger ones in the mainstream. In any case, effectiveness of evaluation or of other policy analysis will necessarily follow rather than lead the growth of the power of the Communities. No current prognosis predicts rapid growth, although the new directly elected parliament may develop some real power, which might be augmented by a good analytical staff. Further, well-conceived Communities evaluation programs might at least provide some models for the member nations.

SOME TENTATIVE CONCLUSIONS

These are different countries—each a democratic country ruled by its own politics. The differences are crucial to this report on policy analysis and evaluation: No analysis will make Belgium into a consensus country or give France the traditions of Britain. Nor will clear thinking provide a parliamentary form of government the artifacts that depend on the checks and balances of the United States. In recent years, members-and-staff delegations of various parliaments have come through Washington and visited the Congressional Budget Office (CBO). That office has a reputation for carrying out good and effective policy analysis, and the parliamentarians want to know how they can obtain such assistance. The real answer, unfortunately, is that they cannot. Congress can get good analysis because Congress has real policy power; as has been pointed out, even the strongest parliaments have the power only to ratify and sometimes be consulted. Analysis cannot change this situation, nor does such a structure provide the basis for bringing in good analysis.

Despite the weight of these differences among the nations, however, some tentative generalizations about policy analysis and evaluation can be drawn.

(1) At the departmental working level—the functional level—the needs and capabilities of the countries do tend to converge. Health provides a prime example here. All the countries except for the United States have national health care systems. These systems are different—the British is quite centralized, for example; the German system is decentralized—and they call forth different institutional forms for evaluation. Nonetheless, all the systems are measured by such indicators as mortality, morbidity, and payments to doctors. Similarly, all the countries including the United States

have problems of too many hospital beds and/or maldistribution of hospital beds according to the needs of different areas and populations. Controlling hospital costs is thus a common problem for policy analysis.

This sort of commonality does not reach across the board to all social problems and programs. Education, for example, is so tied to national culture that the problems differ more from country to country; and even where they do seem common—a number of countries are concerned with the issue of comprehensive schools versus allegedly "elite" institutions, for example—they are highly political. The importance of political inputs to such issues does not necessarily preclude policy analysis, but it may mean that transnational lessons will not be very useful.

(2) At the higher levels of government, however, the most striking commonality remains the failure of Planning, Programming, Budgeting systems. To some extent, the international reach of the failure was due to the fact that it was touted initially as an international lesson to be learned. The adoption of PPB in many countries was based on the early model of the United States, together with the American cultural/political leadership of the early 1960s. Indeed, this was true even for France, which explicitly rejected such U.S. leadership. But perhaps even more important in the adoption of this sytem was the international tendency of public administration to move toward rigidly formalized structures like that represented by the program categories of PPB, and to ignore the fact that the decision systems remain political. One possible lesson of this—at least for the United States—is that the rigid cycle of evaluation implied by Sunset Legislation may fail for similar reasons, as the formal commitment of the Riksrevisionverket to evaluate *all* programs on a cycle has failed in Sweden.

(3) The most important generality, however, is a positive one—that of CPRS. The lesson does not apply to all countries, but for some it is applicable and potentially important.

To be clear, this discussion of CPRS begins with the author's belief that long antedates the beginning of this project: For the United States, at least, a central policy-analytical facility, in or near the Executive Office of the President is needed as a major aid to making policy. Equally clearly, however, there was no difficulty finding evidence backing up this belief. The relevant American political history has already been outlined: the decline of the Bureau of the Budget/Office of Management and Budget; the failure of the Domestic Policy Council staff to turn toward analysis; and the gradual strengthening of the policy analytical staffs within the departments and agencies. It is the last of these continuing events that provides the paradox; the contributions of the agency staffs are not hidden (they are generally agreed to), yet no move to provide a parallel central facility has gone very far. Most recently, President Carter started his administration with the explicit belief that he would make policy in conjunction with his cabinet (and the Eizenstat staff's focus on coordination reflects this). The assumption that such cabinet government was possible in the American system has gradually been abandoned, but this has not been reflected in appropriate changes in White House staffing. Yet it seems reasonable to contend that much of the reason for the failure of the administration to make and hold to strong and relatively consistent policy choices has been the lack of a staff to examine the consequences of such choices.

An American CPRS would necessarily differ from the British model in that the members could not ordinarily cross from one administration to another; in this regard, the American tradition is very political as compared with that of the Civil Service in Britain. The point demonstrated in the United Kingdom, however, is that a CPRS can be helpful to a strong central government. And, despite the vast differences between the British and the American forms, the power of the British Prime Minister to control his or her own government is in practice similar to that of the President of the United States. In the United States, this central power is virtually unchangeable because it is in the written Constitution; given its existence, it needs help, and a CPRS is one form that such help may take.

The same may be true for other countries, aside from Germany and Belgium:

—Despite its federalism, Canada has tight central institutions to which central policy analysis could be adapted and useful.
—France also has centralized government forms. If a decision were made that policy could be illuminated by more central analysis, the decision could be implemented fairly easily. Unlike RCB, however, it would have to be done within established institutions.
—Sweden is clearly looking for such a capability.
—The Dutch quest for a "think tank" indicates a similar search.
—Insufficient observation was made in Norway to automatically draw it within this generalization, but such a need at least seems likely there, too.

The above generalizations are asymmetric. They are stronger for the United States than for the other countries. Since the author is an American, he feels quite sure of his ground. For the other countries, the trade-off between attempted avoidance of writing a purely American report on the one hand and avoiding an impossible arrogance based on the knowledge gained from a short visit on the other has led to a certain ambivalence.

REFERENCE

New Society (1979) "Thoughts on a think tank." November 1: 239

3

The Limits and Potential
of "Program Evaluation"

Georges Ferné

*Organisation for Economic Co-operation
and Development*

At first sight, the world of the social sciences and politics appear two sharply contrasted universes. On the one hand, the world of the social sciences is characterized by continuing demands for recognition of the legitimacy of its quest for knowledge about social realities, its yearning for acknowledgment of its scientific basis, and its tendency to measure its integrity by the extent to which it ignored the demands of power or became critical of them. On the other hand, the world of politics and decision-making has a rationality (or irrationality) of its own. It exhibits a deep-seated reluctance to engage in self-examination or assessment, a preference for ambiguity rather than transparency, and a scorn for long-term reflections and theoretical constructs which do not provide either ready-made solutions to problems or instant recipes for action.

Theoretically, it appears that these two worlds can never meet. They are relevant to different spheres of human concern, and it seems that one could not hope to penetrate the other without harmful effects. Political intervention in the world of science would rapidly turn into manipulation of science—and thus jeopardize the premises of scientific pursuit; excessive preoccupation of scientists with the demands of government would deflect science from its longer-term horizons.

Yet the two worlds *have* met. In the last century industrialization ushered in a new awareness of scientific methods and knowledge as an instrument for progress—whether through reform or through revolution. Much later, in the second half of the twentieth century, the influence of American approaches on empirical research reinforced the conviction that knowledge could be a prerequisite for action. More recently, the growing complexity of governmental problems and responsibilities has increased the need for comprehensive information and understanding in all areas of concern. And the very challenge of these emerging problems of society has caused increasing numbers of social scientists to recognize the value of testing theories and ideas against the practical problems of the day. While acknowledging the legitimacy of long-term theoretical research, established values, and dominant interests, pluralistic societies are increasingly striving to encourage the development of applied social science research which can be expected to contribute more directly to the formulation of policies and their implementation. Hence, the concept of "social science policies" developed.

SOCIAL SCIENCE POLICIES

In recent decades, governmental intervention in the social sciences has increased, prompted by two complementary concerns. First, the social research enterprise developed to meet the conditions required to ensure that sufficient numbers of trained researchers would be available to perform the work and to extend the knowledge and allow for the training of future social scientists. The second concern was with insuring the improved utilization of the social research potential in the formulation of policies.

The sixties were in fact a period of rising expectations directed at social science research. It was thought then that the social science disciplines would provide industrialized societies with the instruments—"social technologies"—required to cope with the destructive aspects of economic growth. Disenchantment followed when practical results (in terms of policy proposals which could actually be implemented, or in terms of outcomes of policies which had been partly inspired by research findings) proved disappointing. The difficulties encountered on the labor market by large cohorts of young social scientists underlined the mismatch between the demands for trained manpower in industrial societies and the numbers and types of specialists produced by the educational system. Identifying the kind of social science needed, how much of it, and under what circumstances, are still unresolved questions which underline the need for reinforced and more systematic government attention in this area.

Similarly, concerns for improved utilization of research findings started off with some simple notions which had to be discarded. For example, it has become obvious that the launching of large programs of research in areas which are thought to be important is not sufficient to ensure that a coherent research design can be elaborated and implemented, and that the results will be conducive to action. Contrary to some assumptions which prevail in political and administrative circles, many obstacles to effective utilization are not inherent in social research but in the behavior of public groups and bureaucratic governmental structures. Research has shown that government agencies have their established practices for the dissemination and collection of information, and that these practices play an essential role in determining what kind of information is actually used, where, by whom, and for what purpose(s) (OECD, 1975, 1976, 1977, 1979). The very notion of "use" must be reinterpreted in light of the fact that social science findings are usually shaped and molded by political forces to respond to their requirements, rather than the other way around. Political conflicts and differences between administrators play a crucial role in this process to allow for the development of meaningful debates about the evidence brought to light by social scientists.

Recognition of these realities constitutes a prerequisite for the formulation of realistic social science policy goals. Social science policy should (1) safeguard the health and balance of the social science research enterprise, which implies the maintenance of a strong disciplinary base as well as the provisions of opportunities for independent research; (2) encourage the development of mechanisms which will ensure that relevant findings are brought to the attention of decision makers at the appropriate time and level; (3) foster research methods and designs to bridge scientific theory and the demands of society; and (4) bring several disciplines together to attack problems which transcend single disciplines. It is in this latter connection, perhaps, that the last two decades have witnessed the most ambitious developments with the rise of social experimentation, of action research, and, last but not least, of program evaluation.

These three approaches have attempted to provide a design whereby social scientists can address directly policy concerns and social issues, often without limiting themselves in analysis in order to become concerned with the application of their research findings. One of the important questions remains whether a high degree of involvement in the social process in question might not lead to a "politicization" of the social scientists at the expense of the scientific aspects of the project. It is not surprising, therefore, that some of the more ambitious claims of this approach are viewed by many scientists as methodologically unsound, especially since it is usually difficult to apply scientific quality control to the work and the conclusions reached in this area.

There is no question, however, that despite these reservations, the development of social experiments, action research and program evaluation has been followed with great interest by many social scientists and policy makers. Action research projects have, for example, been encouraged in several countries, in North America as well as in Europe, and particularly in

Scandinavia. Social experiments have multiplied in the United States, often on a large scale, but other countries have launched their own efforts in this area, albeit on a more modest scale. It is hardly surprising, however, that governments which had to cope with severe budgetary difficulties and were concerned with the need to trim public expenditures have shown growing interest in the methods and approaches of "program evaluation."

PROGRAM EVALUATION:
LIMITS AND POTENTIAL

The development of evaluation research in the United States has attracted a great deal of attention in European countries. It seemed, in fact, to offer a new way to encourage social science research to address the problems of government and facilitate both effectiveness and economy in the use of public resources. As U.S. evaluation efforts became better known, however, questions multiplied: What impact did these projects have on policy-making? What kinds of conclusions did they bring to light? What is their scientific value from a methodological point of view? In which areas could they be most fruitfully applied? And why, if they responded so well to the concerns of social scientists and public authorities, did they remain so rare in Europe?

A preliminary investigation was launched in 1979 by the Organisation for Economic Cooperation and Development, under the aegis of the Committee for Scientific and Technological Policy, to attempt to provide some answers to these questions. A first step was to attempt to identify the most significant evaluations which have been implemented in European countries. It soon became apparent that the most important efforts in this area were still under way and that any assessment would be premature. It was already possible, however, to characterize some of their intents and thus to clarify the complex roles they would be called upon to play in several countries of different political and administrative traditions. The work of Dr. Haroun Jamous, a French political scientist who investigated the practice of several countries in this field, provided the first elements for an "evaluation of evaluations" which is still to come.

This confirmed that, insofar as European countries are concerned, program evaluation, in the strictest sense, is not widespread and the few existing projects are still in progress. The word itself—"evaluation"—is used, in fact, to cover a broad range of approaches which often have little connection with a genuine scientific approach. More than a fad, however, the wide-spread use of this label seems to reflect the existence of a general need for this kind of approach and the quest for "scientific legitimacy" in assessing or analyzing the implications and consequences of public action.

The activities which claim to be evaluations, or which have found their inspiration in American forms of evaluation research, do not have a straight-forward impact on political-administrative structures. It is not so much a question of producing results which will directly affect policy formulation or implementation, but of providing another instrument for policy makers to wield according to their own logic of action. The findings of evaluation research do not differ in this respect from the findings of other types of social research which play a role in policy-making. Their specific feature, how-ever, lies in the ability of public authorities to influence the design and scope of the research itself; in the fact that, once the project is launched, its results cannot be readily ignored; and—most importantly—in the latitude given to the sponsor to assign specific functions to the activities undertaken as "evaluations."

These functions are often more implicit than explicit. Their form and substance are colored by the culture and the political-administrative struc-ture of the country. They may stem from the preoccupation of top echelons within the administration who wish to exercise some form of "monitoring" of the implementation of policies. They may reflect a political wish to oversee administrative performance in certain important areas. They may provide an instrument for a move toward rationalization of the management of government programs. They may also provide a legitimate basis for political debate between interest groups and political forces in order to facilitate the emergence of a consensus.

Most of these motivations do not justify the broad scope of evaluations often advocated in the United States in the 1960s by those who wished to ensure their scientific standards and relevance to the concerns of all groups involved. Rather, under the guise of the evaluation function in Europe, and throughout the different activities which refer to it, broad diverse purposes emerge: creation and development of knowledge; initiation of politicians in new forms of knowledge; control over the bureaucrats by the politicians; assistance to and control over local authorities by the central government; achievement of compromise and consensus; rationalization of public ad-ministration; dealing with crisis situations, putting up with them or using them; reformulation of competences and boundaries between bodies jointly responsible for a vaguely defined or recent field; reformulation or definition of such a field. Evaluation as a goal may become accessory or a pretext for one or more of these aims.

THE FUTURE

Despite its multiple incarnations in Europe in so many diverse activities, the concept of "evaluation" has a surprising resiliency. It is generally accepted that evaluation may be a basic requirement and one which may become ever more imperative. There are many possible explanations for this apparently general conviction, which are not necessarily exclusive of each other: the general economic climate which has prompted a reappraisal of public expenditures in general and social policies and programs in particular; the new awareness in the social scientific community of the need to contribute to the solution of the major problems of our societies; the traditional, natural, and perhaps accelerating inclination of any political-administrative system toward greater rationalization.

At the same time, developments which have taken place in the United States in this area justify a certain caution and the quest for new departures. It has been obvious for some time that some of the most ambitious efforts launched by the federal government have not had the expected impacts on policy, while some scientific circles have questioned their designs and methodologies. The great enthusiasm of the 1960s has faded. Beyond this disillusionment, there remains a more sober recognition of the limits of evaluation research due to the imperfection of scientific approaches to date and to the characteristics of the political process.

It seems now, therefore, that—more than ever—there is a certain convergence between preoccupations expressed by policy makers and social scientists in Western Europe and the United States: a way of evaluating the effects of government decisions and programs by the use of scientific methods is needed. No fully satisfactory approach has yet been proposed, but experimentation can and should continue. The limits of evaluation have become more precisely known. Its potential has been more carefully measured. It still may provide a unique mode of interaction between the world of social science and the world of political decision and action. The search for new methods and means continues as a new aspect of the long-standing and ambiguous relation between knowledge and power.

REFERENCES

OECD (1979) Social Sciences in Policy Making. Paris
OECD (1975) Reviews of Social Science Policy: France. Paris.
OECD (1976) Reviews of Social Science Policy: Norway. Paris.
OECD (1977) Reviews of Social Science Policy: Japan. Paris.

AUTHOR'S NOTE: The opinions expressed in this article are those of the author and do not necessarily reflect those of the organization he belongs to.

PART II

EVALUATION IN THE
ADMINISTRATIVE MACHINERY

The use of evaluation within an administrative situation and the requirements for the application of evaluation research have shaped the evolution of the field far more than discussion on the political context of evaluation and public policy has been able to illustrate. An analysis of the symbiotic relationship between evaluation research and the working of the bureaucracy which provides some guidelines to increase the effectiveness of evaluation research is needed. Gerd-Michael Hellstern and Hellmut Wollman illustrate this point with a case study of the Federal Republic of Germany and explore the relationships of the political reform impetus, the administrative willingness to participate in evaluation, and the emergent forms of evaluation research.

Joseph Wholey stresses the need for a cooperative mechanism between policy makers, managers, and evaluators in the evaluation process. The use of evaluability assessment and the new incentives created by the Civil Service Reform Act may create a climate for better and more useful managerial evaluations. Steven Fitzsimmons draws on his experiences with the transfer of the American entrepreneurial evaluation research model to the West German administrative context. He systematically compares the factors influencing the transfer process and predicts the potential for the extension of the American evaluation research model into the bureaucratic contexts of other nations.

4

The Contribution of Evaluation
to Administration

Gerd-Michael Hellstern

Hellmutt Wollmann

*Center for Social Science Research, Free
University, Berlin*

Evaluation is intended for use, and the demand for evaluation has come mainly from administration. Having a strong administrative tradition, Germany as a rapidly "developing country" in evaluation research is an interesting case study, illustrating the interrelationships among the administrative machinery, the political process, and evaluation research and offering some informed guesses about the perspectives and the utilization of evaluation in such a setting. In describing the connection between administrative needs and responding evaluation tools and strategies, we shall concentrate on the necessity of evaluation to address the special problems created by the administrative process. We shall also analyze the different models and instruments which developed in Germany in response to the various needs of the policy arena and administrative and political environments.

Four questions illustrate the current state of evaluation to administration in this respect:

(1) What was the impetus shaping the evolution of evaluation?
(2) What links will increase administrative and political use of evaluation?
(3) What forms of evaluation have emerged for new assessment tools taking into account the German political and administrative system?
(4) How does the German experience compare with the American one, and what modifications are required?

THE GROWTH OF EVALUATION IN GERMANY

Several years ago, only a few people were willing to consider evaluation research in the Federal Republic as a legitimate enterprise. The spectacular rise in the last few years in the number of evaluation research endeavors was evident from a computer search, with the help of the Informationszentrum Sozialwissenschaft in Bonn. Of approximately 30,000 social science research projects in Germany during the last six years, around 1600 may be considered evaluations. The proportion, as well as the absolute number, of these research projects has been growing steadily to nearly 15 to 20 percent of all research projects in the social science field, quadrupling from 1971 to 1977.

There is a considerable time lag between the American explosion of evaluation research into a major business field and the German evolution of evaluation as a social science research field. Nevertheless, the comparative analysis of the growth and evolution of evaluation in this country helps to clarify the underlying interests in evaluation research and to explain the common reason for such a development. The different uses, forms, and types of evaluation research in Germany may increase the creative use and the development of alternative evaluation research tools. The most astonishing feature of the evolution of evaluation in Germany, next to its growth, is its metamorphosis during the last few years. Evaluation research activities were shaped by different forces stemming from changing administrative and political needs. In response, it had different goals and models. For analytic purposes, three purposes for evaluation may be distinguished:

(1) evaluation as a *rationalization tool* in times of political planning euphoria;
(2) evaluation as an *effectiveness tool* in times of financial difficulty; and
(3) evaluation as an *accountability tool* in a time of need for responsive and well-legitimated government action.

Evaluations were called upon as a "political planning tool" in the late sixties. As a part of a feedback process to increase purposeful coordinated government action, it gained importance as a tool to increase efficiency in a time of recession in the mid-seventies when decisions had to be made about the allocation of scarce governmental resources. Finally, evaluation demand has recently increased due to the need in accountability and responsiveness, as a counterbalance for the destabilized power system, undermined by growing citizen actions and changing political party structure.

Creating Demand

German evaluation research had its beginnings in the reform movement of the late nineteenth century.[2] However, its evolution as a major activity in government and administration may be limited to the last ten years. In the aftermath of the reform movement during the late sixties and early seventies, German evaluation research blossomed. The economic recession in the mid-sixties marked the initiation of great concern and interest in planned governmental intervention (Mayntz and Scharpf, 1975; Johnson, 1972; Ashford et al., 1975). This was ushered in by the "Great Coalition" in 1966, which took the first steps to translate rhetoric into action programs. The introduction of regular state intervention activities had its official foundation in the amendments to the "Basic Law" (the West German constitution) in 1969, in which relatively new tasks for governmental intervention were formally outlined. This intervention was intended primarily to stabilize the economy by extending the range of governmental activities. The main elements are as follows:

—the need for intervention as a federal task was formally recognized;
—new intergovernmental relationships among federal, state, and local governments ("cooperative federalism") were established to regulate and channel this new flow of intervention activities; and
—new rules for financial cooperation aimed at a coordinated economic policy were established to streamline action throughout the different federal levels in the complex and fragmented decision-making structure, characteristic of West German administration.

The policy areas covered by these constitutional revisions were different from those addressed by the American "War on Poverty." Governmental activities were more concerned with promoting infrastructural change than with legislating institutional change or changing social conditions. The areas covered concentrated on policy with a great need for capital investment. According to the amended Article 91a, 91b, and 104a of the Basic Law, spending activities (Reissert, 1978; Spahn, 1978) were in the fields of

—regional economic policy,
—agricultural reform and coastline protection,
—university development and education,
—urban transportation,
—urban development and renewal, and
—hospital building and reforms.

By introducing the new programs, the bureaucratic behavior which traditionally followed "conditional rules" changed to more goal-oriented functional and "programmatic behavior," which emphasized purposeful administrative action and decision-making. At the same time, those changes increased a process of political and administrative centralization, the amount of legislation delivered, led to increased regulation in many policy fields, and increased the size of governmental control (often referred to as *Verrechtlichung*).[3]

Effective demand for evaluation arose for very practical reasons. Stressing the experimental and preliminary character of new programs helped the administration and the majority party to secure the acceptance of innovative changes. Insecurity resulting from the newness of the programs created a demand for ongoing evaluation to optimize the program structure and avoid possible unforeseeable side effects. By requiring an evaluation, Parliament relieved the administration from the burden of proving success of a program in advance. Local reaction to educational reform and urban renewal programs called attention to the lack of information on impact and the proper implementation of the programs. Parallel with the increase of centralization, threats of the state and local levels to systematically displace the foregoing federal goals increased. Evaluations should improve program implementation by providing information on its achievements. The reports of newly installed commissions aiming at rationalization and reform and the evidence of the evaluation research results which were implemented stimulated a new wave of understanding regarding the difficulty in achieving the ambitious domestic reform programs through extensive regulations, the necessary extension for local (or situational) flexibility, and the need for new management and analytical tools.

Evaluation was becoming an important tool in four respects:

—External impact evaluation increased to provide information on the execution of programs in a politically fragmented, multilevel structure.
—Requirements for internal administrative evaluation increased to keep a check on goal-oriented programmatic behavior of the different agencies.
—Assessment of the effects of programs on the victims of change, such as through displacement in the Urban Renewal Program, was increasingly recognized as a necessity.
—As constitutional problems increased, the need for control mechanisms for Parliament to oversee administrative and executive agencies increased.

POLICY ANALYSIS CREEPING INTO ADMINISTRATION

The climate for social science analysis likewise changed. Evaluations, in the heyday of reform between 1969 and 1973, were expected to provide more rational decision-making and streamlining of the administrative and constitutional basis of government and to make "political planning" and "reform" feasible. Social science analysis was called upon to help in meeting ambitious aims of the reformers in three ways:

—as an instrument to change the administrative structure of government,
—as a means to regulate constitutional problems and conflicts arising out of the new power distributions, and
—as a "feeler" for social problems and actions needed.

The work of four commissions may best highlight those problems.

Changing Administrative Structure

The need for change in the institutional and administrative machinery was formally recognized by the establishment of two commissions or task forces. The major purpose of the executive Task Force on Governmental and Administrative Reform (Projektgruppe Regierungs-und Verwaltungsreform) in 1969 was to streamline and rationalize governmental actions, add an analytic capability, and develop coordinating mechanisms and feedback devices to improve the effectiveness of governmental programs.[4] Despite some minor successes, the departmental powers proved too strong to allow for a coordinated overall policy. When the task force was resolved in 1975 only a task sheet remained from the envisioned comprehensive planning system to describe current programs and actions of the different ministries. In 1971, following the establishment of the task force, a parliamentary commission for the reform of the civil service (Dienstrechtsreformkommission) was set up to suggest changes in the bureaucratic personal structure to allow for a more adequate "task-oriented" personal structure, which was hoped would facilitate the implementation of reform programs. Despite a long report in 1973, the translation of the commission's recommendations into effective reform is still not visible. What has remained is the intrusion of "evaluation ideas" into different departments and great concern on the part of the Civil Service Academy for a goal- and result-oriented management system (Verwaltung und Fortbildung, 2, 1979).

Solving Emerging Constitutional Problems

The new activities and domestic reform programs affected not only the operation of the internal administration but, more visibly, the balance of power in the federal system. In 1971 an "Enquete Commission" for the Reform of the Constitution was established. The commission was expected to find new ways to balance the system, to increase parliamentary control, and to find modalities to improve the relationships between the federation (Bund) and the states (Länder). It was hoped that the commission would succeed in institutionalizing some kind of parliamentary control or supervisory procedures of government activities and would be able to find a new balance for the working relation of the federal system between the states and the federation. The promise of the interim report which emphasized different forms of evaluation procedures or regulations to strengthen the supervisory function of Parliament was not met in the final report, which avoided the issue of planning control and evaluation. Despite widespread disappointment, Parliament succeeded in defending its own interests by taking advantage of established traditional tools. Reporting requirements and termination clauses for new programs proved more successful than the plea for institutionalized evaluation procedures. In addition, political changes at the state level brought the political centralization to a sudden halt; the states in control for the implementation of the reform measures were gaining in political weight due to the changing favor of the voters at the state level. The Bundesrat and the Ministerkonferenz of the state governors proved to be the counterweight to any central domestic reform, which often lacked clear goals and rules for implementation.

Responding to Social Needs

A broad mandate to survey the need for change and to set goals for change was received by the "Commission for Social Change" in 1973. In a mammoth approach the commission surveyed the field of social changes and necessary governmental changes with the help of more than 150 (published) reports. The commission recommended changes in nearly all fields, from ex ante evaluation problems in the field of technology assessment to ex post evaluations of governmental programs. But the breadth of their approach and the altered political and social climate by the time the report was delivered in 1975 largely undermined the immediate utilization of the report's recommendations. Their demand for better technology assessment and environmental impact assessment systems, for program-monitoring and continuous evaluation procedures, remained unfulfilled.

The Second Face of Evaluation

"After the reform" in the mid-seventies, the press to establish a rational decision-making base came to a sudden halt, the restrictions on positive planning tightened, and the limits for governmental actions became clearer (Hanf and Scharpf, 1978). The focus of action changed from the executive federal level to the local and state levels. Some of these new directions came from a recognition of the difficulty of planned change in the federal system with varying political forces, from the unanticipated consequences of the measures taken, and from the growing unwillingness to accept further change. The restrictions on the available funds, which drastically limited the range of possible reforms, came from the sudden realization of the limitations on resources, the population decline, and the beginning of the energy shortage. The impetus for evaluation changed from the planning units to the financial budgetary offices to the comptroller general, the BRH *(Bundesrechnungshof)*. The best indication of the changing mood was the recognition of the administrative order coming out of the §7 Budget Law (BHO, Bundeshaushaltsordnung of the new Budget Law in 1973), which provided the first legal basis for ex post evaluation. A major concern for the financial consequences of reform programs developed, especially at the local level. Self-evaluation as a tool for setting priorities with regard to various local tasks and for streamlining the task program (by introduction of "task critique"—*Aufgabenkritik*) became popular in larger local government departments (Banner, 1979). The treasurer became involved in the evaluation of programs to coordinate investment programs.

The Rise of Responsive Management

The new concept of increased financial responsibility and local autonomy merged with a renewed interest in administrative accountability. The growing demand for increased accountability for public institutions is manifested in the growing unwillingness to accept governmental decisions; for example, in the field of environmental policies and transportation. The attempts of political planning and domestic reform became the subjects of attack under the slogan "debureaucratization and private sector control" of governmental activities; attempts were made to deregulate activities and to speed up the decision-making processes. The new mood is reflected in the appointment of "debureaucratization" committees since 1977 at the federal level and in many states which intend to decrease federal paperwork and to increase administrative flexibility and responsiveness to citizens.

In this process, parliament gained new muscles; politicians became increasingly aware of their unused power potential and insisted on reports about the effects and outcome of certain policies and decisions. The willingness to accept administrative actions and reports without questioning diminished. The awareness of the small increments for political change possible given an energy shortage and population decline increased. The political split between the states and the federal level gained in importance. Administration became less concerned with monitoring subordinates; career-oriented administrators became more interested in their own managerial evaluation and became increasingly interested in proving their responsiveness to citizens' needs. As a result of these diverse trends, evaluation needs emerged which responded to the new power distribution. Evaluation became less an administrative tool to regulate subordinates and increasingly recognized as an instrument in the policy-shaping process. Evaluations became more political, and their use as a strategic weapon increased. The growing interest in interactive, process-oriented management tools reflects this new administrative mood. The attempt to add subjective indicators to the "objective" measurement of impact is part of this trend.

The Emergence of Social Science

In order to understand the current boom in evaluation activities, analyses cannot be confined to the field of politics and administration. One has to take into account the dynamic change which has occurred over the years in the field of social science as well. The explosion in the social sciences during the last ten years may be measured by the number of new departments and faculties created, the number of faculty members added, and the mushroom-ing number of students. It has brought changes in the professional perspec-tives of the younger social scientists, who no longer can find their fields in the realm of education, no longer can reside in an ivory tower, and are increasingly forced to work in institutions and organizations outside the universities. They not only enter the administration as a task force for change (like the Task Force for Government and Administrative Reform), but increasingly take up regular posts in the administration, thus providing a necessary link between the social science research and administrative per-spectives. With their entrance into the federal, state, and local government levels they change the framework and background of their agency, often raising the standard of work delivery, increasing the planning and organiza-tional capacity, and providing the kind of receptivity which is needed to use the social science information (Mayntz, 1977).

With the recognition of the need for change and reform, new institutions were founded to engage in applied research (such as The Center for Science in Berlin, the Deutsches Institut für Urbanistik, a national urban institute). Existing governmental research institutions were enlarged (like the National Health Institute); even the states founded their own government research institutions (like the Institute for State Planning and Urban Research in Dortmund). New independent research enterprises sprang up, and universi-ties started to build their own applied research centers. The traditional focus of applied research previously limited to the field of economics changed to reduce the interest in macroeconomic studies. There is now greater concern with the outcome of governmental actions than with tabulating governmen-tal output. Increased demand for an understanding of the administrative process, of the link between intention and outcome, has emerged. This change of focus is reflected not only in the creation of new institutions for the study of public administration in Speyer, Konstanz, Bielefeld, and Berlin, but much more in the new perspective of public administration. The change has been from a legal perspective to one increasingly grounded in the social sciences.

For evaluation, the picture which emerges shows signs of great diversity. The current change is accompanied by a greater concern with program management, organizational development, and procedural change. The new interest in public realities is leading more and more evaluators to question some of their social scientific criteria, with questions of relevance replacing criteria of generalizability. Attempts have been made to combine traditional approaches to an understanding of the sciences with the methodological tools of behavioral sciences. The changing role of social science has led to the fear of increased exploitation of the social sciences—the use or misuse of social science by directing and designing the fields of research. This has led to an intense and critical discussion on the future directions of the social sciences in our society. It may also equally be seen as a new potential for increasing the relevance and influence of the social sciences and evaluation research.[5]

DEVELOPING BASES IN ADMINISTRATION

The overview of the driving forces in the growth of demands for evaluation in Germany illustrates some of its diversity (which partly accounts for its potentials) and its dependence on the administrative and political interests of administrators and policy makers. As in other countries, evaluation in Germany depends on liaisons with the political and administrative process. As a result, evaluation should be organized along traditional channels of information and administrative work production. Government reporting and record-keeping are traditional devices for information processing, cornerstones for evaluation research. The further development of a government reporting (political accounting) system may still prove a strong basis for ensuring evaluation an instant link to parliament. New dimensions for administrative evaluation and monitoring may be opened by the introduction of the computer, which offers new possibilities for joint record-keeping and information systems.

Transmitting Evaluation into the Political Process

The number of official governmental reports which find their way back to Parliament has increased steadily over the last ten years. Whereas the frequency of reporting nowadays is decreasing, the number of required reports is still increasing. These now total around 100, half of which must be delivered at regular intervals. The reports themselves vary greatly in content and are often of limited value as an evaluation instrument, since the information given in the report is, by and large, determined by the agency being evaluated or checked.

Several types of reports may be distinguished, such as comprehensive reports from fields of actions (such as "Planning Reports"), program- or issue-specific reports (for example, "Reports on Housing Problems"), and reports required regularly by law and specific ad hoc reports. These last are increasingly becoming a parliamentary tool to force administrative action. In general, the trend is to move first from analytical to programmatic reports and from there to more evaluative reports. This is best illustrated by the reports in the fields of regional policy, social policy, and agriculture (Federal Ministry of Regional Planning, 1977; Yuill et al., 1980). Most of them appeared for the first time in the mid-sixties as programmatic reports, whereas today they contain some measures of goal-achievement and output production.

Reports alone cannot substitute for more intense evaluation research, nor can they serve as a parliamentary control instrument. However, they can provide an evaluation stimulus, ensure continuing interest in evaluating the policy field, or transmit evaluation research results to a larger public and parliament to keep interest alive in some policy areas. Their constant pressure for evaluation and coordination in the process of report preparation should not be underestimated.

From Administrative Control to
a Computerized Accounting System

Whereas report requirements are often the outside stimulus for evaluation, the collection of administrative data is often the precondition for a successful evaluation. The use of administrative data generated by the processes of application, internal reporting, and spending is very often hampered by the insufficient procedures of recording the data. Only in a few cases have administrative data been systematically used for monitoring purposes. However, with the increasing computerization of administration, the potential use of administrative records and data will become easier, increasing the possibilities for evaluative purposes. Three different approaches may be currently distinguished:

—the building of systematic observation systems from different data sets;
—the use of the financial accounting system to provide information on the flow of resources; and
—the use of particular program statistics to develop a program-related data bank.

"Observation systems" are often part of the federal and state statistical service. These systems contain a set of structural data mostly as background information. They measure, for example, the quality of life (provision of services, financial health) in different communities. These data banks, which are developed mostly outside the regular administrative system, provide only limited information on the administrative achievement in certain programs. Their aim is to provide background information on the state of a region or city, drawing their data from the official statistics. Examples are the observation system of the Bundesforschungsanstalt für Raumforschung und Landeskunde (BflR), the "structural data sheets" of some state statistical agencies, or the indicator system of the Ministry for Labour and Social Affairs. More important for evaluators are attempts to provide some baseline information on governmental spending and to build up program or project statistics. These uses of data banks, however, bring out a major limitation. Both in the states and in such federal agencies as the Department for Economic Cooperation and the Department of Transportation, the uses of data for evaluative purposes so far have been limited by the political sensitivity of the process monitoring its implementation. The system, well known for its high sophistication, includes evaluated observable effects of the highways as data and as part of the decision-making and priority-setting process. But the experience so far also shows how difficult it is to separate such information from various political interests. The past history of the data bank's usage shows how sensitive such a statistical data bank is to political distortion and outside pressures.

Although the agencies recognize the need for a more computerized information system and a more sophisticated evaluation system to maintain monitoring functions, the manpower and the knowledge required to use those computerized recording systems is lacking in many offices and agencies responsible for the programs. Computerized information systems are mainly regarded as increasing the complexity of the information without providing an adequate reduction mechanism or flexible handling of individual cases. For officials, who are empirically knowledgeable but untrained in statistics, computerized project statistics are both too complex and too unsophisticated to serve as a tool for information. Most experienced administrators therefore tend to supplement computerized "early warning systems" or complicated reporting systems by informal controls. They base evaluation activities on the informal mechanism of regular site visits, ratings and judgments by the operating unit, or problem-oriented evaluations by external evaluators for more rigid reviews. Through the use of flexible interrogative technique a better check can be made on possible distortions, and political and administrative constraints can be better taken into account. Political turmoil and clashes can often be better dealt with by early individual consideration of the individual situation than by relying on the formalized, politically inflexible accounting system. In order to improve evaluation systems, one has to find the right balance between the improvement of the recording base and the use of informal scanning and information procedures.

THE DIFFERENTIAL USE OF EVALUATION
IN THE FEDERAL GOVERNMENT

Evaluation research handbooks often give the impression that evaluation is the last stage in the planning-reform cycle: from analysis, planning, programming, implementation, to evaluation. This picture needs correction, because of numerous overlapping and simultaneous actions. In this process, evaluation is a focus which has its source in very different administrative and political activities, such as bookkeeping, accounting, and financial assessment, and which is brought in at very different stages of such planning-evaluation cycles. A large number of heterogeneous approaches stemming from those activities, shaped by different policy arenas and research traditions, have fostered a multiplicity of evaluation approaches at the federal level. For example, the heterogeneity and multiplicity of evaluation approaches may demonstrate the need for adapting evaluation research to the particular needs of the surrounding administrative and political environment. Five different approaches have merged which demonstrate the various uses of evaluation in the federal government:

(1) The most ambitious model of evaluation practice tries to link evaluation to a *comprehensive program-building* process with clear goals and operational objectives. This attempt is best illustrated by the Department of Agriculture.

(2) Less ambitious but still noteworthy is the case of the Department of Economic Cooperation. Here an *institutionalized evaluation office* is responsible for continuous routine and ad hoc evaluation.

(3) Limited in their approach, but easier to institutionalize, are program evaluations which use program-related *monitoring systems* to help shape program decisions. The Regional Economic Policy serves as an example of such a program.

(4) There are numerous *model projects* accompanied by evaluation research mainly to demonstrate the usefulness of the model. The connection of those projects to administration is weaker and the use of evaluation results more uncertain. This approach has often been taken in the field of education and social policy.

(5) The use of *experimental programs* to introduce change is increasing. This approach is mostly limited to fields in which a highly technical problem is involved; for example, telecommunication or transportation. Often administrative and political decisions have already been shaped, and the experimental program is designed only to demonstrate the usefulness of such programs or provide information for program adaptation and implementation.

Evaluation as Program Development

A comprehensive planning program-evaluation system has long been the aim of many administrative reformers. During the heyday of programmatic policy reform in government, the planning staff in the Federal Chancellor's Office tried to develop and implement the first stages of an integrated planning system. According to the federal-level plan, all departments were to be included in a regular feedback system channeled by a "task-data-sheet" *(Aufgabenblatt)*. Despite all initial efforts, the separate departmental administrative interests proved far too strong to allow for streamlined planning and evaluation activities under the auspices of the chancellor. The current practice of the Chancellor's Office is therefore to select only single interdepartmental problem areas for evaluation (Steinhausen, 1979).

The development of an integrated planning and evaluation system seems to have been achieved inside one department, rather than among a group of departments. After many attempts, the Task Force for Governmental and Administrative Reform (Projektgruppe Regierungs- und Verwaltungsreform) finally succeeded in enlisting the cooperation of one "pilot department"— namely, the Department of Agriculture and Forestry (Bieler, 1979).

Case Illustration—Rationalization with No Impact

The Department of Agriculture and Forestry had lost many of its former departmental tasks to the EEC. Public criticism was growing when, in 1973, it decided to introduce a new program structure which would integrate task structure and finance programming. A special evaluation unit was set up to be responsible for conducting evaluation studies and cost-benefit analysis.

In each program section, an authorized planning representative who is at the same time a member of a cross-sectional "planning-group" is responsible for planning programming and evaluation tasks in each program section. Programs and projects for evaluation are selected yearly in a brainstorming session by the planning group or suggested by the various program section. The evaluations are mostly carried out by outside evaluators; one of the main tasks of the evaluation unit is to stimulate discussion and cooperation between the program section and the evaluators. Despite its rational outlook, the system often has difficulty dealing with the political pressures arising in different programs and the need to respond to the complicated decision-making process created by the EEC in the field of agriculture. The transfer and utilization of the evaluation research results therefore still create a bottleneck. Increasing publication is one of the strategies to improve the diffusion and utilization of evaluation research results, however, despite the rational approach to synthesize programmatic, organizational, and evaluation structure, the impact in the political arena has yet to be felt.

Establishing Governmental Evaluation Units

Evaluation activities may be found in all government departments, even at the local level. Very often they are connected with the planning or policy units. At the local level, evaluation-related activities are often carried out by the budget office of sectional agencies (such as in the welfare office). Sectorial evaluations usually prove to be more successful in the acceptance of their findings and the implementation of their evaluation results than their cross-sectional counterparts. Despite many attempts, real evidence of an institutionalization of evaluation rarely can be found. Only a few agencies and cities have their own evaluation office; the earliest and most often cited example of this at the federal level is the inspection (or evaluation) unit of the Department for Economic Cooperation (Bundesministerium für Wirtschaftliche Zusammenarbeit; Lotz, 1979).

Case Illustration–Outside Stimulus, Inside Restrictions

Since the UNESCO Conference on the Effectiveness of Social and Technical Assistance to Underdeveloped Countries in 1954, discussion in the Department for Economic Cooperation (BMZ) has never ceased on how to best evaluate its own program. As a consequence of the UN proclamation of the first Development Decade, the department issued a policy paper in which constant evaluation of its policies was suggested as part of its program. In 1970 an evaluation unit was created which still exists; it forms no part of the administrative hierarchy and reports directly to the concerned program unit and program managers. For purposes of evaluation, projects are chosen partly according to systematic (serial) procedures that cover most of the projects at least once during their respective periods of existence, and projects are selected partly on an ad hoc basis according to special problems brought to light from the regional offices or indicated by the department's "early warning system." This system, called projects statistic, forms a data bank containing, by and large, information on the financial flow and the progress of project activities. The evaluation procedures used by the BMZ largely stem from the World Bank discussion on project appraisal; evaluation is carried out by staff members assisted by some suborganization of the Ministry (the Gesellschaft für Technische Zusammenarbeit, the Organization for Technical Cooperation, GTZ, is particularly important in this regard) and selected experts from outside.

The evaluation is conceived as a "goal-analytical process" which centers around four criteria:

—effectiveness,
—efficiency,
—significance, and
—transferability.

Despite the rather elaborate evaluation system, many of the evaluations are either economic or descriptive. The quality of the evaluations varies, and their validity is often questionable.

The fact that the results of some of the program evaluations have been used as political weapons by the opposition has only served to aggravate an already difficult situation for the special evaluation unit in the department. Willingness to cooperate among the regional and program agencies still remains rather weak; the fear of negative sanctions and repercussions is hard to overcome. However, willingness to cooperate has begun to increase since strict confidentiality for the results of the research was promised and finally achieved to some extent.

The difficulty of including political criteria in the evaluation and of taking into account the dynamic political process in some underdeveloped countries often makes it necessary to alter set goals and objectives, making clear evaluation more difficult. Increased feedback and discussion have helped to increase acceptance of the evaluations. Organized feedback procedures and frequent participation of the program managers are now essential features of the system.

Monitoring

When comprehensive evaluations are not possible, the institutionalization of program-related evaluations is still a possibility. Attempts to continuously monitor programs are increasing. The best examples can be found at the local level, where data are readily available (for example, for the measurement of environmental quality). Data systems for efficient monitoring at the federal level are harder to develop. After the failure of the Central Planning Agency of the Chancellor's Office to establish a regularly updated (Reform) project data bank, some departments developed their own data banks and indicator systems (such as the Department of Labor and the Department of Transportation). A good example of the attempts to introduce some kind of systematic monitoring and evaluation can be found in the field of regional economic policy (Kohn, 1979).

Case Illustration–Monitoring: Stalemate

Regional economic policy is a shared task of the federal government and the states, introduced by Article 104 of the Basic Law in 1969. It aims to secure the same standard of living throughout West Germany and to counterbalance the adverse effects of structural changes. To aid those areas, whose economic potential has lagged considerably behind the federal average, and to mobilize unutilized or insufficiently utilized production factors by stimulating job creation of safeguarding jobs, some 700 million DM a year are spent as investment aids to private enterprises and for infrastructure and industrial sites. In a four-year plan, which is updated annually, progress and planning decisions are reported. To guide the decision-making and to regulate competition between the states, a monitoring system was developed which sought to measure the needs and potential of each region in the Federal Republic. A common indicator was constructed which included measurements of infrastructure, unemployment, and income. All regions falling below a certain level were to be included. The success in reaching a final agreement on the indicator construction created mixed feelings. Critics pointed to the crucial questions of the validity of the indicator regarding to the possibilities of statistical distortion. Using job creation as a tool for measuring success, numerous studies have shown the limits of these current measures. Changes in the indicators may not reflect program-induced change but result of other ongoing processes. Long-term effects may be missed or overrated by the current system, which also may not be able to provide information on the action necessary to guide structural change. Information on side or adverse effects of the program is lacking. The indicator seemed to have been created to fit crucial political needs, with the size and borders of a region largely determining the results of the measurement process. Political bargaining determined the final decision. Monitoring succeeds only so far as consensus can be achieved on the selection of the right indicators. As a consequence, one may state that political decisions cannot be avoided by referring to a (mechanical) technical tool, as has been attempted so far.

The Use of Models

Evaluation has become a major enterprise in the Federal Republic, not only in the field of social policy, but also in education. In both fields, the federal government is limited in its action by the Basic Law. To bring about innovations in these fields, it has often financed model programs to demonstrate the usefulness of some alternative approaches to social and educational problems. A joint federal-state educational commission *(Bund-Länder-Kommission für Bildungsplanung und Forschungsförderung)* decides on most of the model-research program for educational purposes. As a new variation, they now attempt to build up model regions to integrate and combine different models and the so far often isolated and noncomparable projects.

Similar demonstration programs are conducted in the social fields (for example, for pregnancy consultation). Evaluation has played an important part in demonstrating the effectiveness of these programs. For example, at the preschool and primary school levels the federal government spent some 64 million DM in 1978; but the largest and most discussed issue is the introduction of "experimental comprehensive schools." Some 125 million DM have been spent by the Bildungskommission for these projects.

Case Illustration—Action or Evaluation

The Federal Republic tended to produce only a small percentage of students with university educations as compared with other western countries in the sixties. The *Bildungsrevolution* (educational revolution) brought about a major departure from the human-oriented (*"geisteswissenschaftlichen"*) approach to a more empirically oriented approach in education. The Max-Planck Institute (founded in 1963) was one of the forerunners of this development. Preliminary steps for educational reform were taken in the late sixties. In the early seventies most reforms were concerned with implementing new educational systems, as in the preschool curricula programs and the comprehensive school models. Most of the accompanying research projects used a practice-oriented approach, stressing development and substituting action for evaluation.

The evaluation of the German Youth Institute (Deutsches Jugendinstitut) may serve as a characteristic example of such an approach. Most of their efforts went into curricular development evaluation. Rigid evaluation designs were disregarded, since (1) the priorities differed in the different states (the states are responsible for cultural and educational affairs), (2) the program implementation procedures and regulations differed between the states, and (3) the differences in the population of the model schools impeded the implementation of simple experimental design rules.

For their "practice-oriented" approaches they stressed the use of soft designs, using group discussion, expert interviews and parental involvement, communication, and organizational development as their main tools. The immediate success of a curriculum took priority over "scientific rigor." Tests were not regarded as suitable instruments for comparison. Instead, research concentrated on judgmental data-rating schemes, group discussions, and the like. The stress on qualitative approaches to evaluation, the need for success, and the uncoordinated and unconnected evaluation attempts diminished the transfer value of the institute's evaluations. As in other model projects, the model character and the evaluation activity had to serve to conceal the introduction of new programs and to help to make the program "a success." The available evaluation tools in most cases were too rigid to allow for the hidden political aims of the evaluations. More qualitative approaches maintaining the scientific standards of qualitative research procedures are needed to fit this task.

Experimental Programs:
Limited to Technical Issues?

Experimental programs are found mostly in the field of technical experimentation; for example, the introduction of cable TV, new traffic schemes, or noise reduction programs. Some published examples are the "highway speed reduction" experiment and the experiments preceding the introduction of a "phone tact" system (limiting local phone calls in time). One nontechnical experiment with far-reaching implications has been developed in the process of legal reform (Geck, 1977).

Case Illustration—Limits to Reforms as Experiments

For a long time, legal education in the Federal Republic followed a two-stage pattern. The first stage of university training was followed by a practically oriented traineeship. Reform came under discussion in the late sixties and early seventies, accompanied by much resistance in the profession. In order to make reform possible, a federal statute—§5 Richtergesetz (Law for the Judges)—for the first time authorized the states to combine university studies and practical training (one-stage education). Eight universities introduced new experimental programs which were carefully observed by the alerted profession. A steering group was established to evaluate the results of the experiment. A combination of factors made it difficult to set up any kind of reliable evaluation procedures: the attacks by more traditionally oriented faculties, and the sudden student explosion combined with the resulting financial squeeze of the reform models. Most of the research time had to be spent in fighting for the new concept, developing curricula, securing financing, and defending the new program to allow them to work, thus also preventing any kind of systematic evaluation. With termination of the experiment imminent, the different political interest groups still do not agree on what the purpose of the evaluation should be. Should the traditional training system be compared with the new reform models? Or should the reform models be conceived as a form of planned variation? Finally, what should the goals be on the basis of which one could evaluate the models? And how can one terminate the different models, for each shows differing qualities which make it difficult to select the most advantageous? With termination set for 1981, the confusion is still increasing, and political decisions seem to replace scientific experimental evaluations.

THE NEED FOR DEVELOPMENT

No longer is social science found exclusively in universities and limited to teaching and (basic "pure") research. Growing numbers of social scientists are being placed in governmental programs. This change will influence both the program perspectives as well as the relation of administration to evaluation research. Concurrently, administration is changing. It is more receptive now to social science knowledge. More social science information is required to respond to the needs of politics. At the same time, evaluation research must be tailored to the administrative process. New methods have to be developed which are able to respond to the varying political and administrative requirements. So far, social scientists are still used at best for their intelligence, as social bookkeepers of the bureaucracies. They generate information on impacts and process, compile facts, and serve in a monitoring and data-gathering capacity, but they usually fail to play a major role in contributing to the shaping of policies. Political decisions are made elsewhere. Evaluation research has largely failed to have a major impact on governmental or departmental policies and programs. Its use has been limited to soft-issues—education, social policy, economic aid, and manpower policy; even in these areas it has never succeeded in integrating its findings into the political administrative machinery. Some may regard this as a failure; others may regard it as a necessary condition in a democratic society, where research usage should be part of and not dominating the political process. But even then some restrictions have so far limited the wider use of evaluation research.

The lack of adequate methodology. The methodological developments are still borrowed from the (pure) science model. Methodological tools and policy-oriented criteria for policy analysis are slowly responding to the needs of program action and management. The problem of integrating criteria of relevance with the requirements of social science has not yet been solved. Pure scientific methods, still dominate evaluation research. Most quantitative or qualitative evaluation research designs are not able to accommodate the administrative and political *"Handlungs"* structure. Far more expectations of administrators and policy makers are oriented to the use of scientific models, numbers, and figures, even then when only of limited value. Action research models are rarely found. When used, they were often a substitute for nonreflexive usage of social science methods. Reflective methodological mix of different methodological tools is seldom; limitations and administrative and political factors are not taken into account in most research. Only approaches which take into account the administrative and political action (maneuver) room, which are able to integrate the organizational environment of a program, will improve the value of the evaluations conducted. Approaches like evaluability assessment may help in this process.

The inadequate use of theories. Closely related to the inadequate methods is the inadequate use of social theories in evaluation research. If used, they are discipline-oriented or based on a theory-testing model that is inadequate for social action. Well-founded theories and the development of alternative theories are only now evolving; the formation of a theory is only slowly being recognized as part of the evaluation process. There is a need for "basic applied social research" which takes into account the *"Handlungsspielraum"* of the administrative and political system relating basic theory to the action potential.

The lack of administrative receptivity to using social science information. Administration is still largely dominated by legal or technical professionals. Understanding and use of the social sciences are largely confined to statistical reasoning and discussion; the interpretation and translation of social science research into the administrative and political process fails. Evaluation is of use only in a very strict instrumental sense, as justification for their action. The connection between program managers and the departmental research unit is often weak; to strengthen it, more target-oriented research should be conducted. Strategies for incorporating evaluation research into the political and administrative processes must be found.

The lack of trained evaluators. Most evaluators have never worked in administration. They often receive only theoretical or empirical training. Their interest in evaluation differs and often hinders effective evaluation. Career patterns in political and research are different. The potential for an interchange between both systems should be improved.

DIRECTIONS FOR EVALUATION RESEARCH IN GERMANY

Despite all improvements, different forms and usages of evaluation will develop. They all substitute for the political process, but they will increasingly help to shape policies, to improve the management of programs, and to increase the understanding of the consequences and impacts of policies.

If one tries to formulate some "informed guesses" based on our theory of evaluation research as to the future development and perspectives of evaluation research, the need and demand for (outside) evaluation research on the part of politicians and administrators will continue to increase. There are distinct differences between the American and the German political and administrative systems:

(1) As compared with the American federal system with its maze of governmental unit, intergovernmental relations, and dependencies, the West German federal system appears almost "orderly." Governmental units on all levels are less numerous and heterogeneous—for example, the number of local governments was cut from 24,000 to about 8,000 during the communal territorial reform in the sixties and seventies. Their intergovernmental relations are more clearly prescribed as constitutionally fixed systems of matching-grants funding in specific policy areas. Both factors make the implementation process and the outcome patterns more easily foreseeable and calculable in Germany than in the United States and make the need for policy information through outside research less pressing.

(2) While the American administrative system tends to run "experimental" programs through "new" organizations, German administrative tradition and culture tend to implement new policies through established public units and procedures, thus also increasing the possibility of foreseeing the process and its outcome to some extent.

(3) Administrative recording and statistical systems in the United States appear to be in better shape than in Germany, thus allowing at least embryonic forms of internal bookkeeping and program and project statistics. Together with the increasing computerization of administrative data storage, it seems likely that this field will constitute a growing domain of administrative "in-house" evaluation.

(4) German parliamentary evaluations are largely underdeveloped. Given the
    administrative outlook and orientation of the West German political system
    and the lack of the resources of the GAO, parliamentary evaluation will never
    acquire the same importance as in the U.S. context. To improve these evalua-
    tions, the influence of the highly complex system of committees, party frac-
    tions, and congressional research service has to be recognized, as well as their
    different interests in evaluation as part of their power play. Evaluation re-
    search in this context will always take a rather informal and piecemeal ap-
    proach; comprehensive evaluation systems are not to be expected.
(5) A driving force may develop from the interests of the independent Rechnung-
    shof, the Comptroller General's Office, but its research will be limited to
    in-staff evaluations. By evaluating departmental policies, it will increase the
    willingness of others to introduce their own departmental evaluation system
    to be better prepared for the BRH evaluation.

Further growth of the publicly funded "research money market" can be
foreseen, especially if one takes into account the growing interest in evaluations at the state and local levels.

The response on the part of evaluation researchers may be differentiated
as to government-related research institutions, private (commercially run)
research firms, and university research institutes. As far as government-
related research institutions are concerned, it is safe to forecast further
expansion. A case in point for this kind of government-related (albeit independent) research is the Science Center Berlin—Wissenschaftszentrum
Berlin—funded by federal and Berlin money. This organization responds to
the information needs of politics; for instance, by regrouping a major research unit to do large-scale research on labor market policies. A second
example is the German Institute for Urban Studies (Deutsches Institut für
Urbanistik, Berlin, funded by major German cities). These two research
organizations probably constitute the closest German analogy to the Brookings Institution or the Urban Institute in the United States. Yet, a structural
impediment to gaining a comparable visibility and impact vis-á-vis policy
makers and administrators may be seen in the fact that, in contrast to the
United States, where constant circulation takes place among government,
research, and university personnel (Brookings being a conspicuous example), there is hardly any circulation of that sort on the German scene, due to
the fact that the German civil service system makes such an exchange
difficult, if not impossible.

Regarding private (commercially run) research institutions, a further
expansion of research capacities and a sharpening of competition in the
"bidding market" of evaluation research can be foreseen. In the past few
years, some of these private research organizations have specialized in
specific policies and corresponding public bureaucracies, building clientele

relations which may structure the research market to some degree. Due to an interest in reaching some "economies of scale" in terms of computerized data collection and data handling, they may tend to push for further research based on indicators, survey data, and quantitative research designs.

As to the development of evaluation research in university settings, a set of contrasting factors have to be considered. On the one hand, the expansion of research manpower (at least potentially also available for evaluation research) has been dramatic in the course of the university reform and expansion during the sixties and seventies. We illustrate this point with a story: While the entire university community of sociologists could have gathered in a major lecture hall in the late fifties, it took the newly inaugurated, monumental International Congress Center in Berlin to embrace the number and also the self-esteem of this year's meeting of the professional association of sociologists. German social science is more firmly rooted in the tradition of *Verstehen*—sociology (with its implications in terms of research design and techniques, such as historical case studies, the reconstruction of processes on the basis of the actors' perception and interpretations, and also in terms of its openness to interactive research methods such as action research) than its American counterpart. Imbued as it is with a spirit of theoretically derived and supported "societal criticism" (such as the "Critical Theory" of the Frankfurt School), it could be a sort of natural candidate for engaging in a direction of evaluation research which might meet both the administration's need for detailed, process/outcome-oriented research, backed by intensive empirical fieldwork, and at the same time social science's standards of critically detached, theoretically supported analyses. On the other hand, university social science research has undoubtedly had difficulties in claiming and holding its ground in the field of evaluation research due to habitual organizational features of the academic trade which will be hard to change: organizational ineptitude in handling a large-scale research, individualistic reputation and production patterns, and the inability to produce readable and transferable research prose and to deliver it in time. Yet, as noted above, there are indications that policy research at the universities is better suited to cope with the challenges and possibilities (or potential) of evaluation research.

NOTES

The following notes and references are limited to books published in English. Only documents are cited.

1. To stress this point (which has been explored in another paper), the growing reception of Habermas' writings in the United States seems to be a reliable indicator for the growing interest

in the European tradition of social science research methods. The number of new books on qualitative research approaches, the foundation of a special sociological journal with an applied section on qualitative sociological methods ("Qualitative Sociology") may be an additional indication of those developments.

2. Early predecessors to the current evaluation research activities may be found in the social reform movements of the late nineteenth century. The "Verein für Sozialpolitik," the Kathedersozialisten, took an early intense empirical interest in the effects of schooling, housing, and social reform. But to grow into a movement, one has to wait—with the exception of some research in the fifties—until the midsixties and seventies to find systematic and large-scale evaluation research activities.

3. This discussion has been frequently repeated. Attempts have been undertaken to privatize public sector activities in many fields to speed up administrative procedures by deregulating activities (e.g. easing up the procedure for building permissions and the Urban Renewal Law); and at the moment a growing call from the local level is the quest for more global granting ("Pauschalisierung") replacing the conditional grants (a discussion comparable to the American Block Grant Discussion). For a discussion of the Federal Grant System see Reissert and Ashford (1980). For a comprehensive survey of the German subvention practices and problems see Jüttemeier and Lammers (1979). A result of this discussion may be the appointment of the Transfer Commission to analyze the Social Security System at the Chancellor's Office.

4. A short treatment is included in Mayntz and Scharpf (1975). The main results have been published in three volumes, *Projektgruppe für Regierungs- und Verwaltungs- reform beim Bundesministerium des Innern* (1969–1972). In addition, some 20 volumes on special issues and problems of administration have been published informally. Some of them are published as books.

5. The discussion of "what steers the search for truth"; "is modern science largely functionalized?" has been stirred up by Böhme et al. at the Max-Planck-Institut zur Erforschung der Lebensbedingungen der wissenschaftlich-technischen Welt in Starnberg. (1976: 306–336); Böhme, (1977: 319–358, and Pfetsch, forthcoming).

REFERENCES

ASHFORD, D. et al. (1975) Bibliography of Comparative Public Policy in Britain, West Germany, Japan and France. S.I.C.A. Occasional Papers, Hayward.
———— [ed.] (forthcoming) Financing Urban Government in the Welfare State. London: Croom Helm.
BANNER, G. (1979) "Organizing for local government efficiency in Germany." Local Government Studies 3:55–71.
BIELER, U. (1979) "How we have tried to get along with institutionalization of evaluation." Presented at the American-German evaluation research workshop, Berlin.
BOEHME, G. (1977) "Models for the development of science." in Spiegel-Rösing, D.; Solla Price, D. de (eds.) Science, Technology and Society, Beverly Hills, Calif., Sage.
BOEHME, G., W. DAELE, and W. KROHN (1976) "Finalization of science." Social Science Information 15: 306–330.
Bundesakademie für Öffentliche Verwaltung [ed.] (1979) "Ziel- und ergebnisorientiertes Verwaltungshandeln," Verwaltung und Fortbildung (special issue).
Bundesministerium des Innern (1969–1972) Reports I–III, Projektgruppe der Regierungs- und Verwaltungsreform. Bonn.

DORN, H. (1979) "The control of success by the Federal Auditors' Court (BRH)." Presented at the American-German evaluation research workshop, Berlin.

Enquete Kommission (1976) Final report, BT Drs. 7/5924 of 12/9/76.

———(1972) Interim report, BT Drs. VI/3829 of 9/12/72.

FEDERAL MINISTRY OF REGIONAL PLANNING, BUILDING AND URBAN DEVELOPMENT (1975a) The 1975 Urban Development Report. Bonn.

———(1975b) Federal Regional Planning Program, Publication Series Regional Planning 06.002. Bonn.

———(1974) Regional Planning and Development, Overview of the Federal Regional Planning Program, the 1974 Regional Planning Report.

GECK, W. K. (1977) "The reform of legal education in the Federal Republic of Germany." American Journal of Comparative Law 25: 86–119.

HANF, K. (1973) "Administrative developments in West and East Germany." Political Studies 1:35.

HANF, K. and F. W. SCHARPF [eds.] (1978) Interorganizational Policy Making: Limits to Coordination and Central Control. Beverly Hills, CA: Sage.

JOHNSON, N. (1972) Government in the Federal Republic of Germany: The Executive at Work. Oxford: Pergamon.

JÜTTEMEIER, K. H. and K. LAMMERS (1979) Subventionen in der Bundesrepublik Deutschland. Kiel: Kieler Diskussionsbeiträge.

KOHN, H. (1979) "Efficiency analysis in the Federal Ministry for Economic Affairs." Presented at the American-German evaluation research workshop, Berlin.

Kommission für Wirtschaftlichen und Sozialen Wandel (1977) Wirtschaftlicher und sozialer Wandel in der Bundesrepublik Deutschland. Göttingen: Schwartz.

KÖNIG, H. (1977) "Kritische Analyse des Managements finanzieller, personeller und materieller Resourcen in der öffentlichen Verwaltung." Verwaltungswissenschaftliche Informationen 3 (special issue). Bonn.

Landesregierung Baden-Württemberg (1979) Bürgernähe in der Verwaltung. Stuttgart.

LOTZ, R. E. (1979) "The institutionalization of evaluation research—experience from government." Presented at the American-German evaluation research workshop, Berlin.

MAYNTZ, R. (1977) "Sociology, value freedom, and the problems of political counseling," in C. H. Weiss (ed.) Using Social Research in Public Policy Making. Lexington, MA. D. C. Heath.

MAYNTZ, R. and F. W. SCHARPF (1975) Policy Making in the German Federal Bureaucracy. New York: Elsevier.

PFETSCH, E. (forthcoming) "The finalists debate." Social Studies of Science.

REISSERT, B. (1978) "Responsibility sharing and joint tasks in West German federalism," in P. B. Spahn (ed.) Principle of Federal Policy Coordination in the Federal Republic of Germany. Basic Issues and Annotated Legislation. Canberra: National University Press.

REISSERT, B. (1980) "Effects of federal and state grants on local government investment expenditures in West Germany," in D. Ashford et al. (eds.) National Resources and Urban Policy. New York: Methuen.

SPAHN, P. B. (1978) Principle of Federal Policy Coordination in the Federal Republic of Germany. Basic Issues and Annotated Legislation. Canberra: National University Press.

STEINHAUSEN, J. (1979) "Statement to: How we have tried to get along with the introduction of evaluation." Presented at the American-German evaluation research workshop, Berlin.

Studienkommission für die Reform des Öffentlichen Dienstrechts (1973) Bericht der Kommission, vols. 1ff.

YUILL, D., K. ALLEN, and C. HULL (1980) Regional Policy in the European Community. London: Croom Helm.

5

Using Evaluation to Improve
Program Performance

Joseph S. Wholey
U.S. Department of Health and
Human Services

OVERVIEW

My objective is to see evaluation used to improve the design and performance of government programs, my ultimate goal being *demonstrably effective programs*. This chapter examines the implications of successful and
not-so-successful evaluations—and then suggests two ways in which evaluators can contribute to better programs. My reflections are based both on
my work in evaluation research and my experience in policy-making
at federal and local government levels. The opinions expressed are my
own and do not necessarily represent the policies of the United States
Government.

As I use the terms in this paper,

- A government *program* is an organized set of resources and activities directed
  toward a common set of goals.
- *Program performance* includes resources invested, program activities undertaken, and outcomes and impacts of those program activities—including both
  progress toward program objectives and side effects.
- *Evaluation* is the measurement of program performance (efficiency, effectiveness, responsiveness), the making of comparisons based on those measurements, and the use of the resulting information in policy-making and
  program management. Evaluations are intended, in particular, to assist man-

agers in decisions on program regulations, guidelines, and technical assistance—and to assist policy makers in budget and legislative decisions.

The usefulness of evaluation is frequently questioned both by government officials and by evaluators. Policy makers and managers already receive unsystematic feedback on program performance *without* formal evaluation: from telephone calls, letters, meetings with constituents, the press, professional opinion, public interest groups, and officials at other levels of government. In any given instance, the value of systematic program evaluation is uncertain.

When evaluations are completed, government policy makers and managers often find the evaluations irrelevant. They typically complain that evaluations are too slow, are inconclusive, or answer the wrong questions.

My experience suggests that program evaluation is likely to be useful in improving government programs only if decision makers' information needs and intended uses for information are well defined. I therefore advocate two activities intended to help evaluation contribute to better program performance:

(1) My "tactical solution" is to work with program managers and policy makers to ensure that program objectives, performance indicators, and intended uses of information are well defined before evaluations are undertaken.
(2) The proposed "strategic solution" would create the incentives needed to stimulate program managers (a) to identify and get policy-level agreement on the sets of program objectives and performance indicators in terms of which their programs are to be assessed and managed, and (b) to manage program activities to achieve acceptable/improved program performance.

LACK OF IMPACT ON PROGRAM PERFORMANCE

Program managers are likely to use information to improve program performance only if there has been prior agreement (1) defining "improved performance" and (2) indicating how information will be used to improve program performance. I will begin with two evaluation efforts from my own experience: one successful; the other unsuccessful.

Legal Services Program[1]

For some time, the national Legal Services Program used a subjective peer review system in project refunding decisions (for example, decisions to impose special grant conditions). In this system, site-visit teams interviewed project staff and others in the community, rated staff attorneys, and then rated the quality and effectiveness of each of the local legal services projects in meeting national program goals (Duffy et al., 1971). For a typical project, a two-person team visited the project site for approximately two days. For larger projects, a larger evaluation team or a longer site-visit was required.

During each site-visit, evaluators contacted a wide range of people in the community, ranging from judges to the Black Panthers or other militant groups. The evaluators interviewed people from local welfare departments, housing authorities, and other groups aware of the legal problems of the poor. The evaluators attempted to get a wide range of subjective appraisals of the value of project services. In addition, the evaluators asked each staff attorney to select every fifth case from his or her last one hundred cases for reading and review by the evaluators. The evaluators selected three or four of the cases for discussion with the attorney; the attorney was asked to select three or four other cases that were also discussed.

The evaluators then rated individual staff attorneys on their performance with regard to each of the following factors: empathy with the community, interaction with the community, competence in routine cases, and competence in sophisticated cases. In the end, the evaluator gave an overall rating to each attorney. Each member of the evaluation team assigned ratings independently, though the evaluators did some of the data collection jointly.

At the end of the site-visit, each member of the evaluation team rated the project as a whole. The evaluators then pooled their ratings, and the leader of the team prepared a site-visit report according to a standard format. The site-visit report included a one-page summary, prepared before the evaluators left the site and submitted immediately to the central office in Washington. The Office of Legal Services used the resulting information in project refunding decisions.

Atlanta Public Schools

One of the most instructive examples of my evaluation career is that of an evaluation system that was *not* used to improve program performance in the Atlanta Public Schools (White et al., 1974; White, 1975). In 1971–1973, Bayla White, Sara Kelly, Dona Kemp, Joe Nay, John Waller, and I developed and tested a system for monitoring the relative performance of elementary schools in the Atlanta School system.

For each grade in each school, the students' average scores on standardized achievement tests were plotted against the proportion of students participating in the free (and reduced-price) lunch program.[2] Visual displays were then prepared presenting the standing of each grade in each school relative to curves locating average and close-to-average performance for all Atlanta schools. We then had a "signaling system," a quick, automatic way to pick out the schools that were doing very well or very poorly compared with what would have been expected, given the proportion of children in the school receiving free lunches.

White and Kemp (1976) note, however:

> Despite their acceptance of the underlying principle of comparing perform-
> ance among similar schools, Atlanta personnel found it difficult to use the
> signal information in operational decision making. We found only a few
> instances in which the information about relative performance was used to
> trigger the diagnosis of performance or reshape program activities.

> (*Note:* In this study, we adopted a "hands-off" policy. We were told by the
> federal funding agency that we were not to "coach" the recipients of our
> performance information on how that information should be used in managing
> the school system, because the federal agency wanted to learn whether simply
> providing information would make a difference in the management of the
> school system. We later felt that we had made a strategic mistake in not
> ensuring that we would be able to help management to use the evaluation
> data.)

Some Lessons Learned

What can we learn from these evaluation efforts—and from the many
others that we could have examined? Research on program evaluation indicates that evaluation is likely to lead to better program performance only if
the program design meets three conditions (Horst et al., 1974; Wholey et al.,
1975; and Wholey, 1979):

- *Condition 1: Program objectives are well-defined;* that is, those in charge[3] of
  the program have agreed on a set of realistic, measurable objectives and
  performance indicators on which the program is to be held accountable.
- *Condition 2: Program objectives are plausible/realistic;* that is, there is
  evidence that program activities have some likelihood of achieving progress
  toward program objectives.
- *Condition 3: Intended uses of information are well-defined;* that is, those in
  charge of the program have agreed on how program performance information
  will be used to achieve and demonstrate improved program performance.
  These are also the conditions indicating that program managers are ready to
  manage their programs to achieve and demonstrate better program performance ("manage for results").

In the Legal Services Program, evaluation produced relevant information
for use in specific management decisions. Prior interaction between evaluators and program managers had produced understanding of management's
objectives, appropriate performance indicators, and intended uses of
information—and an environment in which evaluation findings would be
used to improve performance.

In the Atlanta Public Schools, on the other hand, evaluators went off by
themselves and produced an information system that later proved to be

largely irrelevant and almost useless. School system policy makers and managers had not agreed on the program objectives and performance indicators on which their programs would be held accountable; evaluators had little understanding of how information would be used in specific management decisions.

USING EVALUATION TO IMPROVE PROGRAM DESIGN (THE TACTICAL SOLUTION)

Evaluation often fails to improve program performance because program objectives or intended uses of performance information are poorly defined. Why not directly attack these problems, having evaluators work with program managers and policy makers to ensure that Conditions 1, 2, and 3—definition of objectives, plausibility of objectives, agreement on intended use of information—are met before evaluations are undertaken? Evaluators know how to measure program performance and test causal links between program activities and intended results; managers and policy makers know what problems they are experiencing and what types of decisions they face. Given a choice of possible actions and information purchases, managers and policy makers may be able to select evaluation efforts that will lead to better programs.

Over the last five years, U.S. and Canadian governments have become increasingly interested in a process that uses the strengths of evaluators, program managers, and policy makers to

(a) document the objectives and expectations of program managers, policy makers to whom the managers are accountable, and those who deliver services at the local level;
(b) estimate the likelihood that measurable progress will be made toward program objectives;
(c) document intended uses of information on program performance; and
(d) identify changes in program activities or uses of information through which managers and policy makers could produce better designed, more effective programs.

This evaluation process, known variously as "evaluability assessment," "exploratory evaluation," or "accountability assessment," has been used to document and improve the designs of a number of U.S. and Canadian government programs and is being further developed and tested on a fairly broad scale by the U.S. Department of Health, Education and Welfare (HEW), the Canadian Auditor General's office, and a number of other agencies in both countries (Wholey, 1979; Rutman, 1980; and Auditor General of Canada, 1978). Evaluability assessment is being used to stimulate agreement on realistic, measurable program objectives, appropriate program performance indicators, and intended uses of program performance information before full-scale evaluations are begun.

Appalachian Regional Commission

In the Appalachian Regional Commission (ARC), for example, evaluators worked with managers and policy makers to achieve consensus on new program designs more likely to lead to demonstrably effective performance. Evaluability assessment of the Appalachian Regional Commission health and child development program began with collection of data on management's intentions and on program reality. In this evaluability assessment, the evaluators

- reviewed commission data on each of the 13 state ARC-funded health and child development programs;
- made one-day site visits to five states to aid in selection of two states to participate in evaluation system design and implementation;
- reviewed approximately 40 pieces of documentation considered essential in understanding congressional, commission, state, and project objectives and activities (including the authorizing legislation, congressional hearings and committee reports, state planning documents, and project grant applications);
- reviewed 50 to 60 other pieces of documentation including ARC contract reports, local planning documents, project materials, state documentation, and research projects;
- interviewed approximately 75 people on congressional staffs and in commission headquarters, state ARC and other state health and child development staffs, local planning units, and local projects; and
- participated in workshops with approximately 60 additional health and child development practitioners, ARC state personnel, and outside analysts.

Analysis and synthesis of the resulting data yielded a "logic model" that presented program activities, program objectives, and assumed causal links among program activities and objectives. The measurability and plausibility of program objectives were then analyzed and possible redefinitions of the program design were presented. Here the evaluators moved beyond sterile critiques of program design and suggested how managers and policy makers could establish realistic, measurable objectives and use program performance data to improve performance. Schmidt and Scanlon (1976) reported:

The Phase I Urban Institute report presented both an overall ARC program model and series of individual models, each concerned with an identified objective of the program. The report outlined a series of information options, expressed in modeling terms, any one of which could be developed into a specific study or evaluation system. In reviewing the report, then, ARC staff had to explicitly choose among alternative courses of action. The review process used was a series of intensive discussions, with ARC and Urban

Institute staff participating, in which we focused on one objective and program model at a time. In each session, we attempted to reach agreement on the validity of the flow models presented in the report, the extent to which the objective was important, and the extent to which any of the information options ought to be pursued.

This evaluability assessment was completed in approximately six months, at a cost of approximately $50,000. Another two months of work with the Appalachian Regional Commission and state and local groups resulted in ARC decisions to systematically monitor the performance of all ARC health and child development projects and to identify and evaluate the effectiveness of "innovative" health and child development projects.

Twelve of the thirteen ARC states have since adopted the performance monitoring system voluntarily. Representatives of those states report that project designs are now much more clearly articulated and that they believe the projects themselves have improved (Schmidt, 1979).

Bureau of Health Planning and Resources Development

In an evaluability assessment for HEW's Bureau of Health Planning and Resources Development, all of the key elements of evaluability assessment were again present: the evaluators explored the objectives and expectations of managers and policy makers, explored the reality of program operations, and identified evaluation/management options for more effective program performance (Wholey et al., 1977a).

In the evaluability assessment of the Health Planning program and three subprograms, evaluators reviewed documentation available in the Bureau of Health Planning and Resources Development, in local Health Systems agencies (HSAs) and State Health Planning and Development agencies, and from prior research and evaluation work. In exploring the bureau's intended program, the evaluators reviewed:

- 7 documents indicating congressional intent (the law, committee reports, congressional debates);
- 26 draft or final program regulations and guidelines;
- 30 reports, monographs, journal articles, and speeches;
- 25 memoranda prepared at bureau, agency, or department level;
- 10 program letters transmitting information to local and state health planning agencies;
- 7 documents describing bureau organization and staffing; and
- 8 Requests for Contracts (RFCs).

The evaluators interviewed all nine key managers in the Bureau of Health Planning; each of these managers was interviewed once at the start of the evaluability assessment (for one hour) and again when preliminary findings were available (for two additional hours). These managers were briefed and interviewed, individually and collectively, at the completion of the evaluability assessment.

The evaluators interviewed one staff member in the Office of the Secretary, two budget examiners in the U.S. Office of Management and Budget, and five House and Senate legislative and appropriations committee staff members. The evaluators also visited one HEW regional office, one regional Center for Health Planning, two State Health Planning and Development agencies, and three local Health Systems agencies.

To focus on evaluations that would be useful to bureau managers and staff, the evaluators presented assessments of three internal programs over which HEW managers had direct control: "Rulemaking" (production and dissemination of health planning program regulations and guidelines), "National Program Administration," and "Development and Dissemination of Discretionary Technical Assistance Products."[4] The evaluability assessment focused on (1) realistic objectives for the bureau's internal programs; (2) appropriate measures of performance for those programs; and (3) evaluation/management options the bureau should consider to improve the performance of these three programs.

The evaluability assessment documented the fact that the bureau's major programs were being managed to produce specific federal, state, and local products but that bureau managers had not agreed on outcome-oriented performance measures for any of these programs. It further indicated that none of the bureau's major programs appeared likely to achieve significant progress toward bureau objectives. Next, the evaluability assessment identified 14 evaluation/management options which appeared to have the potential for improving the performance of these three programs.

In order to assist managers in reacting to the evaluation/management options, the evaluators prepared a decision paper which (1) summarized the findings and conclusions in the three evaluability assessment reports; (2) described the 14 evaluation/management options open to managers and staff; and (3) summarized the next steps to be taken in deciding which options should be selected for further development and testing (Wholey et al., 1977b).

The evaluators then met with the nine bureau managers individually to brief the evaluability assessment findings, and to get their reactions to each of the findings, and to get their judgments on the priorities to be given to each of the evaluation/management options. The evaluators then prepared and the bureau director distributed three additional reports for consideration by bureau managers:

(a) a report (Urban Institute, 1978a) summarizing bureau managers' reactions to the evaluability assessment findings and the 14 options for the bureau's internal programs;

(b) an illustrative management and evaluation report (Urban Institute, 1978b) defining the bureau's internal programs, expectations, and possible new performance measures, and presenting hypothetical data showing results achieved to date and results expected in terms of these performance measures; and

(c) a preliminary draft bureau evaluation plan for fiscal years 1978 and 1979 (Urban Institute, 1978c).

Finally, the evaluators met with bureau managers in a group to present and test the tentative bureau consensus on evaluation/management priorities.

As a result of this and several follow-up meetings with the evaluators, bureau managers agreed on new measures of success for each of the bureau's major internal programs:

- For the "Rulemaking" program, bureau managers decided to monitor not only *planned vs. actual schedules for production of regulations and guidelines* but also *the opinions of Health Systems Agency and state agency staffs as their timeliness, understandability, usability, and practicality.*

- For the bureau's "National Program Administration" program, bureau managers decided to monitor the extent to which each Health Systems Agency and State agency:
  (a) *produces realistic plans for making measurable changes in the health care system;*
  (b) *demonstrates progress toward the measurable state/local objectives for the health care system;* and
  (c) *demonstrates progress toward specific federally defined objectives for the local/state health care system.*

- For the bureau's "Technical Assistance" program, bureau managers decided to monitor not only *planned vs. actual schedules for production and dissemination of discretionary technical assistance products* but also *Health Systems Agency and state agency reactions on the usefulness of selected technical assistance products.*

At the close of the evaluability assessment, it appeared that it had helped bureau managers to set realistic, measurable objectives for the bureau's major internal programs. It was not yet clear whether the evaluability assessment would help the bureau to refocus program activities and improve program performance.

The three evaluability assessments took approximately five and one-half months and 12 person-months of professional staff effort, approximately four person-months per evaluability assessment. Another three months and 1.5 person-months were required to get bureau management's responses to the three evaluability assessments.

The bureau has since completed the design and testing of a system for monitoring the performance of Health Systems agencies and state agencies—and is about to implement the system. The bureau's monitoring system includes the following elements (Bureau of Health Planning, 1979):

- telephone surveys of a sample of Health Systems agencies and state agencies to assess their progress in achieving specific objectives;
- follow-up site-visits to a subsample of those identified to validate information collected through the telephone surveys and to collect additional information on actual or anticipated effects of HSA/state agency activities; and
- development of case studies of successful strategies or methods employed by a sample of HSAs/state agencies.

Current Activities in the
Department of Health, Education and Welfare

In the Office of the Secretary of Health, Education and Welfare (HEW), we have initiated evaluability assessments of 10 programs. These evaluability assessments are cooperative efforts carried out by agency staff and OS evaluation staff. The intended products are sets of agreed-on objectives and performance indicators on which the programs will be held accountable— and on changes in program activities and uses of program performance information that will lead to demonstrably effective programs.

Our goal for FY 1980 is to help program managers to identify and get policy-level agreement on realistic measurable objectives and appropriate performance indicators for 20 HEW programs—and to demonstrate the value of the evaluability assessment process for achieving program manager/policy maker consensus on the sets of program objectives and performance indicators on which specific programs will be held accountable.

On the basis of the demonstration efforts to date, three other HEW agencies (the U.S. Office of Education, the Health Resources Administration, and the Health Services Administration) are beginning to develop and carry out evaluability assessments. The Office of Education, for example, is testing the usefulness of evaluability assessment in meeting the congressional requirement to identify specific measurable objectives for all its programs.

Further, the Department's FY 1980 Guidance for Evaluation Activities (Champion, 1980) encourages HEW managers and evaluators to "give high priority to activities designed to clarify program goals, identify appropriate program performance indicators, and document what is known about program performance in terms of those indicators," and asks each agency to prepare a schedule indicating the dates by which each program will "have a documented statement of agreed-upon measurable objectives, important side-effects, and the performance indicators on which the program will be held accountable."

CREATING INCENTIVES FOR RESULTS-ORIENTED MANAGEMENT AND IMPROVED PROGRAM PERFORMANCE (THE STRATEGIC SOLUTION)

Neither evaluability assessment nor other management/evaluation processes are likely to lead to better program performance unless a prior condition is satisfied:

Condition 0: Program managers are determined to achieve and demonstrate better program performance.

As I see it, evaluators can use evaluability assessment and other evaluation processes to help those rare program managers who wish to manage gain results related to program goals—or evaluators can go further to help create conditions that will stimulate the demand for results-oriented management and improved program performance (Scanlon, 1977). Throughout government, there is policy-level concern over the performance of programs—but there is little consistent progress toward better program performance.

To achieve and demonstrate better management and better program performance, four steps would be necessary:

(a) defining what "good performance" would mean in each program in terms of realistic, outcome-oriented objectives and performance indicators that would measure the extent of progress toward the program's legislative goals and agency priorities;
(b) establishing systems for measuring program performance (and intraprogram variations in performance);
(c) establishing program performance targets which are realistic in terms of resource availability and past performance in the program or related programs; and
(d) managing program resources to achieve improved program performance.

In many programs, there is uncertainty over even the first step: determining which directions would indicate better program performance.

In the United States government there are isolated efforts to improve program performance (for example, current efforts to reduce fraud and abuse), but there has been less policy-level attention to a root cause of poor program performance: the failure of government policy makers and managers to set realistic, outcome-oriented objectives which would adequately reflect progress toward their programs' legislative goals and agency priorities. Except in rare instances, there has been little real demand for results-oriented management or improved program performance. Neither the executive branch nor the Congress holds managers accountable for setting or achieving outcome-oriented program objectives.

There is a promising new development, however. The Civil Service Reform Act of 1978 is intended to create an environment in which pay and other incentives for government managers will be directed toward

(a) "providing a competent, honest, and productive work force,"
(b) "improving the quality of public service," and
(c) "improving the efficiency, effectiveness, and responsiveness of the Government to national needs."

Among the means to these ends are establishment of a Senior Executive Service, providing for merit pay systems and cash award programs, establishment of new systems of performance appraisal, and personnel research and demonstration programs. Civil Service Reform is directed at better management and ultimately at improvements in program efficiency, effectiveness, and responsiveness. Under the Civil Service Reform Act, federal managers and their staffs are to be held accountable for results—that is, for producing efficient, cost-effective programs which provide better services to the American people.

Implementation of the Civil Service Reform Act provides the United States government with an unusual opportunity to produce demonstrable improvements in the management and performance of federal programs. Government agencies can use currently available incentives (such as public recognition and cash awards) and new incentives available under the Civil Service Reform Act to recognize and reward program managers and their staffs for

(a) clarifying program goals and getting policy-level agreement on a set of realistic program objectives, important side effects, program performance indicators, and performance targets that would appropriately reflect progress toward the program's legislative goals and agency priorities; and
(b) demonstrating acceptable or improved program performance in terms of the agreed-on set of program objectives, performance indicators, and performance targets.

Evaluators should work with government policy makers to ensure that Conditions 0, 1, 2, and 3 are satisfied. In broad outline, the proposed effort would include the following elements:

(a) Federal agencies would develop an official list of agency programs.
(b) Federal agencies would develop timetables for identification and agreement on the set of program objectives and performance indicators on which their programs would be held accountable.

(c) In implementing the Civil Service Reform Act, federal agencies would require program managers, within a reasonable period of time, to identify and get policy-level agreement on the set of realistic outcome-oriented program objectives and performance indicators on which their programs will be held accountable.

(d) Each program manager would also be required, within a reasonable period of time, to produce documented evidence of the extent to which his or her program is being implemented satisfactorily and is producing the intended results.

(e) As soon as program performance is defined in terms of realistic measurable objectives and performance indicators that would appropriately reflect progress toward the program's legislative goals, federal agencies could use pay and other available incentives to reward program managers and their staffs for clarifying program goals and for demonstrating acceptable or improved program performance in terms of the agreed-on set of program performance indicators.[5]

Evaluators will be assisting in implementation of the Civil Service Reform Act in the U.S. Department of Health, Education and Welfare and in other federal agencies.

CONCLUSION

Given the increasing complexity of the problems government is asked to address, it is more important than ever to understand what government programs can realistically be expected to accomplish; to direct government activities to efficiently achieving realistic, agreed-on, outcome-oriented program objectives; and to recognize and reward managers and staffs for achieving progress toward agreed-on objectives related to problem goals.

In this chapter I have suggested two ways in which evaluators might help solve the problems faced by government managers and policy makers:

(1) assisting managers and policy makers in clarifying program goals, identifying the objectives and performance indicators on which the programs can realistically be held accountable, and developing evaluation/management options for changing program activities in ways that will enhance performance; and

(2) assisting government policy makers in developing and implementing systems that will create the incentives needed to stimulate managers and their staffs (a) to identify and get policy-level agreement on appropriate objectives and performance indicators, and (b) to manage program activities to achieve acceptable/improved performance.

At this moment, I am optimistic—optimistic that evaluators can work with managers and policy makers to improve program design and performance. Tomorrow will be better for evaluators, for managers, and for the citizens both groups serve.

NOTES

1. The descriptions of this and other evaluations are from Wholey (1979).

2. Atlanta students' performance on standardized tests was strongly correlated with the proportion of students receiving free (and reduced-price) lunches; that is, the proportion of students from low-income families. Other factors such as students' race, mobility, and attendance were not consistently or significantly correlated with achievement. See White and Kemp (1976).

3. For a specific program, "those in charge of the program" are typically six to twelve key people. In some cases, this group includes U.S. Office of Management and Budget examiners and key legislative and appropriations committee staff members.

4. The bureau's internal programs are typical of a large number of federal programs. See Wholey et al. (1978).

5. Incentives to be used could include personal recognition, public recognition, honor awards, cash awards (including bonuses for senior executives under the Civil Service Reform Act), quality increases, increased responsibility, removal of constraints, delegation of authority, allocation of staff, support for budget proposals, and support for legislative proposals that would enhance program performance.

REFERENCES

Auditor General of Canada (1978) Study of Procedures in Cost Effectiveness. Extracts from the 100th Annual Report of the Auditor General of Canada to the House of Commons.

Bureau of Health Planning (1979) Development and Implementation of HSA/SHPDA Performance Monitoring Systems. Hyattsville, MD: Health Resources Administration. (unpublished)

CHAMPION, H. (1980) FY 1980 Guidance for Evaluation, Research, and Statistical Activities. Washington, DC: U.S. Department of Health, Education and Welfare.

DUFFY, H. et al. (1971) Design of an On-Site Evaluation System for the Office of Legal Services. Washington, DC: The Urban Institute. (unpublished)

HORST, P. et al. (1974) "Program management and the federal evaluator." Public Administration Review 34 (July/August): 300–308.

RUTMAN, L. (1980) Planning Useful Evaluations: Evaluability Assessment. Beverly Hills, CA: Sage.

SCANLON, J. (1977) The Management Incentive Program: A Proposal to Make One of the Nation's Most Significant Resources, the Federal Workforce, More Efficient and Productive. Washington, DC: The Urban Institute. (unpublished)

SCHMIDT, R. (1979) Personal communication.

_____ and SCANLON, J. (1976) Appalachian Regional Commission Health and Child Development Program: Interim Evaluation System Design. Washngton, DC: The Urban Institute. (unpublished)

_____ (1971) "Comparison of the simplified and traditional methods of determining eligibility for and to families with dependent children." Report to the Committee on Finance, United States Senate. Washington, D.C.

United States Comptroller General (1977) "Finding out how programs are working: Suggestions for congressional oversight." Report to the Congress.

Urban Institute (1978a) Evaluability Assessment for the Bureau of Health Planning and Resources Development: Bureau Managers' Reactions to Findings and Evaluation/ Management Options. Washington, DC: The Urban Institute. (unpublished)

———— (1978b) Bureau of Health Planning and Resources Development: Bureau Program Performance: Activities, Objectives, and Results (Preliminary draft for bureau consideration). Washington, DC: The Urban Institute. (unpublished)

———— (1978c) Bureau of Health Planning and Resources Development: Preliminary Evaluation Plan: Fiscal Years 1978 and 1978 (Preliminary draft for bureau consideration). Washington, DC: The Urban Institute. (unpublished)

WHITE, B. (1975) "The Atlanta project: how one large school system responded to performance information." Policy Analysis 1 (Fall): 659–691.

———— and KEMP, D. (1976) "Performance information: does it make a difference? Presented at the American Educational Research Association Convention, San Francisco, April.

WHITE, B. et al. (1974) The Atlanta project: How One Large School System Responded to Performance Information. Washington, DC: The Urban Institute.

WHOLEY, J. (1979) Evaluation: Promise and Performance. Washington, DC: The Urban Institute.

WHOLEY, J. et al. (1978) Evaluation Planning for the Bureau of Health Planning and Resources Development: Draft Case Study. Washington, DC: The Urban Institute. (unpublished)

WHOLEY, J. et al. (1977a) Evaluation Planning for the Bureau of Health Planning and Resources Development. Washington, DC: The Urban Institute. (unpublished)

———— (1977b) Evaluation Planning for the Bureau of Health Planning and Resources Development: Decision Paper. Washington, DC: The Urban Institute. (unpublished)

———— et al. (1975a) "Evaluation: when is it really needed?" Evaluation 2(2): 89–93.

———— (1975b) "Social research and public policies." Presented at the Dartmouth/OECD Conference, Dartmouth College, Hanover, New Hampshire.

AUTHOR'S NOTE: An earlier version of this paper was presented at the Conference on the Future of Public Administration, Quebec, Canada, May 1979. At that time the author was Deputy Assistant Secretary for Evaluation in the Department of Health, Education and Welfare prior to its being renamed, in May 1980, the Department of Health and Human Services.

6

The Transfer of Public Policy Research from the United States to the Federal Republic of Germany

Stephen J. Fitzsimmons

*Abt Associates Forschung
Gesellschaft fur Social- und
Wirtschaftswissenschaften
mbH, Bonn*

How transferable are various American assumptions about the types of
public policy research and evaluation which can be conducted, the ways in
which it can be conducted, and the impacts it can and should have on policy
makers?

Based upon experiences gained through the actual transfer of one public
policy research organization from the United States to the Federal Republic
of Germany, this chapter will address some differences between the two
countries and their implications for both present and future policy research in
the Federal Republic. Our experiences, and the corresponding adaptations
we made to an "American Model"—adaptations in the organization, planning, staffing, acquisition, and performance of research in order to build a
public policy research organization—suggest some tentative answers to the
questions posed.

These comments are divided into three sections. First is some background on events which led up to the establishment of this organization in
Germany and on its subsequent development. Second, some hypotheses
about differences between the two nations, and their implications for the
conduct of such research in the Federal Republic, will be discussed. Finally,

some predictions on the future of this type of research during the next several years will be made.

There are pitfalls in generalizing about differences between these two countries; one is faced with the question of whether differences within are greater than differences between. The word "hypotheses" should be applied, since these observations are restricted to personal experiences; other researchers might reach different conclusions. The differences discussed are often matters of degree.

Value judgments that one country is "better" than the other on a given point are not inherent; rather, important differences do exist, and they have implications for those scientists and policy makers who share a desire to apply social research to the improvement of government and society.

My first contact as a social scientist with the Federal Republic of Germany occurred about six years ago. I came to Germany in connection with a study for the Federal Ministry for Research and Technology (BMFT). My research organization, Abt Associates Inc.[1] of Cambridge, Massachusetts, was contracted by the ministry to investigate the possible application of the concept of "technology transfer teams"—a concept developed for America's National Aeronautics and Space Administration. These teams were designed to bring scientists, manufacturers, and potential consumers together to explore the possible transfer of space program technology innovations to the solution of urban government (technology intensive) problems. Our organization had been selected because it had done much of the research and development work on this topic for NASA, and it was hoped that together with a German research firm we would be able to apply similar concepts and procedures in the new setting.

Abt Associates, along with a number of other private and quasi-private research organizations (such as Brookings Institute, Mathematica, National Opinion Research Center, Rand, Stanford Research Institute, Urban Institute) represents an American *organizational innovation* of the past two decades; namely, the organization of scientists and related specialists into research teams that perform highly specialized, applied research activities designed to assist policy makers (executive, legislative, and judicial) in decision-making. In a sense there were simultaneously two types of "transfers" involved here. First, the contract itself was exploring new approaches to the application of hard technologies to public sector problems. Second, the organizational approach to public policy research represented by the firm was being tested in another nation—a form of "social technology" transfer.

BACKGROUND

At the outset of our technology transfer project, we were also interested in the possibility of developing other research projects in Germany, particularly in social and economic policy research. We sensed that Germany would be an especially hospitable environment for the type of policy research conducted in the United States, for several reasons: its economic strength, population size, commitment to effective social progress, and a deeply ingrained tradition of basic research. However, we knew little about either the propensity of the federal and state governments to support this type of research or about the existence of organizations in Germany already doing such research. We recognized, however, that if we wanted to participate in policy research in the Federal Republic, we would probably have to locate an operation in Germany. Significant social research in the policy arena cannot be effectively conducted from afar.

A number of government agencies and research institutes were visited in order to learn about their interests, activities, priorities, staff, and organizations in which research was conducted. Reinhardt Bartholomai, then with the Labor Ministry, introduced me to innovative researchers in other agencies. He had just completed Germany's first social indicators report (1974), which described the real problems of obtaining cooperation among federal agencies, of agreeing on what research was needed, and on settling jurisdictional disputes. Detlef Affeld, then with the Youth Family and Health Ministry, discussed the harsh realities of trying to obtain data and conduct evaluations that cut across the interests of various public and private groups in light of their need for intergroup cooperation. Ulrich Pfeiffer of the Housing Ministry, and Helmut Kohn of the Commission on Economic and Social Change, who were supervising a range of applied social research projects, both stressed the need in Germany to move away from purely disciplinary research and "categorical program research" toward interdisciplinary, cross-program research (for example, economists and sociologists studying integrated labor and education policies). Aside from these substantive and political concerns, these public officials all observed the difficulty in finding organizations skilled in the delivery of interdisciplinary policy research which was tailored to agency needs. In short, Germany seemed, in certain of these respects, to be similar to the United States. However, there were two major differences. First, given the intellectual resources of the agencies and the strong commitment of the political parties to effective social programs, there seemed to be far fewer pilot programs and social experiments in Germany than would be expected. This was especially notable in light of the huge federal investments being made in social programs and the discussions on expanding these programs and creating new ones. Second, there appeared to be a relatively small community of research institutes whose primary concerns were with the broad spectrum of applied public policy research. Related to this, it was difficult to ascertain how much funding was actually being devoted to this type of research.

During subsequent visits to Germany and discussions with more than one hundred policy makers and researchers in federal and state agencies and in universities and research centers, a variety of other differences between the two countries became apparent. These differences might require that various adaptations be made in the "American Model" of a public policy research organization if it were to function effectively in Germany.

In 1977, our organization began operations in Germany. During the first few months much time was spent locating staff and advisors with interest and experience in public policy research. We also sponsored a conference on the future need for social programs and research in the Federal Republic. Members of government, universities, and research centers from both America and Germany presented papers on expected social programs and research in the 1980s. The experience in bringing together perspectives from both sides of the Atlantic clearly indicated the potential for transfer of ideas in both directions. However, when Americans discussed social experiments, elaborate research designs, and massive data bases, with comparable measure across states, it was often remarked: *"Das geht uberhaupt nicht in Deutschland!"* This comment, as we shall see, was a reflection on some differences between these two countries.

Based upon our experiences to date, Germany has proven to be an exciting place for policy research. Our staff, which now consists of more than 25 employees and consultants, is composed of German social scientists trained primarily in economics, sociology, and political science, with interests in applied public policy research. Most are skilled in research design and quantitative methods. At the present time we have acquired more than a dozen research projects from both federal and *länder* agencies. Many of the techniques regarding both the management of such projects and the research methodologies applied have been transferred from the parent corporation. Our research bears topical similarity to that of the parent corporation (in such areas as housing, unemployment, environmental protection, regional development, social impact assessment, and innovation and technology policy). However, in all cases the German policy and institutional context required adaptations in the conduct of the research. Moreover, we have seen only limited examples of research opportunities in large-scale, systematic program evaluations. Finally, there is presently only limited opportunity to work with "pilot programs," "social experiments," and "social impact assessments"—all of which represent the most innovative aspects of such research in the United States. These differences were, in fact, symptomatic of a variety of other differences in the society, its institutions, and its research orientations, all of which have a bearing on this type of research.

ENVIRONMENTAL IMPLICATIONS FOR PUBLIC POLICY RESEARCH

Perhaps the first thing a person interested in public policy issues notices when comparing these two countries is the differences in citizen awareness of public issues and their participation in political processes. While both countries have an active and free press, one sees and hears in Germany more frequent and more thorough discussion and debate of issues on television and radio, as well as in the press, than in many American cities. The difference is one of degree, but it appears fairly large. Not only students, but German adults as well, have maintained sustained interest in politics over the past couple of decades. While Americans become interested and active in specific issues (such as nuclear power plants, unemployment, health costs, and right to life), interest on any given issue often appears to have a relatively short duration for the larger electorate. This pattern does not restrict itself to domestic matters. Perhaps because of several hundred years of intense interaction with many other European cultures, German citizen interest in and awareness of activities in other countries is generally far greater than that of the average American, who often seems unaware and uninterested in what is going on in the rest of the world. This is also reflected in political participation in Germany which is quite active at the federal, state, and *länder* level. Perhaps one of the most striking behavioral indices of this phenomenon is the rather regular participation of between 80 and 90 percent of Germans in their federal elections, in contrast to the poor turnout of American voters when electing their representatives. Germans clearly are not apathetic about their government, parties, and the obligations of citizens.

Persons with an interest in policy research, then, generally find a more knowledgeable and active citizenry in Gemany. Much of this activity, it should be noted, operates through the various political parties. Here a second difference emerges. Americans seem to be far more active than Germans when it comes to mobilized public participation. Examples in recent years include the Black and Chicano movements, environmental protection, women's liberation, and tax rebellion. The German counterpart to this phenomenon—*Burgerinitiativen*—however, escalated rapidly in the late 1970s. In this respect, it is probably best to conclude that the styles of participation differ between the two groups of citizens. But there are some differences in the ways in which citizens look at things as well.

SOCIETAL DIFFERENCES IN OUTLOOK, COMPOSITION, AND PROGRAMS

For a long time Americans have been preoccupied with whether or not something "works." Naturally, certain values are stressed, such as individual freedoms, equity, honesty, and responsibility. But whether in business, government, or private life, Americans have always prized the "practical" approach to problem-solving. Teamwork is very much a part of this culture. Germany, which shares many of these basic values, appears to also possess some notable differences. One difference is that there is a profound interest in ideology. Within the democratic framework, the major parties are in a constant process of debate over the directions the society should take. The Social Democratic Party, the Christian Democratic Party, and the Liberal Party advocate different relationships among the state, the private sector, and the individual, and there is profound concern with the question, "What is the right thing to do?" Strong leadership is stressed in defining social goals. The corollary to this for public policy research is that studies in the United States are oriented more toward questions of how well a program is working (for example, is it efficient, effective, and relevant?). Researchers in the Federal Republic typically operate within the context of party-dominated agencies, and the legislative process has determined that a particular policy is appropriate; research tends to focus on issues such as whether a program is being implemented as it is supposed to be, how many persons receive services, and the like.

America and Germany also differ markedly in the composition of their society. In the United States, the population is made of descendants of immigrants from many races, lands, and cultures. The recent influx of Hispanic peoples (many of whom retain their mother tongue) and a rise in cultural awareness of Blacks is complemented by consciousness-raising among the various ethnic descendants of earlier settlers. Moreover, groups composed of women, the elderly, and youth have been stressing their differences and rights for special attention. The culture is heterogeneous. By contrast, and despite the large influx in the past decades of guest workers (who do not have the right to vote), Germany is a more homogeneous culture. Regional differences do exist, as, for example, between the Prussian culture in the north and the Bavarian culture in the south, or between rural and urban Germany; however, a strong basic culture with a long tradition is clearly present and thriving. Public policy research in the United States tends to be heavily preoccupied with issues of cultural differences as these influence both necessary policies and program diversity designed to reach different types of people. With the exception of the *Gastarbeiter* studies, most German public policy research operates under the assumption of cultural similarity, and issues arise as to differences among particular subgroups within the culture.

More in the realm of social differences, Germany has implemented the concept of the "social net" wherein the family, or individual, receives considerable support from the state in cases where self-support is a problem (for example, unemployment benefits, retirement programs, or health insurance). While the United States has programs with similar intent, they provide relatively less support to eligible citizens. Thus, considerable public policy research in the United States has been preoccupied with programs to serve the approximately 30 million poor people and to enable future generations to "escape from poverty" (for example, the Headstart and Follow Through programs). There is little demand for such research in Germany, although certain groups, such as the elderly, do seem at times to have very limited discretionary income.

These differences between the two societies have an impact on the nature of programs and policies implemented by the government. In the United States there is heavy emphasis on innovation in programs—attempting to discover ways of effectively serving different groups. Questions are asked as to "what works with whom." This orientation has led the U.S. government to embark on a variety of demonstrations and model programs and in recent years to attempt carefully studied "social experiments" in which controlled variations in a program are studied. These allow for, and have been accompanied by, more rigorous applied social research than has heretofore been possible. In contrast, the German government debates programs and laws in the Parliament; once decided, these federal programs tend to be implemented uniformly across the states.[2]

In Germany there are many examples of innovative, creative, and effective social programs at two distinct levels. First, a number of the national programs are well thought out (for example, job training and development for youth and various aspects of the social security program). The United States could learn a great deal from Germany about conceptualizing programs. Second, there are examples of pilot programs in Germany (such as emphasizing the provision of health care, which focuses on the patient as a human being, or providing community-based group therapy to single parents, or exploring new concepts in child care). These programs are developed at the community level and represent a protest against more established practices.

DIFFERENCES IN LEGISLATIVE PROCESSES

America has a representative form of government, wherein all Senators and Congressmen are elected by voters. Germany has a parliamentary form of government (and in recent times is generally governed by a coalition of parties). The legislative process in the United States essentially operates so that various reference groups—Republicans, Democrats, Liberals, Conservatives, pro-labor, and pro-business—influence legislation (for social programs) through a process of advocacy and compromise. Liberal Democrats and Republicans ultimately may vote together to override their respective conservative party members. In the Federal Republic, on the other hand, often intense debates erupt between the major two coalitions: following long party caucuses, the decision to fund a program is often decided by party dominance. A given policy enacted reflects that the ideology of the party has prevailed. Each party spells out in considerable detail why its program is the best for the citizens of the country. These differences have a number of consequences for the role of public policy research. Such research in the American context is frequently expected to provide feedback to the executive and legislative branches concerning what has happened following implementation of programs and policies. In recent years, probably more negative findings than positive ones have been reported, but the two political parties are concerned with whether or not their rationale or assumptions appear to be correct. In the Federal Republic, policy makers are far more interested in research that reports findings which support their contention that a program "is a good thing to do." Reports of research projects which reflect poorly on programs may not be released by agencies. Research on issues which is expected to potentially produce damaging findings may not be funded. Moreover, where several actor groups are involved and have very different objectives (as in the health field and among doctors, insurance companies, and the different states), obtaining support for "objective" research appears to be especially difficult. In this respect, the public policy researcher in Germany has a more difficult time securing sponsorship for broad-based, quantitative research than does his counterpart in America.

SUPPORT FOR PROGRAM EVALUATION AND POLICY RESEARCH

An important difference can be seen between the two governments in terms of legislation concerning program evaluation and public research policy. First, the U.S. Congress in the 1960s passed legislation requiring that programs initiated as a part of the Great Society program be evaluated and that the results be reported to Congress. Second, under the National Environmental Protection Act (NEPA), Congress required that Environmental Impact Statements (concerning economic, social, and environmental impacts) be produced prior to implementation of most federally supported investments. (Here the future with no project, versus project alternatives, is studied.) Considerable funding was appropriated to support such activities, and in 1978 more than $1 billion was allocated for external research on the programs of the government (and allocated across a broad spectrum of program areas). While there has been some legislation concerning Environmental Impact Statements in Germany (modeled partially after U.S. legislation), the German Parliament has not made such major allocations for the funding of public policy research (as Americans think of it). Rather, funding is directed more toward basic and disciplinary research on various social and economic matters. Comparable inter-nation figures are hard to find, but based upon our own analysis of the budgets of German federal agencies for research (as distinct from research *and* development), we estimate that Germany shortly may be funding social and economic research at a level of about DM 1 billion annually; and of this, between DM 75 and 150 million are available for various grants and contracts (the remainder being allocated to special research centers supported by federal and state agencies). These figures, however, do not distinguish between disciplinary and basic research on the one hand and distinctively policy-oriented research on the other. Thus, due significantly to legislative enactments, the research communities and the substance of their investigations differ considerably. The United States performs both absolutely and relatively more of this type of research through a greater diversity of research centers, and this research is more evenly distributed across various program areas. The United States has developed a greater number of institutes whose primary function is public policy research. Germany, in contrast, has relatively more single-purpose research centers which conduct less research that is directly targeted to policy decisions per se.

THE ROLE OF EXECUTIVE AGENCIES

In the United States, the federal government is the initiator of a broad range of social programs (in education, health, housing, welfare, employment, and so on). In many cases, regional, state, county, or local government agencies carry out program implementation. They may have varying degrees of control over program content, but the guidelines, standards, and requirements are in many cases federally mandated. In the Federal Republic, above and beyond various federal programs (such as unemployment compensation and housing assistance), the states appear to play a far more active role in determining the content, participation, and policy of many programs. Thus, German programs and policies vary from one state to the next. However, such differences have little to do with "planned variations;" rather, they reflect differences in local conditions, values, and political party dominance. It follows logically, therefore, that the nature, extent, and emphasis of the applied research activities in the states vary correspondingly. The public policy researcher in the United States has many opportunities to conduct systematic, comparative research (with a comparable data base) in programs across many states (and often among various cultural subgroups); survey and case study research can be combined—often funded under one contract with one research sponsor. In Germany, much research on social programs must be conducted within the state context (although there are some instances of cross-state evaluations). Moreover, unsystematic variations in program objectives, procedures, and contexts in available data, and often meager funds for program evaluations, mean that German policy researchers are placed at a distinct disadvantage. Case studies are often the only feasible form of research. The amount of systematic data available for analysis of differential program effects, under varying conditions and upon different groups of people, is at the present time very limited.

Although highly impressionistic, there appear to be some subtle differences in the perceived roles for policy makers in the two countries—perhaps corresponding to different bureaucratic functions. In the United States, many of the officials seem to have a "mission-oriented" attitude toward their jobs. Charged with program or policy implementation, they generally assume an active role, taking steps to ensure that things are happening, conducting site visits, facilitating communications among various participating agencies, and so on. Many Germans seem preoccupied with legitimate *"Kompetenz"* (authority) and have a more control or "monitoring-oriented" attitude toward their jobs—that is, they focus on documenting program inputs and compliance with procedures. This is especially true where states play a role in a program's implementation. Given this difference in orientation, there is a corresponding difference in attitudes toward program research. The public policy researcher in America is often asked to perform analytical research, using quantitative data, sampled according to fairly rigorous criteria. Considerable emphasis is placed on determining why programs work or fail to work with various recipient groups. In the Federal Republic, emphasis tends to be more on descriptive research, focusing on the number of recipients, the amount of funds expended, and services provided.

There are also differences in who supervises applied social research. In the United States, most of the federal employees I have worked with are trained in the social sciences (economics, sociology, and political science) or in allied areas (public administration, public health, education, or social work). These public officials frequently are heavily involved in designing the research requirements. In Germany many persons, especially senior officials, have been trained in law or a field akin to business administration. As such, their orientation seems more legal and procedural than on research per se, and some of them are less interested in or familiar with standard empirical research methods and techniques. The policy researcher in the United States frequently finds himself working in a more collegial relationship—speaking the same research language as that of his sponsor. In Germany, social scientists often find that the sponsor views many words and concepts as foreign. Communication tends to take place on different levels in the two countries vis-á-vis policy research.

A related issue concerns the interchange of university and government employment opportunities on a temporary basis. This has occurred in the United States for many years with heavy participation of social scientists in government. While there certainly are many professors who consult with German agencies, the "cross-employment" phenomenon is largely nonexistent. The typical university faculty member will never be an employee of a federal agency, and vice versa. While in both countries there is some tendency to think of professors in "ivory towers" (not understanding the problems of the "real world"), the participation of American university professors in government serves at minimum to heighten their understanding of internal policy matters of the federal agencies; likewise, the government researcher who spends a few years teaching and doing research has a better understanding of why scientific rigor is important to policy studies. In short, there appears to be a larger gulf between government and academia in Germany.

There is also a difference in the general attitudes of federal agency staffs in the two countries toward the use of data. Despite various exceptions, many American agencies (such as the Census Bureau, Agriculture, and Labor) seem quite disposed to the provision of data for use in research projects. The Census Use Studies are good examples of active efforts to make data available for local research purposes. In contrast, in Germany agencies are somewhat less disposed to share data with researchers; furthermore, the data are stored in more diffuse places (and under a greater variety of authorities). Cooperation among various data holders is frequently hard to obtain (even by the agencies themselves!). The average American policy researcher has a much easier time on this score than does his German counterpart.

UNIVERSITY DIFFERENCES

Two issues appear to have implications for applied research. The first is that the American departments are, in general, somewhat more oriented toward empirical research, while the German departments are somewhat more oriented toward theoretical considerations. There are, of course, notable empirical centers in Germany and notable theoretical departments in the United States. However, there is a greater emphasis in the United States on the development of empirical models of various phenomena, whereas in Germany there appears to be a greater concern (at least among graduate students) with the development of heuristic models. (Economics may be an exception, for there is considerable empirical testing of models in Germany in this field). German scientists seem to have "thought through" their models and concepts somewhat better than the Americans, but then have trouble obtaining data to test these models. Americans seem to do better in testing their models, but then have trouble explaining their results!

These differences in emphasis have manpower implications as well. In establishing our institute in Germany, we have encountered some difficulties in locating staff who have had actual experience in the design and conduct of research (wherein they have actually collected and analyzed their own data). To be sure, several German departments stress this, but many do not. German students seem to be well versed in the theory of their disciplines. But going beyond the *Diplom* (roughly equivalent to the U.S. Master's degree— depending on the field), in their doctoral studies, German students simply have less formal coursework focusing on research methodology and actual data-gathering than do their American counterparts. My experience in the United States was somewhat the reverse: students were well prepared on the empirical side but had weaker backgrounds in theory. To the extent that public policy research requires recent doctoral graduates who can move quickly into empirical research activities, there is a proportionately smaller pool of candidates to draw from in Germany, and the training time required to get up to minimum proficiency is greater.

RESEARCH CENTERS

The effect of legislation requiring various forms of policy research in the United States (much of which is large in scale and interdisciplinary in orientation) has been to foster the development of a large number and variety of research centers in the private and quasi-private sector (as well as special policy institutes in various universities). In Germany, where demand has been much less and where government heavily funds more disciplinary and sector-specific research, the vast majority of research is carried out by universities, federally supported research institutes, and specific state institutes. Germany appears to be richer in its number and diversity of single-purpose research organizations within the public sector, with somewhat less emphasis on applied research; while America seems to offer a much broader range of research organizations specifically concerned with applied, analytical policy research across various program areas.

Within this context of funding—and specifically with respect to social research—the United States government has now funded, through competitive procurements, numerous large evaluations and social experiments— many of them amounting to millions of dollars per study. Most of this research has been conducted under contract mechanisms which allow the government to play an active role in the conduct of the study. In contrast, in Germany, the majority of federal agencies appear to use the grant mechanism wherein there is less specification of exactly what research approaches will be taken. Regularly funded research centers, in fact, can and do receive large grants each year for their ongoing research. However, many grants to individual professors or to departments are relatively small in amount and short in duration. The public policy researcher in the United States, then, has been given more opportunities for large-scale, systematic research than have been available to researchers in the past few years in Germany. Conversely, the United States has witnessed in the past decade a considerable reduction in the availability of grants, especially of the smaller variety, while in the German university departments and public research institutions grant opportunities appear to be relatively greater than in the United States at present.

Policy researchers also face different legal situations in obtaining data. As indicated above, U.S. federal agencies seem to encourage sharing of data, and this has been true of many agencies for many years. The passage of the Freedom of Information Act and the Right to Privacy Act formalized many procedural aspects and furthered access to data (especially access to anonymized microdata). German government agencies are regulated by a data protection act, as well as by a host of internal regulations concerning conditions for access to information. In general, American researchers simply have a much easier time obtaining data and information they need for their research or which is useful as auxiliary information. In Germany, where data are to be obtained covering different aspects of a program area, complex negotiations often have to be conducted with four or five separate entities (and some of the success of such negotiations appears to be a function of obtaining good rapport with a data holder, above and beyond the legal adherences). One further difference is that a requirement does not exist in Germany that, after 90 days, all studies must be made available to the public. There are a number of cases of completed studies not being released by agencies, which will not permit publication of study findings without permission. As a result, professional growth through publication, as well as information, is curtailed. Often, German researchers will not accept work with such a "publication permission" clause, but many others must accept those conditions if they wish to obtain contracts to conduct research.

Work laws also affect the characteristics of research centers. In the United States the union movement as yet has had only limited presence in the research firm, and there are few external checks on American organizations in terms of hiring and dismissal.[3] In contrast, German research organizations (like all German employers) are covered by national employment security laws. An organization needs to be relatively assured of a steady stream of work (as through longer term contracts) before hiring any staff member. To get around this requirement, it is a common practice in Germany to issue strict "time contracts," which means that a staff member must leave the organization after a number of years (usually five). Thus, public policy research centers in the United States, which do not afford employment security, can staff up for special projects with a little less hesitancy than does the German organization. This partially explains why the flow of employment among research centers, university departments, and government is more constrained in Germany than in America. Also, and again partially as a result of these employment security laws, German research centers appear less growth-oriented than their American counterparts; stability is valued more than growth.

Finally, there are also differences in the characteristics of the center as an operating institution. There is a somewhat longer history of social research being applied in the public policy context in the United States than in the Federal Republic. In addition, the volume, project size, and diversity of projects handled by the policy research centers has been greater. Researchers have been given some sizable research challenges (for example, with the application of quasi-experimental designs, use of extremely large samples in longitudinal studies, and so on). As a result, the need to innovate is constantly present; teamwork (especially interdisciplinary teams) has been a critical factor; organizations have been growth-oriented, and in a sense very entrepreneurial; and, over the past decade, management concepts for such operations have emerged (involving everything from various line and staff management functions, complex labor planning systems, accounting systems developed for a labor intensive research industry, and so forth). Many new journals have emerged, reflecting a response to interest in policy research findings and interdisciplinary interest. In short, a new institution has developed and established a variety of widely shared practices. While there have been a number of major research projects in Germany (such as social indicators research, the income transfer study, and national housing surveys), these have occurred largely within the existing institutional framework, albeit with some interuniversity linkages. A strong emphasis continues on theoretical study directions with less emphasis on management questions (such as research teams, research project management, budgeting, and client involvement throughout the course of research) which characterizes much U.S. policy research. For example, the operations research procedures for project planning seem less widely applied by German groups in project implementation. Perhaps the best way to sum it up is that while each of these characteristics is found in various German research organizations, they are not typically found in combination across a large number of organizations. In short, it does not appear that the "critical mass" has yet been achieved in the public policy research community. Large-scale, sustained funding has not been available to enough organizations long enough for this to have occurred. For these reasons, the American model of the policy institute is not as typical today in Germany. Much of this has to do with the funding of research.

DIFFERENCES IN RESEARCH PROCUREMENT

A great deal of the U.S. contract research is advertised in the *Commerce Business Daily*. This is supplemented by various announcements and notices in professional newsletters. Information about available sources of funds is widely disseminated. Moreover, several years ago Congress and the executive branches placed considerable stress on the importance of geographical diversification of funding, so that universities, private institutions, and state and regional centers around the country are reasonably equitable (albeit competitive). While several agencies in the Federal Republic do issue public announcements for social research opportunities (notably the housing, development, and education ministries), this practice, and the centralized availability of information on research grants, appears to be the exception rather than the rule vis-à-vis research project funding. Thus, in contrast to the highly competitive situation in the U.S., German research is still funded in more of a "closed shop" environment. It is not unusual for individual research centers and university departments to be funded over many years on a variety of projects. While this promotes good understanding of the problems (and the orientation of the agency providing the funding), it can also limit the extent to which new ideas and concerns over more innovative research strategies can emerge.

The procurement process appears to move much more slowly in Germany than in the United States. American researchers are accustomed to receiving notifications of award within a couple of months of proposal submission (perhaps involving a final round of negotiations) and then starting the research process within one or two months. In the Federal Republic the time lapse between notification of award and actual receipt of a signed contract can vary from two weeks (exceptional) to three to seven months (normal) to two years (extreme). To deal with this problem, agencies sometimes give "verbal work orders" which allow research centers to start work before a contract is received. In one case a colleague turned in the final report after one year without having ever received a signed contract!

Finally, in contrast with the United States, the majority of contracts in the Federal Republic seem to involve initial sole-source submissions: the ideas on what to investigate and how to investigate are often initiated by the supplier. This is especially true where the government agents are lawyers and less experienced in the research procedures. While American professors are continually submitting grant applications in selected agencies, funded research in America is determined far more by the demand side. In both countries, agencies have "research windows" within which grant applications must fall, but German scientists probably have a greater freedom in determining the way in which projects will be carried out while at the same time having less opportunity to obtain funding for large projects.

Table 6.1 summarizes these hypotheses. It is important to remember that the emphasis here is on differences in degree, rather than absolute differences. Also, differences have been stressed which appear to be relevant for the transfer of the organizational procedures associated with public policy

TABLE 6.1

INSTITUTION	NATIONAL DIFFERENCE		POLICY RESEARCH DIFFERENCE	
	America	Germany	America	Germany
SOCIETY	Pragmatic traditions	Ideological traditions	Concern: Does it work?	Concern: Is it the right thing to do?
	Heterogeneous	Homogeneous	What works with whom?	Equity of distribution
			Diverse programs	Standardized programs
			Trend toward pilot and experimental programs and evaluation	Community-based pilot programs, with limited evaluation
	High poverty population	"Social net" with low poverty population	Emphasis on "anti-poverty" research	Little need for such research
LEGISLATION	Compromise of Interests	Dominance by Party	Congress wants feedback/ rationale	Party wants support
	Congress requires evaluation, and future impact assessment	Tendency of parliament to cut funds for social research	High demand for policy research	Moderate to lower demand for evaluation and impact studies
EXECUTIVE	Many programs run by federal agencies	Many programs run by *länder* agencies	More systematic, comparative research	More case studies
	Mission oriented	Control oriented	Analytic research	Descriptive research
	High exchange of staff between government and universities	Low exchange of staff between government and universities	Government/university *tend* toward congruence	Government/university *tend* toward divergence
	Government social scientists supervise research	Government lawyers supervise research	Focus on research methodology and analysis	Focus on process and description

	Government agencies frequently stress information assistance	Government agencies frequently stress information control	Ease of access to information	Difficult access to information
DIVERSITY	More empirical emphasis	More theoretical emphasis	More empirical models with robust data	More heuristic models with strong theory
	Students trained in research	Students trained in theory and logic	Large policy research manpower pool	Small policy research manpower pool
RESEARCH CENTERS	Heavily dispersed through public, private, and quasi-private sectors	Heavily concentrated in public sector	Heterogeneous research mechanisms; more multi-purpose centers	Homogeneous research mechanisms; more single-purpose centers
	Many large contracts above and beyond grants	Large grant mechanism research vs. smaller contracted research	More large-scale applied research	More middle- and large-scale basic or discipline research
	Funding of surveys and panels	Funding of descriptive research and case studies	Large analytic capacities	More descriptive capacity
	Research covered by Freedom of Information and Privacy Acts	Research covered by Data Protection Act	Easy access to research reports and data	Difficult access to research reports and data
	Absence of strong work laws	Presence of strong work laws	Easy flow of staff among research centers and other employers	Much lower turnover in staff
	Long history of applied social research	Shorter history of applied social research	Management techniques well developed for evaluations and social experiments	Management techniques still emerging

Continued on next page

TABLE 6.1 Continued

INSTITUTION	NATIONAL DIFFERENCE		POLICY RESEARCH DIFFERENCE	
	America	*Germany*	*America*	*Germany*
			Growth oriented Diversity of research areas	Stability oriented Continuity of work areas
	Innovation oriented	Scholarship oriented	Greater acceptance of new methodologies	Greater expectation of consistency and throughout in approach
RESEARCH CENTERS (cont.)	Entrepreneurial and growth oriented	Stability oriented	Rapid growth and diversification	Slow growth and single-area research
	Team efforts on problem-oriented research	Leader centered on disciplinary-single-program research	More interdisciplinary	More disciplinary
PROCUREMENT	Well-publicized, coordinated, and open procurements	Low amount of publicity, uncoordinated and restrictive procurements	Extensive research competition	Competition with "closed shop" framework
	Internal agency research activities run in parallel coordination	Internal agency research activities run in sequential coordination	Short period from award of research to start-up (1–2 months)	Long period from award of research to start-up (3–12 months)
	Agency determined	Agency and supply determined	Targeted research	Less targeted research
			Policy researcher contributes ideas during project	Policy researcher contributes ideas before project

research centers, American-style. What do these differences mean in the aggregate? First, we have always known that the findings of public policy research in America were not directly transferable to Germany, and vice versa. Obvious differences in population, culture, institutional functions, and political process all mean that the methods used to study a problem could possibly be transferred, but that the findings on various issues (for example, how to reduce unemployment) often would be less applicable. What these differences suggest is that the various assumptions underlying the organization and conduct of research are also subject to modification when crossing the Atlantic. German public policy centers differ in how they approach staffing, training, organization development, acquisition of work, and the conduct of research. Their longer term goals also tend to be somewhat different in terms of growth and breadth of policy research which they seek to incorporate within one center. Second, and seemingly a contradiction, it is precisely the American style of policy research and policy research management (as distinct from methodological innovation) which has, at this point in time, some valuable contributions to make to the research scene in the Federal Republic. There are two elements involved in resolving this paradox.

First, both American and German public policy research environments and organizations are changing. American applied research capacities have markedly strengthened in the past decade (especially in social experiments and environmental impact assessments and in terms of research management strategies); it has also become clearer as to where such research can have policy impacts and where a situation places severe limitations on utilization. Simultaneously, there are significant changes taking place in German governmental agencies, universities, and in the marketplace itself which are favorable to this type of research—some changes are already well under way. America has a great deal of experience to offer in development and management of such research, and Germany is more ready to apply such approaches than at any time in the past. Second, Americans and Germans who wish to facilitate the cross-transfer of policy research procedures need to work together in both countries to bring it about. Short-term visits by German social scientists to such institutions in the United States are useful, but not enough. Short-term visits by Americans to the Federal Republic are not enough. Americans have too much to learn about the German political, social and cultural context to do this in a short time. Germans will have difficulties seeing the entire research organization picture to be able to learn these techniques in the United States (especially management) in a couple of months. Prolonged exposure and application appear to be the only feasible solutions to effective cross-applications.

CHANGES IN DEMAND FOR POLICY RESEARCH—
PRESENT AND FUTURE

During the past few years in the Federal Republic there has been a notable increase both in the demand for government-sponsored policy research and evaluation and in the supply of institutes and individuals responding to this rising demand. We will see an acceleration of these parallel trends during the coming decade. Among the trends already discernible are the following.

(1) There has been an increase in the percentage of the total research budgets of various federal and state agencies allocated specifically to evaluation of programs and analyses of various policies. However, certain agencies and states are well ahead of others in this respect; that is, while the trend is not yet "uniform," it seems to be established.

(2) There seems to be a growing specificity of topics related to policy studies for which researchers are being sought; in other words, policy research is becoming more targeted in its questions.

(3) While much of this evaluation activity concerns already existing programs, there is some funding available concerning the probable future impacts of alternative programs (or policies) under consideration. Related to this are plans for evaluations to begin with new program initiatives.

(4) A growing number of German universities are stressing empirical research, thereby increasing significantly the supply of new graduates prepared to conduct applied, empirical social research.

(5) Given the limited number of available university positions and increasing opportunities for graduates to work either in government or in various non-university-based institutes, an increasing number of social science graduates are seeking employment in these alternative settings.

(6) Increasingly, social scientists are working with the research divisions of the federal and state agencies (either as regular employees or as professors with consultant status). These individuals, in turn, are raising the quality of requests for research proposals (and ideas) in terms of the specification of research questions, design and data-gathering procedures, and analysis planned to complete the research. They are also able to interact on a more collegial basis with external research centers than was typical for the earlier generation of government employees trained in law or administration.

(7) There has been a shift in certain agencies (housing, development, and education) away from heavy reliance on sole-source submissions and toward public, competitive procurement for contracts and grants. Research projects are therefore being awarded to the growing diversity of research centers (which are evolving in response to this demand).

Looking toward the 1980s, a number of additional changes relevant for policy research in response to three phenomena will occur. First, the economic growth of Germany appears to be settling into a rather stable pattern (between three and four percent a year). However, due to various legislative entitlements established by the parliament in the 1960s and early 1970s (in a period when Germany's economic growth rate was considerably higher), demands on the treasury are continually rising (related to retirement payments, unemployment compensation, welfare funds, defense expenditures, health payments, and energy investments). Parliament has passed two recent increases in the Value Added Tax rate to support these demands. Thus, competing, often incommensurable needs for scarce tax revenues are forcing the parliament to set more stringent priorities in order to avoid further unpopular tax increases. Second, and quite naturally, changes in the composition and characteristics of the population, as well as in public values and priorities, are generating pressures for new policies and programs for the 1980s which, if passed into law, will further force competition for scarce funds among various government agencies. Third, the whole phenomenon of relatively broad-based *Burger-Initiativen* (citizen action groups) is becoming an important political factor in the German policy-making environment. In contrast to a decade ago, when student groups often typified public protests, today we see a more broadly-based, organized public speaking out on various issues. Recent examples include the anti-nuclear power plant protests, the environmental movement, and, to a lesser extent, the women's movement; all of this constitutes a public role which the parliament can ill afford to ignore. Thus, a combination of rising costs of existing programs, demand for new initiatives responsive to emerging public needs, and active citizen involvement together will mean growing pressure to improve the efficiency of many existing programs, trim or eliminate others, and figure out how to start new initiatives within reasonable cost constraints. In many cases, it will not be apparent which programs should be kept, how to improve them, or, in the case of new initiatives, what program concepts are likely to be most effective. This context leads me to the following expectations.

(8) There will be a marked increase in the use of applied social research in the 1980s as part of the government information-gathering and decision-making process. While by no means the dominant force, such research will take on a more robust role in supporting decision-making in government and, through better coverage in the mass media, contributing to the public debate.

(9) Based upon some of the longer term and heatedly discussed social issues, certain areas will emerge as major research themes. These will

include a heavy emphasis on various employment issues (youth, women, the "second generation" *gastarbeiters,* job retraining, job enrichment, and alternate career planning), education (including integrated curricula in the public schools, vocational education in the firm, adult and continuing education, and technology impacts on regular media forms), health service delivery and cost factors, urban development, transportation system developments, aspects of crime and the criminal justice system, family problems, and population research. Much of this research will concentrate on problem definition, specific group needs, and the programs suited to bring about social changes within reasonable costs.

(10) This research will be "problem-centered," and we can expect to see increasing emphasis on collection of empirical data, careful sampling procedures, large-scale social surveys, and interdisciplinary research. Greater emphasis will be placed on communication of results in a manner understandable to legislators and to the public.

(11) In the most progressive federal agencies and states, alternative pilot programs and, in limited cases, social experiments (that is, subjects receiving a service under a random design, rationalized as the most equitable approach, given more applicants than available services) will be increased. Though they may be limited in number, they will constitute the most significant opportunities for policy research. They will provide examples of the ability to generalize findings to a larger population and show the value of more analytic designs relative to policy questions.

(12) Given concern about budgets, research projects will examine such issues as participation rates in programs and unit costs, as well as related questions of cost effectiveness, cost efficiency, and program administration and outreach practices.

(13) When the present research on Germany's income transfer programs, being conducted by Professor Krupp and his colleagues, is released, a clearer picture will emerge of how Germany is achieving its social net—who are its various beneficiaries and possible inequities, and where various problems may exist. This will, in turn, set further research projects into motion which will look at how well individual programs seem to be performing. In the longer run, there may be some revisions in benefit formulas, eligible population, and the like.

(14) Applied social research budgets of the various agencies will be forced to expand as a percentage of total research budget, and this will be somewhat at the expense of more traditional research. There will be a rise in the number and diversity of interdisciplinary research centers, but will further a shift in the applied direction of many of the university research centers in order to accommodate this more targeted research. Good performers (those whose work is seen as relevant, high quality, and is delivered on time

and within budget) will do especially well, as government agencies (with increasingly sophisticated research management) become both more critical and more demanding of their research providers. To cope with these pressures, research centers will have to improve their own management (especially with respect to staffing, training, project assignment, general management, and keeping within contract budgets).

(15) Social and environmental impact assessments (that is, looking beyond economic impacts) of alternative projects which are still "on the drawing boards" represent a major form of research which should become increasingly important during the next three to five years. Both parliamentary concerns and *Burger-Initiativen* will speed this emphasis.

(16) While major changes in the ideological battle styles between the major party coalitions are unlikely, the parties and their representatives in the various ministries will become more receptive to evaluation research. I doubt, however, that the various attitudes toward "objective" research on major political priorities will change much. Political pressures from the public, press, and special-interest groups may, however, lead to exploration of alternative programs designed to achieve similar goals, cost effectiveness and efficiency questions, and so forth.

In short, the assessment of many of the present and future research trends in Germany's public policy research is optimistic. Such research will gradually increase as a source of information in the policy-making process, although political considerations will continue to be the dominant factor in decision-making (as is true in the United States). An active free press and public interest pressures will make it increasingly difficult for politicians to ignore important findings.

Among the countries of Western Europe, Germany appears to be likely to cross the threshold and achieve the critical mass necessary for the development of a highly active and viable public policy research community. However, the institutional, cultural, intellectual, and ideological forces of the culture will play powerful roles in determining the style, content, subject matter, and priorities of this research. Rather than being a reflection of American-based assumptions, this public policy research community will be "Made in Germany."

NOTES

1. Abt Associates was established in the United States 14 years ago. It is devoted to the application of social sciences, operations research, and knowledge of social programs to the evaluation of government programs and policies.

2. In one notable respect, however, there is considerable diversity in public programs. This exists where the states themselves are responsible for program implementation (notably in health and education). Unfortunately, it is very difficult to obtain similar data on programs across *länder,* so that while the potential for comparative research on different programs exists in the Federal Republic, it is at present largely unrealized for policy analysis purposes.

3.The Equal Opportunity Act affects who is hired, but usually not the general policies of hiring and termination per se.

REFERENCE

BARTHOLOMAI, R. (1974) Gesellschaftliche Daten 1973. Bonn: Presse- und Informationsmat Bundersregierung.

AUTHOR'S NOTE: The author would like to express his appreciation to members of the West German federal and state agencies and research organizations, whose willingness to share their time, ideas, and counsel has contributed to insights presented in this chapter. In addition, both the American and German staff of Abt Associates have contributed many ideas. Finally, members of the Abt Associates Forschung Scientific Advisory Board have been very helpful. They include: Dr. Clark C. Abt and Professors Kenneth Arrow, Daniel Bell, Hans Jurgen Krupp, Renate Mayntz, Erwin Scheuch, Carl Christian von Weizacker, and Rudolf Wildenmann. However, the points made in this article, and opinions expressed, are solely the responsibility of the author.

PART III

IMPROVING EVALUATION
RESEARCH STRATEGIES

Evaluation research strategies have evolved parallel with traditional paradigms of scientific research. The experimental design as ideal model is being increasingly challenged by more interpretive designs based on interaction, qualitative, and ethnographic research paradigms. Those conflicts have largely negated the combined force which a careful mixture of research approaches may provide. Jealousy and competition across disciplines have made discussion of cross-fertilization more difficult. As a result, the benefits of stimulation, combinations of research traditions have been limited. Martin Rein, an advocate and pathbreaker for a more qualitative research design, challenges the narrow focus of much of contemporary evaluation research. He provides a framework for a comprehensive evaluation strategy which integrates the task of process and outcome evaluation. On the basis of a case study, some of the most experienced European evaluation researchers, Professors Franz-Xavier Kaufman and Klaus-Peter Strohmeier, reiterate this thesis and stress the need for mixing theory-based tradition characteristic of European research with the experimental tradition in evaluation research developed in the United States. They stress the importance of more responsive and relevant research strategies. Manfred Küchler's case study aptly illustrates that the reflected use of quantitative models may still help to approach the casual questions in evaluation research without the need to rely on experimental models.

7

Comprehensive Program Evaluation

Martin Rein
Massachusetts Institute of Technology

THE CONTEXT OF PROGRAM EVALUATION

Most evaluations take as their primary task a focus on programmatic outcome. The critical aim for an evaluation study is the specification of whether the program works—that is, whether the original intent was carried out.

I think this "reading" is not correct. There is more to evaluation than the study of effects, or the analysis of the extent to which intent is realized. This makes clarity of intent critical; yet, a decade of experience with evaluations makes it clear that programs change in midstream. Even if programs did not adjust to changes in the environment as they evolved, and if they rigidly conformed to the prespecified set of legislative intents, over time the users themselves would change their ideas about the preferred results.

Experience in implementing a program often leads to a change of mind about what the program can or should do. A review of outcomes helps in understanding intentions. In this sense, the beginning and the summative review of a program are parts of the same process. This suggests that the meaning of the outcome is different after the effort of getting there because at a later point in time a new context of events emerged. Having discovered what the outcome looks like, one can then reassess whether that objective seems either more or less important than when the program began.

A recent General Accounting Office report, "Finding Out How Programs Are Working: Suggestions for Congressional Oversight," cites some difficulties involved in attempting to make a one-time, or summative, assessment of a program's achievements. The report observes that "what is desirable is often altered with the passage of time by circumstance or the availability of additional information. . . . Early overspecification of program goals or measures for oversight questions may lead to questions being asked that are simply unanswerable from inspection of the program as it actually operates."

The idea that we cannot specify in advance the destination of the chosen journey also seems counterintuitive. As Wholey states, "if you don't know or care where you get to, then it doesn't matter which way you go." These insights naturally draw us to the further specification of our goals.

The United States Senate resolved to work on the problem of goal clarification. A Senate resolution required the specification of legislative intent so that Congress could judge programmatic effectiveness during appropriation or reauthorization decisions. The GAO was asked to assist, which it did by testing the feasibility of goal specifications in an intensive examination of two cases. It concluded that "the results of the dry run did not produce an optimistic forecast that the resolution could do what it intended." Why can't government be clear about what it is trying to do? The GAO report explains, "People in groups [that is, interest groups] are often interested in and will accept only certain measures of outcomes. These may be of no interest and/or completely unacceptable to other people and groups." A wide range of oversight questions seems plausible "depending on where interests are accepted by the analyst" (U.S. Comptroller General, 1977). In summary, then, the GAO found that people change their minds over time. Different groups of people want different things, and much depends not on intent but on the way the program is in fact implemented. Because of these considerations, programs can be evaluated from a variety of perspectives.

What is the scope of evaluation of effects? This question takes on special urgency because specifying aims depends on a variety of factors that ranges from the source of knowledge about the subject to the micropolitics of legislative committees. The constructive message of the GAO report appears to be that a useful evaluation essentially requires learning about the experience of the program from two perspectives: why the program did what it did and what outcomes it achieved by taking account of a broad range of measures that reflect different interests. The report somewhat optimistically recommends that learning can effectively occur through improved communication among the responsible legislative committees and agencies. The GAO puts its faith in Congress' potential for learning from what might be called the "doctrine of the three C's": communication, clarification, and consensus. Presumably, in a spirit of open and trustful communication, the intent of the various competing groups will become increasingly clarified, and this clarification will eventually lead to an agreement on purposes. "More frequent communication will not only provide more assurance that the objectives and effectiveness measures are agreed upon but that policy makers have realistic expectations as to what information will be forthcoming from the evaluation."

I accept the insights of the GAO appraisal of the problem, but I doubt that the "three C's" strategy will work in practice except in unusual circumstances where the commitment to consequence overrides partisan interests. But what are the implications of the GAO diagnosis for those who carry out the evaluations? In order to be able to learn from experience, one must be able to look at the experience as a whole. Studies of intent, implementation, and the measurement of outcome are parts of the experience. Hence, a perspective broader than outcomes, yet including outcomes, is essential.

The difficulty of achieving agreement on detailed aims that can be operationalized in the legislative process rather than at a later stage by evaluators is now widely acknowledged. This difficulty arises partly because of conflicts of interest and the requirement of smoothing over such conflicts in the effort to reach consensus. We can also pose a new and less familiar question: "In whose interests are evaluations carried out?" Once stated, the question seems obvious. However little systematic attention has been given to an analysis of the interests in evaluation, I believed that the way in which inputs, process, and outcomes are evaluated depends on what we want to do with it. That interests dominate inquiry is not surprising.

The interests relevant to evaluation are positional interests in the policy development process. We can usefully identify four of the main interests based on different positions in the process: oversight, administration, consumer, and evaluation. The list is obviously not exhaustive.

Most evaluation studies arise from the interest in oversight. Congress and other legislative bodies want to know if public funds are spent for the program for which they were intended and are not being used as a substitute for locally financed programs; therefore, they request audits. They also want to know about the costs for a given program rather than for some alternative. These studies are carried out by the Congressional Budget Office. Finally, they want to know if they are getting their money's worth—whether the program is doing what it is supposed to be doing. The type of study used in this case is program evaluation mandated by legislation. The oversight interests in accountability are common to the different kinds of evaluations. Is the claim made against scarce governmental resources legitimate?

To appreciate how selective the oversight interest is we need only identify another type of interest, that of the administration of a program or an interest in getting something done. In this setting, political and administrative feasibility dominate. An administrator is interested in ways to achieve compliance without sacrificing morale. For some administrators the critical question is how to acquire resources to assure the growth and vitality of their bureaucracies. The interests of the practitioners are not the same as those of the administrator; the kinds of evaluation they would undertake would be informed by a different set of questions, including how to protect themselves against intrusive systems of accountability which reduce their scope for the use of professional discretion.

An evaluation to satisfy consumer interests would be different from ones that satisfy the administrative and oversight interests. The critical evaluation of public policy on behalf of consumer advocate groups illustrates the point. Client satisfaction, safety, and investment dominate their interests.

Can we posit a harmony of interests, when all interests are in pursuit of the public interest? It seems more likely that people view the world from their special position in it. Where they stand determines or strongly shapes what they see and what they want to know to increase effectiveness.

Evaluators also have interests. Basically, they want to carry out evaluations with the tools they have. The evaluator imposes order on the world in the context of his disciplinary interest so that he may study it with the techniques and concepts he commands. One celebrated example is the evaluation of the Head Start Program. Evaluators knew something about the measurement of cognitive competence but much less about social competence. As a result, they imposed the objective of the development of intelligence on the program that enabled them to evaluate the program with the tools they had on hand.

Briefly, there is no way to achieve understanding without the bias of interest from which an inquiry begins. This does not mean that there is no objective reality. Rather, it means that programmatic posture and disciplinary interests shape the questions that are asked and the methods used to find the answer.

In summary, then, evaluations cannot separate the programmatic interests that commission the study from the disciplinary interests that organize the inquiry. To appreciate the role of the separate interests we need only consider a given institution, such as a university, and imagine the kind of evaluation studies that would be useful to the boards of overseers, the deans of the schools, the heads of departments, the faculty, and the students. While there are some topics on which all might agree, each interest would raise quite different questions that they would like to have answered by the evaluator. But each question raised by the various interests would be answered differently, depending on the disciplinary interest of the evaluator. Economic, sociological, and psychological studies would yield different insights. In the analyses that follow, I shall try to give examples of how interest affects the process of evaluation. However, my main objective is to make the case for a comprehensive evaluation. In particular, I want to comment on something typically taken for granted in most evaluations: the programmatic unit to be evaluated.

I propose four elements that are necessary in evaluation. We must examine what the program is, what it does, what results these inputs yield, and through what processes these outcomes come about. I shall elaborate each, cite some examples to illustrate each approach, and offer some preliminary suggestions about the research design appropriate for each.

WHAT IS THE PROGRAM?

We assign names to the activities we evaluate, and these names help to specify what we are evaluating. These names comprise the social definition of what evaluators call "the program." However, the social definition of a program is only the starting point for analysis. We cannot assume that a program is what it is socially defined to be. A program such as manpower training may be defined as an investment in human capital, but in practice it may also be seen as a transfer program, replacing lost wages.

An important aspect of an evaluation, then, requires an examination of what the program is. To find out a program's intent begins with the program's rhetoric. Getting beneath the rhetoric to the realities of intent is another question. Defining a program is difficult because no one agrees on the activities to be included and on the intent to unify these activities into a coherent entity, the program. The "unit" or "activity" to be evaluated is not self-evident and defined by the legislation. Rather, it is uncertain and, therefore, problematic.

To begin with, we must determine how interests contribute to bounding the unity of activity into budgetary categories. To do so we briefly review the different intellectual approaches to the problem of budget classification proposed by the General Accounting Office, which represents the legislative interest in auditing, and the Office of Management and Budgets (OMB), which represents the executive interests in the preparation of the federal budget.

Budget classification is essentially an evaluation procedure in which governmental activities are sorted into a set of categories. The underlying logic for this procedure is that similar activities should be grouped together, and the positional interests shape the selection. I would like to illustrate this point with some specific examples.

An early discussion of the question of budgetary classification was published by Murray Widenbaum, drawn from his experiences with the federal budget. He summarized the statistics reported in the budget which examine the distribution of the same activity across different administrative agencies. Thus, the answer to the question, "How much money is spent on student aid for university students," is not simply in the Department of Health, Education and Welfare (HEW) budget (renamed Health and Human Services [HHS]), which was responsible for the administration of educational programs. In fact, the bulk of the money for student aid is distributed by the Social Security Administration as part of the dependent's allowance for children of aged, disabled, and deceased workers covered by the program. Widenbaum's generalization led to the development of a table, in which function (health, education, income support, training and employment, and so on) was cross-tabulated by department (HEW, Veterans, Labor, Military, Agriculture, Housing and Urban Development). Inspired by Widenbaum's insight, OMB introduced this kind of analysis in the *Special Analysis of the Budget*. When he cross-classified income support by function, he found that in 1976, 65 percent of income support was spent by HEW and 35 percent by other agencies (that is, almost $60 billion; OMB, 1976). In the example above, a grid was constructed of different administrative groups classified by the same activity. This approach has a more general application, whereby the same activity can be assumed to have multiple purposes, and overlapping rather than mutually exclusive categories are provided. For example, a manpower training program can be classified both as income support and as investment. Other functional goals such as health (psychological well-being) might also be added. From these functions and purposes one could construct a social policy grid based on function by purposes, on the assumption that the same function serves multiple aims. Of course, carelessly adding across the totals would lead to double counting, but adding the rows and columns separately could yield considerable new insights.

The Office of Management and Budgeting approach to budget classification stems from a different interest and, hence, embodies a very different analytical scheme. OMB approaches the budget classification task by developing mutually exclusive categories. If a program has multiple goals, only the primary goal is used in the classification and the secondary goals are ignored. If a program has ambiguous or conflicting goals, the classifier must make a judgment or inference about intent. OMB describes the logic of this procedure as follows:

> The functional classification focuses on the end of ultimate purposes of governmental activity. The stress is on what the federal government seeks to accomplish rather than on the means of accomplishment, what the government purchases, or the clientele, or geographic area served [OMB, 1975].

The skeletal framework on which the budget classification system is based is a set of appropriation accounts and the variety of activities that are associated with these accounts. The accounts are grouped under a set of functions and subfunctions.

When we take a disciplinary interest in budget classification, we find, surprisingly, that the concept of "program" is not a key analytical concept. In fact, it is never defined in the budget. However, accounts distinguish between direct and reimbursable programs. This is a very special use of the term "program." Its meaning derives from the budgetary context of its use. The concept of "activity" is closer to the common meaning of the term "program," but "activity" should not be confused with the concept of a program because a single activity may contain several programs. For example, under the appropriation account, Elementary and Secondary Education, there is an activity called "grants for the handicapped, migrants, the educationally deprived, and grants to the states for administrative purposes."

But what methodology can be used to infer the true intent of an activity, which is not self-evident or obvious after a review of the legislative history? The GAO, in its report "Finding Out How Programs are Working," offers this advice: "The evaluators must determine from the rhetoric of policy exactly what was intended." Guided by such advice, the evaluators may be able to show only after much effort, time, and measurement that the world is quite different from what it was thought to be. In the public arena, evaluators will have difficulty distinguishing a program failure from a misdesigned evaluation that accurately measures programmatic effects if they naively accept the legislative rhetoric as the program's "true" aims.

The same issues arise in budget classification, where the efforts to identify the "ultimate purposes of governmental activity" must address the difficult question of how to infer "true intent" from rhetoric. A specific example might help to illustrate the point at issue. The Basic Educational Opportunity Grant activity is classified under the subfunction "higher education," and the activity "comprehensive education and training (CETA)" is classified under the subfunction "training and employment." The logic of the classification depends upon the assumption that these activities are sorted by their ultimate purposes—education and employment. However, we could also argue that it would be useful to separate distal and proximal purposes. The most immediate purpose of student aid and training is to provide individuals with cash income. Tuition and training costs should be reclassified under the function "income security." A thoroughgoing reclassification of activities would lead to a very different distribution of expenditures by function and by account and therefore a very different understanding about the allocation of public priorities. It would also mean a functional reorganization of the agency's organizational structure.

If we further extend our disciplinary interest in understanding not only the activities of direct federal budget but also the allocation of resources, we are led to a different system of classification. Perhaps the best example of such an effort is the work of the late Richard Titmuss, the "father" of critical British social policy. Titmuss's seminal essay on the classification of activities is based on the argument that activities having similar effects, regardless of their formal intent should be grouped together. He suggested that occupational welfare, fiscal welfare, and social welfare should be grouped together (Titmuss, 1954). His purpose in this recategorization of the activities of the welfare state was to show that, with a broader definition of welfare, society would recognize that income redistribution had not been achieved and that a substantial amount of reverse redistribution had developed; that is, more welfare outlays are spent on the middle- and upper-income groups than on the poor.

Budgetary classification is a useful plan to begin an examination of what constitutes the meaning of "program." This is an extraordinarily important step in evaluation that has not received the attention it deserves. A first step in advancing understanding in this area would be a systematic effort to reclassify accounts from different intellectual perspectives. As OMB explains, "There is no single best way to classify Federal activities. The functional structure chosen for the budget is the classification deemed most useful for the specific purpose of budgetary exposition" (OMB, 1975: A-4).

"WHAT DOES IT DO?"

Let us turn from a discussion of the nature of intention (how it might be understood and classified) to a discussion of the evaluation of the activity as put into place or implemented. Here I distinguish between the program as intended and the program as carried out. Each requires a different procedure of evaluation.

In a discussion of programmatic inputs a primary concern is with how a program is put into operation in the field. Evaluators are led to undertake input studies when they are not certain that the program's conception has in some measure been realized in practice. Obviously, there is a continuum between full realization (compliance) and the complete failure at realization (non-program). The case for a rigorous study of input rests on the assumption that most programs are seldom, if ever, fully realized as conceived.

The study of "non-events," programs never realized in practice, was identified in the mid-sixties by Herbert Hyman and Charles Wright. Drawing their examples from programs carried out in developing countries and during World War II, the authors give the following perceptive observation:

> All too often a program is simply a statement on paper of what planners in an agency hope to do that has never been fully translated into action by the field staff. Taking the word for the deed, an evaluator may try to observe the effects

of the non-existent treatment. By contrast, no experimenter could ever deceive himself so greatly as to make observations of the effect of a non-existent stimulus, since he would know that he had not yet initiated the procedure [Hyman and Wright, 1967].

As an example of a program that was never realized, they cite a study of the relationship between motivational appeals and mass action during World War II. Persuasion was to take the form of a series of posters that were to be distributed by a national voluntary oganization. In fact, thousands of posters were printed. However, although these posters had been printed and shipped all over the country, they remained in local depots for lack of volunteers to distribute them. In the example cited, the investigators did not proceed with an evaluation because they discovered the failure of an input.

The typical situation is not the non-event, but the partial event. There is reason to believe that a fragmented government system encourages the substitution of resources. An increase in federal resources to provide a new programmatic initiative may lead to a reduction in expenditures of local resources available from ongoing programs. The result, then, is no additional outlays and expenditures but only a substitution of federal for local money. A federalist government, where many social programs are financed by the federal government and carried out at the local level, provides a great incentive for substitution. If we believe that substitution is a serious problem, we should develop a methodology appropriate for its study, or use the methodology developed in the traditional audits carried out by the GAO. If the audit becomes an important technique for evaluation, however, the traditional distinctions among auditing, monitoring, and evaluating must be sharply redefined. Since social bookkeeping is an essential element in program evaluation, we should turn to the discipline of accounting to look for methodological guidance.

In addition to compliance, input studies must address the more subtle problem of progressive transformation of broad aims into concrete practice. Four different types of input can be distinguished: inputs as conceived; inputs as distributed; inputs as received; and inputs as experienced.[1]

The study of *inputs as conceived* assesses the relationships among the theory underlying the program, its programmatic design, and the translation of the design into programmatic inputs, as conceived by the designers. An implicit assumption in this formulation is that a program is an intervention designed to address a problematic situation. "Delinquency" is a problematic situation accompanied by the theory that frustrated opportunity is its cause and opening pathways of opportunity for those so deprived will reduce its occurrence. The theory must be translated into a concrete method for opening opportunities. These may be the design of a program for manpower training or community action. In practice, budgetary, political, administrative, and conceptual constraints influence the conception and design of specific kinds of training and educational programs that could open to relieve the frustrations that in theory produce delinquent behavior. A study of inputs as conceived traces the "fit" of problems, theory, design, and projected resources that are needed to realize the design. At the conceptual level we are dealing with inputs thought necessary for achieving a transition from our understanding of the problem to a strategy for addressing it.

Underlying the intervention, then, is a theory concerning the kind of activities most likely to reduce or eliminate the problem. A program is a theory and an evaluation is its test. At the empirical level, an evaluator attempts to understand whether the theory, the design, or the implementation led to the outcomes. An input study addresses only one of these questions—the movement from design to practice. It tries to understand the extent to which the design as conceived was realized or frustrated because of the difficulties in implementation.

The study of *inputs as distributed* focuses on the dissemination of resources in the aggregate administrative units. The Brookings Institution performed the classic study of the distribution of inputs. This study was to monitor whether the distribution of public-sector-financed jobs led to the displacement of local public jobs (displacement meaning the use of federal money to pay for local public employees' salaries which local government would have paid had there been no federal program). This kind of study does not evaluate outputs, in that it does not inquire into the effects of public service employment or unemployment. It is an impact study of federally financed jobs.

The Brookings project reviewed two approaches to the study of inputs: existing statistical analysis from published data and a new monitoring survey carried out by Brookings. It first used previously published regression analysis which estimated the extent of displacement by comparing actual and predicted displacement. These studies concluded that two-thirds of the jobs were displaced.

The monitoring study estimated the extent of displacement by fieldwork. It used techniques such as direct observation, review of budget and employment conditions, and assessment of demand for services. The monitoring study reached a different conclusion than the statistical study. It found that only one-fifth of positions were displaced and concluded that the public service employment program "was significantly more stimulative than substitutive . . . funds are not fully absorbed over time into general funds of state and local government" (Nathan et al., 1979).

Inputs can be distributed differently in different settings. Even in the same setting the flow of resources can vary at different times. These variations in the input over time and across space are a critical task of input evaluation.

The study of *inputs as experienced* focuses on the meaning of the program for those who use it. Most of us who teach in universities know that some of the most distinguished professors listed in the catalogue never teach courses because they are preoccupied with their own research, or they act as program administrators and are not available to students. The student may experience this gap between potential and actual realization as disinterest.

It may not always be necessary to study inputs as experienced; however, in certain programs they are important. It may be necessary to understand how clients experienced their assignment to an experimental group and what meaning the program's stimulus has for them. For example, did clients in a negative income tax experiment fully understand the practical implications of different marginal tax rates and guarantee levels? The experiment may have assumed that the subjects rationally responded to different inputs, but they may not have experienced these inputs as the program had intended. In this situation the subjective understanding of the experience by those who receive it is an important input of the program itself.

Inputs as received is a logical extension of inputs as distributed but shifts the focus from aggregate inputs to individual inputs. An Urban Institute study of a national program for Women, Infants, and Children (WIC) is a good example. The political decision to replace direct distributional nutritional programs with food stamps was at issue. Output studies showed that infants enrolled in the program showed increases in weight, height, and hemoglobin concentration and a decline in anemia. The Urban Institute report cast doubt on the outcome studies by finding that the foods were used by all members of the family—80 percent of the households used WIC foods for family diets. The study also found that although two-thirds of the health clinics surveyed provided nutritional counselling, only 12 percent of the participants indicated that they learned anything about improving their nutritional intake (Nelson, 1979). The study contributed to the repudiation of the medical evaluation of the output inquiry. The Urban Institute findings that targeting food was ineffective because the family pooled food and that nutritional instruction failed to change the pattern of family sharing showed that the inputs as distributed were not the same as the inputs as received. Hence, analyses of results based on such problematic inputs must be questioned.

In summary, each type of input study requires a somewhat different methodology. Inputs as conceived must undergo a conceptual analysis. The study of inputs as distributed takes an institutional analysis of the flow of resources between the funding and the receiving body. Inputs as received is an analysis that monitors the resources individuals actually received. The study of inputs as experienced takes a subjective study of service users, designed to elicit the impact of meaning on behavior.

LINKING INPUT STUDIES TO OUTCOME STUDIES

To illustrate how input and outcome studies are linked, I review an outcome evaluation that failed to take account of the inputs (Cunningham, 1977). The study tried to evaluate the impact of two different theories on how to determine eligibility for an income support program, a new system of declaration, and the traditional comprehensive investigation. The declaration system had been modeled after the income tax system and consisted of simple eligibility forms to be filled out by the clients. No routine verification was made of what the clients claimed was the situation. However, a percentage of welfare cases was checked for error and fraud, much as the Internal Revenue Service audits taxpayers' accounts. By contrast, the full investigation approach required extensive interviews with clients, home visits, and independent verification of the client's situation. Birth certificates were used to confirm the age and number of children; cross-checking with the Social Security Administration and the Internal Revenue Service was employed to determine whether a client was earning money in the labor market. On the assumption that these two distinct program models were implemented in practice, Cunningham proceeded to study how the different eligibility determination procedures affected outcomes such as error, fraud, and acceptance rates. She discovered a significant correlation between eligibility procedure and error.

Cunningham assumed that eligibility procedures represented two distinct inputs into administrative practice. An input study by the Government Accounting Office (GAO) revealed that, in fact, there was very little difference in practice between the two procedures for determining eligibility. This was largely because the procedure for full verification was time-consuming and workers took shortcuts and developed a simplified procedure in order to cope with the heavy demands on their work schedule. By contrast, workers were reluctant to accept the simplified eligibility procedures, because they did not trust the clients. They periodically subjected many cases to a full investigation. The net result of these two different processes was that the two types of programs were practically indistinguishable. A program that looked different in principle was much the same in practice (U.S. Comptroller General, 1971).

In retrospect, we can now appreciate that the Cunningham study used a crude scale in ranking agencies by their procedures for determining eligibility. Moreover, a weak correlation existed between error and eligibility procedure, which led the author to reach the unsupported inference that the two are related to each other. An input study would have warned the investigator that the scale developed in ranking states on the degree of stringency and leniency of eligibility determination procedures was of doubtful validity.

PROCESS STUDIES

Initiative for process studies arises when ambiguities appear between the theory of intervention and the sequence of events following from the program to its effects. A process study tries to lay out the process as it developed. An outcome study shows a strong correlation between income guarantees and labor force participation rates: a process study documents the process of events and motives that led the one event to produce the other.

Process studies, which seek to understand the way things go together, contribute to a theory of "fit." The vocabulary of fitting and congruence, however, has not been fully developed. The inference is a leap from empirical observations to an insight about congruence.

For example, many observers have noted that school classes function differently among different social classes. In a class of black youngsters from the lower social stratum, there is a considerable amount of "horsing around." In a class of middle-class blacks the children are performance oriented and authoritarian. A white class is organized like a corporation with committee work and reports. One might infer from these findings that school classes conform to the social stratification in society. That is to say, the class activity "fits" the group for whom it was designed.

Why, one might ask, do schools "fit" the outcome of class structure? What are the processes by which this accommodation takes place? Perhaps the school administrators cue themselves to parental demand. Perhaps teachers preselect themselves for certain schools. Some teachers cannot function in the way they consider appropriate in ghetto schools. They want to teach youngsters autonomy, and they are unable to accommodate to an environment in which this way of teaching is inappropriate.

A process study commits the investigator to learn about the intent of the actors. Documenting the disparity between the intended and the realized is very much at the heart of the sociological imagination. There are many ways in which this could be done. For example, a study could show that a reception center designed for new migrants does not serve them, but serves permanent residents. A housing program designed for self-help for the poor ends up being used by others as a way to find housing to rent. An institutionalized program designed to be a halfway house for mental patients en route to the community in fact accommodates community residents who cannot function in the local community. The examples can be multiplied, but they share a sense that the task of analysts is to expose incongruities. I want to distinguish the empirical study of process from the theoretical interpretation of function, which asserts that schools "fit" the class structure—that is, they are functional for the prevailing stratification system.

LINKING OUTPUT STUDIES TO PROCESS STUDIES

The 1970s was a decade for large-scale social experimentation. The largest and perhaps the most sophisticated are the income maintenance experiments. The findings of the Seattle-Denver experiment, the last of four experiments in the income maintenance field, has caused a storm of controversy because of its provocative finding that income support contributes to marital instability and to the reduction of work effort. (The latter finding was expected and, therefore, less controversial.)

The primary goal of the income maintenance experiment was to obtain information on the costs of alternative designs of income support programs. Controlled experiments were assumed to provide the most reliable information about cost. That the funding contributed to the reduction of work effort was important because it could significantly influence the cost of the experiment. For example, it is not so impressive that male heads of two-parent families reduced work hours between one and 11 percent and that female heads reduced work hours by about 15 percent; and that women in two-parent families reduced their work between zero and 31 percent. When the findings are linked to program costs, however, the meaning of the work reduction becomes dramatic. The results show that when a program's benefits are set at three-quarters of the poverty line and with a 70 percent benefit reduction rate, the loss of work effort accounts for 58 percent of the total cost of the program. By contrast, in an experimental program that paid benefits at the poverty level with a 70 percent benefit reduction rate, reduced work accounted for only 17 percent of the cost.

Over time, the question of comparative cost has receded from the political agenda because the political possibilities for implementing a negative income tax which provides unrestricted cash grants to able-bodied males in poverty has proved stubbornly difficult to legislate. But while welfare reform, proposed in the experiments, has passed from the center of political attention—at least for the moment—the findings of the study remain of great interest.

Commenting on the finding, Henry Aaron observed that, "the less generous program would usually cover lower-income people who worked less to begin with. A decrease in their work effort would be proportionately greater than a similar decrease in work effort of a group that initially worked more" (Aaron, 1978). But Aaron's comments do not help us understand how work effort declines. After all, many blue-collar jobs do not permit a full-time worker to work four or five hours a week less than a full work week. Nor do the comments help us understand why the participants in the experiment decided to work less. We need to understand the subjects' point of view compared with that of the control groups. How did the clients interpret the payments they received? How much did they understand about these experiments; what conclusions did they draw from their understanding; and how did these conclusions influence their work efforts? A combined input-process study would provide the answers. It is extremely useful to have an effect against which to measure these processes because it provides a firm anchor about what kinds of processes need to be explained.

The need for a process study becomes even more pressing when the findings are puzzling. The experimental finding that income guarantees lead to marital instability is especially puzzling. The experiment showed that

> rates of family instability were about 60 percent higher among blacks and whites who received assistance than among those who did not. . . . However, during the third year of the experiment, the effect from white families declined causing white families in the experimental group to be actually more stable than their counterparts in control groups, although by a statistically insignificant amount [Aaron, 1978: 38].

In addition, the rate of family instability apparently increased more in plans with lower benefits than in plans with higher benefits. The results are so counterintuitive that the need for process studies is urgent.

Several theories but very few data have been advanced to interpret the findings from the income maintenance experiment. The researchers can distinguish between an income and an independence effect. They believe that a larger amount of income helps families to achieve their aspirations more fully; the independence effect works in the other direction. The guarantee provides a source of support and induces one or the other parent to separate. The independence effect also seems to dominate the action of some groups, but only at certain times in the experiment and not at others. However, we know almost nothing about how the independence effect works. Does it promote irresponsibility on the part of the father who decides to leave and the let the government meet his family obligations? Or perhaps it is the wife who decides that income support provides a viable alternative for a frustrating and inadequate marriage.

Several other theories surrounding the income maintenance experiment exist as well. To account for why low benefit produces more marital disruption, Aaron proposed a welfare discount effect. He posited "that families do not value a dollar of income from welfare as highly as they value a dollar of income from any other source . . . because of the stigma or administration associated with regular welfare programs."

Rainwater (n.d.) expanded the range of options and posited two other effects: an anomie effect in which destabilization arises because family members do not know how to use the additional money allotted to them; and a role-definition effect, where destabilization occurs because the husband's role as main breadwinner is redefined. Rainwater lucidly made the case for linking process and output studies:

> An understanding of the process by which the experimental effect comes about is crucial for any sensible interpretation or debate about what the effect means for policy. Even a clear understanding of the processes certainly will lead people with different values to have a different valuation of the effect. (Some persons have argued that the independence effect is a desirable policy goal.) But at least at that point the value issue becomes clear, where as long as there is no understanding of the process it is likely to be confounded by a different interpretation to what really went on in the experimental families.

These imaginative interpretations are, of course, only guesses. There is no way to answer the question without a process study.

NOTE

1. This formulation on the nature of input studies is an extension of the concept developed in an unpublished essay by Robert S. Weiss, "Input Studies and Process Studies as Alternatives and Complements Throughout Evaluation" (Boston: The Laboratory for Community Psychiatry, 1979), mimeo.

REFERENCES

AARON, H. (1978) "Welfare research and experimentation." Hearing before the Subcommittee on Public Assistance of the Committee on Finance, United States Senate, 95th Congress, 2nd sess., November 15, 16, 17.

CUNNINGHAM, M. (1977) "Eligibility procedures for AFDC." Social Work 21: 21–26.

HAVENS, H. (1979) "Program evaluation in support of public policy." Presented at the International Conference on the Future of Public Administration, Quebec, Canada, May. (mimeo)

HYMAN, H. H. and C. R. WRIGHT "Evaluating social action programs." p. 744 in P. Z. Lazarsfeld, W. H. Sewell, and H. L. Wilensky (eds.) The Uses of Sociology. New York: Basic Books.

NATHAN, R. P. et al. (1979) Monitoring the Public Service Employment: The Second Round. Washington, DC: Brookings Institution.

NELSON, J. (1979) "The special supplemental food program for women, infants, and children (WIC): A case study of policy making." Washington, DC: National Academy of Science. (mimeo)

OMB [Office of Management and Budget] (1979) The Functional Classification in the Budget. Executive Office of the President. Technical Paper Series BRD/FAB 79-1. Washington, DC: Government Printing Office.

———(1978) Special Analysis Budget of the U.S. Government Fiscal Year 1978. Washington, DC: Government Printing Office.

———(1975) "The functional classification of the budget." Technical staff paper.

RAINWATER, L. (n.d.) "Observations of marital instability in Seattle and Denver income-maintenance experiment." (mimeo)

TITMUSS, R. (1954) The Social Division of Welfare in Essays on the Welfare State. New Haven: Yale University Press.

U.S. Comptroller General (1977) "Finding out how programs are working: suggestions for congressional oversight." Report to Congress.

———— (1971) "The comparison of the simplified and traditional methods of determining eligibility for and to families with dependent children." Report to the Committee on Finance, U.S. Senate.

WIDENBAUM, M. (1969) The Modern Public Sector. New York: Basic Books.

8

Evaluation as Meaningful
Social Research

Franz-Xaver Kaufmann
Klaus-Peter Strohmeier
Universität Bielefeld

PROGRAM EVALUATION AS
"APPLIED BASIC RESEARCH"

Scientific program evaluation research must be seen in the focus of two different, but not necessarily contradictory, perspectives: On one hand, in as much as evaluation attempts to discover causal empirical relationships, it falls under the standards of a logic of (causal) scientific inquiry. Accordingly, strong emphasis must be placed on the complexity, completeness, and causal closure of a system of theoretical hypotheses from which the direction and the nature of a causal process under study can be derived.

It is more or less accepted, according to the logic of scientific inquiry, that an empirical statement about something (as a cause) having affected something else (as an effect) can only be accepted insofar as it confirms an underlying theory (Stegmüller, 1960; Popper, 1964; Opp, 1976; Simon, 1970; Luhmann, 1970). Treating an empirically confirmed relationship between variables as causal will be justified only by the underlying theoretical propositions, not just by the kind of research operations applied.

On the other hand, program evaluation research is applied social research, which is intended for application outside the scientific community.[1] In that perspective it differs from general or basic social research. Its underlying theoretical presuppositions are never "grand" social theory, but theories of the short- or middle-range type. And the "causes" and "effects" are not just "empirical realizations of generally conceptualized social phenomena" (Weber, 1964), but political or policy-induced variables (Kaufmann et al. 1978). As applied social research, program evaluation is not only committed to high technical standards; but also, to be incorporated into political processes, its results have to be precise and communicable. These two perspectives, both the more practical and the methodological, must be kept in mind in examining the applicability and adequacy of different research designs for the handling of a specific evaluation research problem. Neglecting either of them will lead to methodologically and practically irrelevant research results.

This chapter discusses the relationship between theory and method in program evaluation research; later it will describe two standards, "object adequacy" and "problem adequacy" of a research design. These might help to ensure that program evaluation research be theoretically relevant and practically (politically) useful social research.

PRINCIPLES OF EXPERIMENTAL EVALUATION

The expanding literature about methodological issues in evaluation research documents the predominant type of theory about how and why social programs come to effect as the almost classical "impact model" of the following type (Hellstern and Wollmann, 1977):

$$\text{a PROGRAM} \xrightarrow{\text{initiates}} \text{a CAUSAL PROCESS} \xrightarrow{\text{that produces}} \text{EFFECTS.}$$

Factually, this impact model expresses a very simple causal hypothesis, assuming that the program and nothing else will bring about the desired effects, and that, controlling for intervening factors, a direct causal relationship between the program and the dependent (target) variable will remain. Distinguished authors, such as Suchman (1972), Weiss (1972), Campbell (see Campbell and Stanley, 1966), and Scheuch (Scheuch and Rüschemeyer, 1965) have assigned the experimental research technique the highest degree of validity and precision. The simple impact model usually is the grounded theory that underlies the "real experiment" as a technical device in program evaluation research.

"Real" experiments allegedly come nearest to the exact technical devices of the experimental natural (or physical) sciences (Suchman, 1972; Scheuch and Rüschemeyer 1965). There are firm reasons, which, at least, question that methodological position which has so far been prominent among evaluation researchers (Lazarsfeld, 1965). Before expressing the problems of a strictly experimental technical approach, we want to summarize the basic principles of experimental program evaluation.

In the natural sciences, experimental research can be characterized as the creation of conditions that allow initiating a succession of manipulating changes in the object under study in an ideally innumerable number of cases, practically undisturbed by irritations from external factors. Consequently, applying experimental techniques assumes that it is possible to reproduce theoretically closed systems for practical research purposes.

The "real" experiment in evaluation research appears at the first glance weaker and, on the whole, not similar to the allegedly ideal natural science experiment. Actually, it is completely different.

—Randomly selected units (persons) from a program's target population are assigned to a control group and to at least one experimental or "treatment" group. Random assignment (or other devices, such as "matching") allows the exclusion of systematic bias from the composition of groups, ensuring that potentially intervening variables will either be randomly distributed or can otherwise be regarded as constant.

—Control and experimental groups are then submitted to a first measurement (before-treatment) in which their values on the target variable which are expected to be influenced by the program are measured.

—The experimental group(s) is (are) submitted to a treatment (or, in the case of several groups, to different treatments), whereas the control group gets no treatment.

—At the end of the program (and sometimes in between) additional measurements are taken to identify changes in the dependent (or target) variable. If significant changes from earlier measurements can be observed and if significant differences between groups can be identified, the program and the different modes of treatment under study can be said to have brought about the observed changes (Suchman, 1972; Jones and Borgatta, 1972; Breedlove, 1972).

"OBJECT ADEQUACY" OF EMPIRICAL DESIGNS

Differences between the evaluative experimental technique and the allegedly ideal experimental model of the natural sciences are obvious and self-evident. There is no point in discussing how the social science use of experimental designs can be improved in order to reach natural science standards of validity and precision; this would be a vain effort and, moreover, according to the object of empirical social research, an inadequate attempt. The "social world" as the object of social scientific inquiry is different from the concerns of the physical sciences, and inadequate research standards would not help us (Lazarsfeld, 1965). It is this fundamental gap between the object of research and a growing "complex of exactness" among sociological re-

searchers that made König (1968) call empirical social scientists to a higher
consciousness of the "object adequacy" *("Gegenstandsadäquanz")* of their
research operations.

This argument has also been stressed by interactionist methodologists
who, however, equate "object adequate" with "nonquantitative" (Blumer,
1973; Wilson, 1973; Matthes and Schütze, 1973). Tentatively, one could
well use these two positions—the one with the "complex of exactness"
(König, 1968) on one side and the anti-quantitative entirely "qualitative"
approach on the other—to group both general social science and evaluation
research into two discrete categories. Nonetheless, neither of them can
factually claim to be more "object adequate" than the other. "Object adequacy" is not achieved simply by choosing between two paradigmatic
branches of empirical social research which are too often regarded as mutually exclusive. A presupposition that social research be either "qualitative"
or "quantitative"—either "valid" and "exact" or "invalid" and "weak"—
erects false barriers that hinder the progress of scientific research (and its
practical uses are part of that progress).

It is true that the concerns of social scientific inquiry, the "social world"
(Blumer, 1973), differ from those of the physical sciences; therefore, we
need not bother as social scientists to reach factually inadequate standards of
exactness. However, this cannot mean that access to any phenomenon in the
social world can be gained only by working on it qualitatively—for example, by means of direct observation, contextual analysis, or narrative interviewing (for the latter see Schütze, 1976). Moreover, we would extend the
criterion that research operations be "object adequate" also to the problem of
deciding whether to use a qualitative or a quantitative approach (or both) in a
given research situation.

In a very broad sense, all social scientific research devices, "weak" or
"exact," "qualitative" or "quantitative," can be called "object adequate"
insofar as they allow a researcher to deal with a phenomenon within his or
her social world of research objects. The specific character of the object
under study additionally imposes advantages and restraints that make one
technical procedure of research appear more adequate than another. A direct
experiment as a special research technique will be adequate only when the
causal process investigated is as simple as the "impact model" as a basic
causal theory suggests. Other, more complex social processes may well
demand the use of technically nonexperimental, even nonquantitative, research designs or a mixture of techniques with varying degrees of rigor.
Program evaluation research can be regarded as a specific and fruitful challenge to social science researchers. Its specific concerns do not easily fit into
the (mutually conceded) "claims" of either qualitatively or quantitatively
orientated researchers, but, instead, are far less conventional.

An evaluation researcher asked to identify the implementation process of a specific program is well advised to use qualitative research devices, such as documentary analysis or interviewing of key persons involved in the implementation. When evaluating the impact of a program, the approach depends entirely upon the type of program studied and the theoretically assumed relationships of variables and their complexity (the impact model). In this case, the researcher might use an experimental or quasi-experimental design to identify program effects (Hellstern and Wollmann, 1977). Only recently, evaluation researchers have conceded that qualitative approaches are adequate and informative procedures for empirical research (Campbell, 1974). Hellstern and Wollman (1977) also emphasize the use of applying multiple research techniques of both qualitative and quantitative approaches to a given research problem.

It is still an indicator for a widespread, but nonetheless erroneous, methodological orientation that, where real experiments are factually impossible, alternative research designs are labeled "quasi"-designs. However, the value of a research technique, in our view, does not lie in its similarity to an allegedly ideal experimental technique. König (1968) has made the point that all analytic scientific inquiry is experimental, in that it follows a basic method of "experimentation." The principle is to keep factors constant while varying others to see the results. We call this the principle of "controlled variation" (Smelser, 1967). All sorts of analytical research techniques, including real experiments and even a *Gedankenexperiment* in the Weberian sense, are under certain conditions distinguished technical realizations of this basic methodological principle.

The selection of the empirical approach will always depend upon the character of the research object and the theory that is to be examined empirically.

"PROBLEM ADEQUACY"

Our understanding of "object adequacy," developed in the preceding section, comprises methodological standards that are applicable to all empirical social research. In the special case of program evaluation, however, it would suggest that there is no such thing as an absolute ranking of designs, going "downwards" from the direct experimental to other, perceptibly weaker, devices in terms of validity, "hardness" of data, and results. Instead, "experimental" in the sense of "controlled variation" is a basic criterion distinguishing analytical scientific research from other (for example, descriptive), fact-collecting types of research. The various research techniques existing in the social sciences are all technical realizations of this basic experimental method—each of them is adequate, provided it is applied to a specific type of objects. Object-adequate research designs alone will not, however, make an evaluation "problem-adequate" as to the political problem of concern.

Donald Campbell (1974) considers "evaluating the outcomes of deliberately induced political innovation" as the main objective of program evaluation research. This definition may hold for the United States; however, it is problematic when applied to Germany. Evaluation research as a specific mode of interaction between the social sciences and the political system (Kaufmann, 1980) has been imported into the Federal Republic from the United States. Consequently, the methodological and theoretical affiliations that most West German evaluation researchers adhere to have also been imported. Nevertheless, there remain crucial differences in the structure of the political systems and their modes of initiating, implementing, and improving policy. Our political system is by no means experimental, neither in the sense that political innovation would play an important role in state activities nor in that it would be implemented in a way that followed the logic of scientific experimentation (Kaufmann and Schneider, 1975). Experimental reforms as well as established policies in the Federal Republic will be implemented, delivered, and administered grounded on legal regulation. Our political process is basically regulated by law and only secondarily by attainment of goals. The administration through which a policy program is implemented commits itself to a principle of "legality" *(Rechtmäßigkeit);* that is, the compatibility of an individual administrational action with general legally codified norms. This particular structure and function of the German political process, (policy being nonexperimental and policy regulated by general law), pose particular problems to evaluation research that we will discuss in this section.

The primacy of "legality" *(Rechtmäßigkeit)* in German policy can be most consequential for empirical research on the impacts of policy. Legal regulation determines which target population under specified conditions and in specific modes use a program (whether established or innovative) and receive associated benefits. No one who fits those legally defined conditions can be excluded from using a program, for example, by being assigned to a control group. Conversely, nobody who has the right to use a program can be urged to submit himself to a treatment.

In a situation in which a potential client submits himself to a "treatment" in a social program, the way in which (and the conditions under which) he does so necessarily become a subject for evaluation. Unlike a physical scientist, who creates an experimental setting and can observe a successive relationship between changes in specific variables, the evaluator of a social program is essentially unable to assume causal closure with an empirical research design. Human beings (or social units in general), can "allow" themselves to be effected by a treatment. One can say that the disposition or motivation of clients to use a program is an essential prerequisite for it to come to effect. It is here more appropriate to consider "causal" relationships not in a deterministic sense but as contingent.

That basic motivation of a client to participate in a program, however, is not just a matter of entirely voluntary individual decision. It has systematic and objective bases in the client's life situation and personality. An evaluative research design will then be problem adequate when it allows reconstruction of conditions for those meaningful social processes of self-selection among potential clients and determines their influence in a program.

With established programs in the Federal Republic a purely experimental approach is not possible. Even with reforms where one might employ experimental evaluation techniques, one would be unable to identify the complex sets of influences in the social settings of the program and their impact on effectiveness. The experimental design does, in fact, allow an adequate empirical reconstruction of the simple impact model mentioned earlier. However, it is the impact model that provides an oversimplified view of reality, especially when nonexperimental, legally regulated policy is evaluated.

It is true that results of experimental research are easily communicable. However, their information value for political purposes is relatively limited. In fact, direct experiments would be able to demonstrate only how programs work without the influence of the social reality in which they operate. The interest of policy makers in program evaluation goes further (at least, it ought to) than just wishing to know if a program works or not; normally, it also includes potential ranges of program effects, the conditions under which programs are used, and the utilization by the target population.

Initially we remarked that causal relationships identified through scientific investigation are confirmations of a theory from which the nature of the causal process and the causal character of the observed relationships will become plausible. In evaluation research, this theory describes a social or political problem addressed by a program. In this sense, problem adequacy is not only a property of the empirical research operations, in as much as they allow identification of the influences of the social settings in which programs normally will work. In fact, problem adequacy also characterizes the problem-solving or policy-improving capacity of an evaluation study.

Object-adequate and problem-adequate evaluation starts from a theoretical "impact model" that is sufficiently differentiated and informative to conceptualize cause-effect relationships within a heterogeneous social field. Finally, it will conclude with a theory, empirically confirmed, that informs both the politician and the administrator how their social programs work and which effects they have under specified circumstances. Insofar as meaningful evaluation research is committed to general standards of methodology, it will fulfill the professional norms of quality, such as a sufficient amount and quality of theoretical conceptualizations, as well as object- and problem-adequate research procedures. The more comprehensive the underlying impact model and the more object-adequate and problem-adequate the empirical investigations, the less is the probability that evaluation results, as empirically grounded theories, will vanish in a drawer (Hellstern and Wollmann, 1978; Blankertz, 1976) somewhere in a government agency and be used only for the purpose of political legitimization. The latter, however, is most likely to happen when evaluation limits itself to merely delivering data, no matter how exact, instead of theories or models of reality. Evaluation research as applied basic research performs a scientific reconstruction of the conditions through which and the modes in which social programs operate.

Initially we said everyone involved in a program will do his personal subjective evaluation and, in terms of practical theories or definitions of the situation, will have a conception about how and why "his" program works. Improving policy through evaluation serves to correct those everyday conceptions of reality where they need to be corrected. Evidently, in that respect, social scientific evaluation will only then gain a policy-improving function or become "professionally effective" (Breedlove 1972) when it is able to confront those practical, everyday interpretations of reality with an empirically grounded scientific reconstruction of the way in which social programs work.

EVALUATING ESTABLISHED PROGRAMS

An eventual policy-improving function of an evaluation study will depend upon the quality of its grounded theory or "impact model"; that is, the way in which it conceptualizes relationships in the social field in which policy programs operate. We will exemplify the need for a complex impact model and for "object-" and "problem-" adequate research strategies by introducing the basic theoretical propositions and a few selected results taken from an evaluation study we conducted for the Federal Ministry of Youth, Family and Health Affairs (Bundesministerium für Jugend, Familie und Gesundheit) between 1974 and 1978 (Kaufmann et al., 1978, 1980).

The policy question appeared very simple at first glance: "What is the impact of the State's established policy programs[2] for families with young children of preschool-age upon the socialization process in the family?" The programs or policies considered comprise the following heterogeneous activities:

(a) financial benefits, such as
   —monetary family allowances *(Kindergeld)*
   —monetary housing allowances *(Wohngeld)*
   —monetary subsidies that grant a minimum living to the very poor *(Sozialhilfe)*

(b) social services, such as
   —nursery schools *(Kindergarten)*
   —adult education for parents *(Elternbildung)*
   —advisory services *(Erziehungsberatung)*
   —health services *(Mütterberatung)*.

Literal equivalents in the United States are difficult, but the common factor is that all policies potentially influence the life situation of children. They are all established programs, some of them for decades. For an evaluation researcher the policy question appears unanswerable in its original formulation. Instead, we had to translate the simple political problem into a workable scientific research problem:

(a) What do we have to evaluate? Rather than an innovation, or something that has not existed before, we must evaluate policies that to a great extent have shaped the everyday world of the family in our country. Achinger (1958) stated that the social world, the reality in which we all live, has broadly been effected and is continually influenced by social policy. Everyone knows what a "Kindergarten" is, although they may have never attended one.

(b) How do we measure the "impact" of social policy as a part of social reality upon the socialization process? The "programs" we studied have no explicit and operative "program goals" (which a less rigorous evaluation might adopt as dependent or target variables (for educational programs, see Blankertz, 1976).

As social scientists we asked ourselves, "What effects can be expected if the programs were to improve the life situation and developmental conditions of young children in the family?" In accordance with recent trends in socialization theory, and sociologically elaborating Bronfenbrenner's "Ecology of Child Development" (1974), which emphasizes the predominant influence of children's enduring environment upon developmental processes, we have identified parents' communicative and regulative activities (their "performance" in their social role as parents) as the key variable of the socialization process (see, for details, Kaufmann et al., 1979, 1980; Herlth and Strohmeier, 1980). Parental activities decide the quality of a child's home environment, and the modes in which a child gains access to the outside social and physical world are also a result of parents' regulative activities. Thus, the dependent variables in our study were not questionable measures for the problem at hand, as children's IQs for example, but specific modes of parental competence and behavior.

(c) How can the (causal) links between the policy programs and parental performance be conceptualized in an impact model? Primarily, it cannot be taken for granted that there are any causal links. Simple impact models only allow the conclusion that a program has or has not worked. Our interest, however, was directed at the "causal processes" that explain the observed "effects" or "non-effects." We have developed a theoretical framework to represent the "impact model" that, taking into account the actual research literature, conceptualizes the "environment dependency of the family socialization process."

The basic theoretical proposition is that families need "social resources," such as knowledge on socialization (see Lüscher, 1977), goods, money, housing, and social services (medical care and day care), to bring up children in qualitatively sufficient ways (according to a child's social chances). Some of those "social resources" are "internal resources"; that is, families "have" them by virtue of parents' education or occupation, the structure of the family, and the personality of its members. Others, however, are "external resources," such as goods which families have to gain from the "socioecological context" of their environment. External resources are transferred into the family via temporary interaction of its members within other social systems, such as the employment sector, social networks, and social agencies and social services. Thus, the social policies being evaluated and the agencies providing the services must be treated as environmental systems which offer special kinds of external resources—money, advice, child care, parent education, and so on. As such, the use or nonuse of specific services by a family represents a distinctive familial property—"selectivity" of participation—in specific social systems in the socioecological context. This theoretical assumption also considers the special characteristic of "programs" (they are conditional and they are not more than just offers) that can be but do not have to be accepted.

A theoretical impact model such as ours has two main functions. It can explain under which conditions people actually use programs designed for them and the extent of the utilization. On the other hand, it can identify factors influencing the dependent variables apart from the program(s) evaluated. Furthermore, it clarifies additional conditions under which programs work and in what ways self-selection of clients explains eventual program effects measured. This type of impact model performs the analytical reconstruction of a concrete social field in which policies realistically work. It contains variables on different analytical levels. We have thus decided to use a multi-level and multiple-research-methods design. The relevant variables needed were measured on an individual (family), an aggregate (socioecolo-

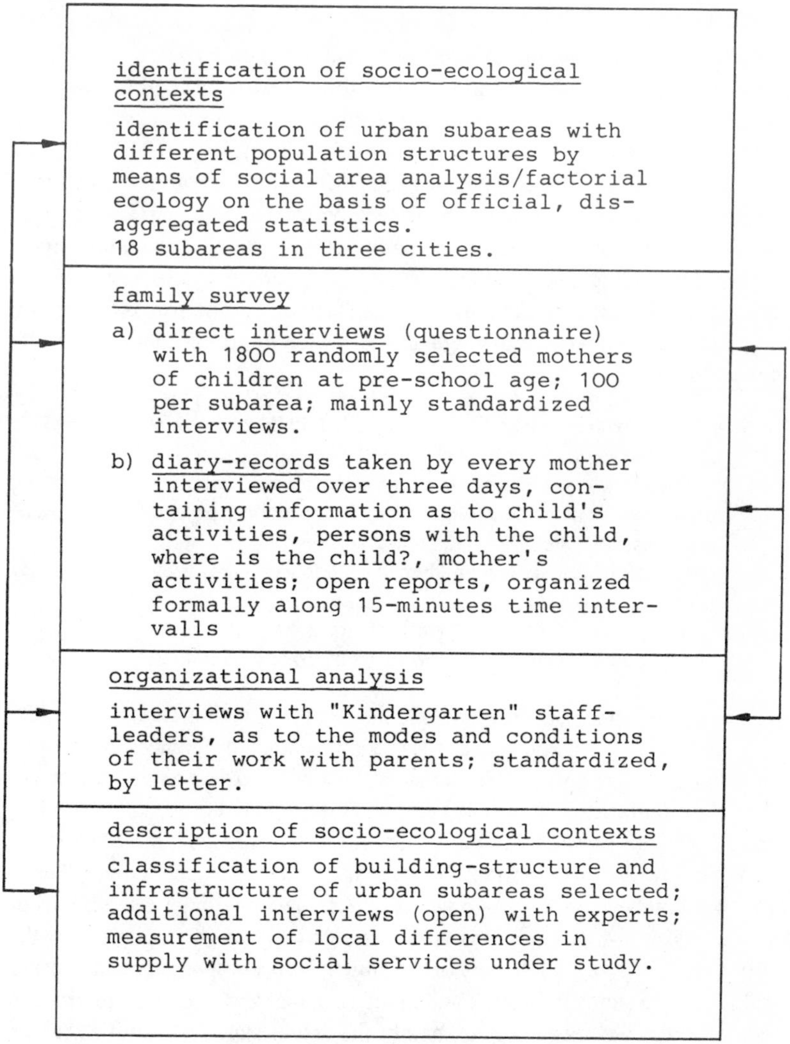

<u>identification of socio-ecological contexts</u>

identification of urban subareas with different population structures by means of social area analysis/factorial ecology on the basis of official, disaggregated statistics.
18 subareas in three cities.

<u>family survey</u>

a) direct <u>interviews</u> (questionnaire) with 1800 randomly selected mothers of children at pre-school age; 100 per subarea; mainly standardized interviews.

b) <u>diary-records</u> taken by every mother interviewed over three days, containing information as to child's activities, persons with the child, where is the child?, mother's activities; open reports, organized formally along 15-minutes time intervalls

<u>organizational analysis</u>

interviews with "Kindergarten" staff-leaders, as to the modes and conditions of their work with parents; standardized, by letter.

<u>description of socio-ecological contexts</u>

classification of building-structure and infrastructure of urban subareas selected; additional interviews (open) with experts; measurement of local differences in supply with social services under study.

FIGURE 8.1   Analytical Levels of Research and
             Research Instruments

gical context), and an organizational level—the kindergarten.

The scheme presented in Figure 8.1 compiles the different levels of research and the research techniques, qualitative and quantitative, applied. "Bows" denominate research procedures with cross-validating function; that is, variables were redundantly measured in different procedures.

Finally, we would like to demonstrate the influence variables in the structure and life situation of families have upon clients selectively submitting themselves to different modes of political treatment, and the ways in which the same variables determine the impact of a treatment. We use data about the use and impact of nursery-schools (kindergarten). The nature of our dependent variable, competence and performance of parents in their role as parents, suggests that we concentrate upon what a kindergarten does with parents, how far it affects the "parent-child-system" (Bronfenbrenner, 1974). Depending upon the degree to which parents are involved in the activities of the kindergarten (that they can factually participate is assured by legal provisions), we can distinguish four different groups that receive different "treatments."

> B = Parents who do not and will not send their children to a kindergarten. This group will serve as a control group with no treatment.
>
> A1 = Parents whose children attend a kindergarten but who themselves do not participate in parents' activities (formal assemblies, pedagogic discussion, activities with parents and children, and the like).
>
> A2 = Parents who send their children to a kindergarten and irregularly take part in parents' activities.
>
> A3 = The group with the most intense treatment: the child attends a kindergarten and the parents regularly participate in kindergarten activities.

Actually, we can expect differences in the composition of groups B, A1, A2, and A3. Figure 8.2 demonstrates these compositional differences in a profile of subgroups' mean scores on life situation and family structure indicators. The only similarity of the control group to the treatment groups (A1 to A3) is the age of their preschool children. On all other variables it has a markedly different profile. Nonuser families have the lowest socioeconomic status; a low percentage of mothers are working; families live under the worst economic and housing conditions and have relatively many children. On the other hand, a growing intensity of "treatment" is accompanied by increasing values on the status indicators and in the financial and housing situation. In other words, we see that it is mainly the social status of families (as an indicator of specific types of life situations; (see Strohmeier and Herlth, 1979) through which the different modes of participation can be explained.

We have chosen four indicators to demonstrate the effects of those different modes of parents' participation in the kindergarten upon their behavior as parents:

—the number of *children's books* available in the family;

—frequency of *children's* playmates allowed to visit the family home;

—frequency of *intensive mother-child interaction*—that is mother spending more than half an hour in intensive communication (play, reading a story, and so on) with her preschool child; and

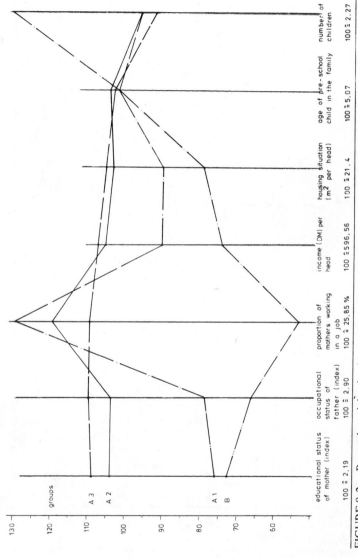

FIGURE 8.2: Parental participation in nursery-schools ("Kindergarten") on the background of families' structural and situational properties

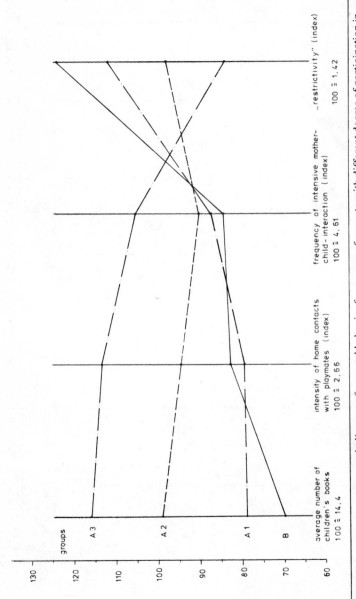

FIGURE 8.3: Average scores on indicators of parental behavior for groups of parents with different degrees of participation in nursery-schools ("Kindergarten")

—parental *"restrictivity"*—that is, parents not allowing their children to play with "dangerous" objects such as a saw or knife.

Figure 8.3 shows profiles across the mean scores on those indicators for the four "treatment categories" introduced above.

There is almost no difference between "control group" B and group A1. They are the most restrictive, and we find them below average on the other dimensions. The scores for group A2 are almost average (100) on every dependent variable, whereas the profile of group A3, the one with the most intensive treatment, is significantly over average.

It is most likely, however, that these results are merely effects of the composition of groups as demonstrated in Figure 8.2. If, however, we select only those families from our sample for which intensive participation in the kindergarten would, according to their structure and life situation, be most untypical (that is, families with social status lower than average, number and age of children more than average, in financial and housing situations being both worse than average) and if we apply the same kind of analysis to these "problem families," significant differences can be found. Note, however, that in Figure 8.4 the values taken as 100 are the respective means of this subgroup of "problem families" and not, as in Figure 8.3, those of the entire sample.

Figure 8.4 illustrates that among "problem families" only those in which parents participate in a kindergarten's parental work most intensively (A3) show scores on the dependent variables that indicate (compared with other families in similar life situations) relatively favorable conditions for children. Thus, Figure 8.4 confirms an assumption that even depressed and underprivileged families show an effect of the treatment, provided it is extremely intense. However, it still must be demonstrated how and under which circumstances it will come to these effects.

We have analyzed the kind of causal processes involved here by means of multivariate (path) analysis. Thus, we had to differentiate the assumption that with depressed families compensatory effects of the kindergarten can be expected. They can be, provided certain minimum standards of living are fulfilled. Families with a middle-class background showed no demonstrable effects. Families from the lowest working-class strata, segregated in low-ranking social areas (which, nevertheless, were not marginal, such as homeless families or ethnic strangers) with a very low per capita income and with the lowest standards of accommodation and many children (even if the parents have participated in the kindergarten in a highly intense manner), have hardly benefited from the treatment as far as the quality of parent-child interaction at home is concerned. Only "restrictivity" appeared slightly influenced by the treatment itself and not by only the depressed life situation of the families. The simple reason for that apparently was that, in those families, minimum standards in their life situation were not available to form the

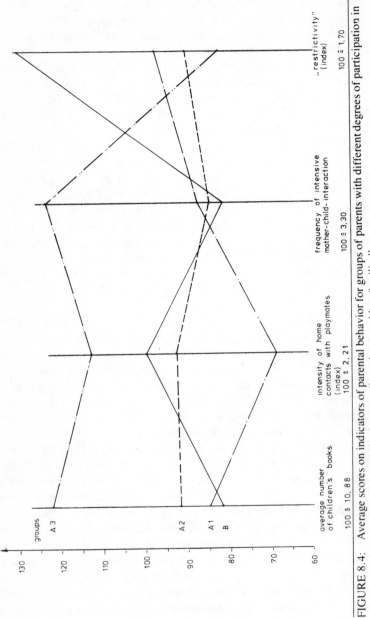

FIGURE 8.4: Average scores on indicators of parental behavior for groups of parents with different degrees of participation in nursery-schools ("Kindergarten"). only: *"problem families"*

basis upon which parental participation as a political treatment can bring about the desired compensatory effects. Consequently, working-class families which at least fitted those minimal standards appeared broadly effectuated by the program.

SUMMARY

Our study comprises a critical discussion of "traditional" approaches in social scientific evaluation research which more or less follow the experimental model of the natural sciences. The evaluation of political intervention, however, demands research designs that do *not* presuppose causal closure of processes studied. The scientific value and the practical use (the policy-improving function) of an evaluation do not depend upon a research design's formal exactness but, instead, result from its "object" and "problem adequacy." Depending upon the object of research, we suggest deliberate application of qualitative or quantitative research techniques; certain research problems may demand a combination of both.

Different from social policy in the United States, political intervention in the Federal Republic is generally implemented on the basis of permanent laws and not in the form of revisable "programs." To be "problem adequate" evaluation research in Germany demands empirical designs which have to be more complex than those merely applicable to the evaluation of limited political "programs." Possible research strategies are demonstrated using the example of our own research project on the effects of social policy upon the socialization process. Rather than simply measuring how far program-defined goals may have been attained, we suggest a complex and theoretically confirmed "impact model" enabling us to analyze the modes in which political intervention hypothetically comes to effect and considering subjective and objective factors that explain the utilization of programs (or social services) by their target population. This comprehensive approach consequently leads to more than just the identification of global "casual" relationships. In fact, it allows us to demonstrate how far the effects of political intervention are influenced by the social context in which policies normally operate.

NOTES

1. Ideally, the results of applying evaluation research in the political process perform a policy-improving function (Kaufmann, 1977, 1980). In fact, under specific conditions of interaction between science and politics, evaluation research can also have a "killer function" as well as merely a "legitimizing" function. "Applied" social research, consequently, is not a distinct concept. When the application and applicability of research results are discussed in this chapter, we concentrate upon the first of the above-mentioned types of application—improving or rationalizing policy.

2. We hesitate to use the term "program" because it does not characterize the legally regulated (and not explicitly goal-oriented) type of established policies of concern. The proper term, *"Sozialleistungen,"* however, cannot be adequately translated as "social services." We prefer to use the term "program" or "policy(ies)" synonymously in the meaning of monetary or personal aids and services delivered to families by established state agencies.

REFERENCES

ACHINGER, H. (1958) Sozialpolitik als Gesellschaftspolitik. Von der Arbeiterfrage zum Wohlfahrtstaat. Reinbek bei Hamburg: Rowohlt.

BLANKERTZ, H. (1976) Was heißt "Erfolg" oder "Scheitern" von Bildungsreformen. GFPF-Materialien, 8:29–46.

BLUMER, H. (1973) "Der methodologische Standort des symbolischen Interaktionismus." pp. 80–146 in Arbeitsgruppe Bielefelder Soziologen (eds.), Alltagswissen, Interaktion und gesellschaftliche Wirklichkeit (vol. 1). Reinbek bei Hamburg: Rowohlt.

BREEDLOVE, J. L. (1972) "Theory development as a task for the evaluator." pp. 55–70 in E. J. Mullen et al. (eds.), Evaluation of Social Intervention. San Francisco: Jossey-Bass.

BRONFENBRENNER, U. (1974) Wie wirksam ist kompensatorische Erziehung? Stuttgart: Klett.

CAMPBELL, D. T. (1974) "Qualitative knowing in action research." Presented at the meeting of the Society for the Psychological Study of Social Issues, New Orleans, September 1.

_____and J. STANLEY (1966) "Experimental and quasi-experimental designs for research on teaching." pp. 171–246 in N. L. Gage (ed.), Handbook of Research on Teaching. Chicago: Rand McNally.

_____(1977) "Methodische Vorstudie für die Analyse der städtebaulichen und stadtstrukturel-len Wirkungen ausgewählter Sanierungsmaßnahmen nach dem Städtebauförderungsgesetz (final report). Unpublished manuscript. Berlin.

HELLSTERN, G. M. and H. WOLLMANN (1978) Sanierungsmaßnahmen. Städtebauliche und stadtstrukturelle Wirkungen. Bonn-Bad Godesberg: Schriftenreihe "Stadtentwicklung" des Bundesminsters für Raumordnung, Bauwesen and Städtebau.

HERLTH, A. and K. P. STROHMEIER, (1980) "Sozialpolitik und der Alltag von Kindern." In L. Vaskovics (ed.), Der Mensch als soziales und personales Wesen (vol. 6). Sozialökologis-che Einflußfaktoren familialer Sozialisation. Stuttgart: Klett.

JONES, W. C. and E. F. BORGATTA, (1972) "Methodology of evaluation." pp. 39–54 in E. J. Mullen et al. (eds.), Evaluation of Social Intervention. San Francisco: Jossey-Bass.

JUHOS, B. (1960) "Welche begrifflichen Formen stehen der empirischen Beschreibung zur Verfügung?." pp. 101–158 in E. Topitsch (ed.), Probleme der Wissenschaftstheorie. Festschrift für Victor Kraft. Vienna: Springer.

KAUFMANN, F.-X. (1980) "Social policy and social services: some problems of policy formation, program implementation and impact evaluation." In D. Grunow and F. Hegner (eds.), Reponsiveness of Social Service Organizations to Clients' Needs. New York: Praeger.

_____(1977) "Sozialpolitisches Erkenntnisinteresse und Soziologie. Ein Beitrag zur Pragmatik der Sozialwissenschaften." pp. 35–75 in C. von Ferber and F.-X. Kaufmann (eds.), Soziologie und Sozialpolitik. Sonderheft 19 der Kölner Zeitschrift für Soziologie und Sozialpsychologie. Opladen: Westdeutscher Verlag.

_____and SCHNEIDER, S. (1975) "Modelleinrichtungen—ein Instrument für experimen-telle Reformverfahren in der Sozialpolitik?" Neue Praxis 3: 206–218.

KAUFMANN, F.-X., A. HERLTH, and K. P. STROHMEIER (1980) Sozialpolitik und fami-liale Sozialisation—zur Wirkungsweise öffentlicher Sozialleistungen. Stuttgart: Kohlham-mer.

KAUFMANN, F.-X., A. HERLTH, H.-J. SCHÜTZE, and K.P. STROHMEIER (1979) "Wirkungen öffentlicher Sozialleistungen auf den familialen Sozialisationsprozeß." pp. 181–211 in K. Lüscher (ed.), Sozialpolitik für das Kind. Stuttgart: Klett.

————(1978) "Sozialpolitik und familiale Sozialisation. Schlußbericht des Forschungsprojekts "Wirkungen öffentlicher Sozialleistungen auf den Sozialisationsprozeß." Unpublished.

KÖNIG, H. (1968) "Beobachtung und Experiment in der Sozialforschung." pp. 17–47 in R. König (ed.), Beobachtung und Experiment in der Sozialforschung. Praktische Sozial forschung (vol. 2). Cologne: Kiepenheuer und Witsch.

LAZARSFELD, P. F. (1965) "Wissenschaftslogik und empirische Sozialforschung." In E. Topitsch (ed.), Logik der Sozialwissenschaften. Cologne: Kiepenheuer und Witsch.

LUHMANN, N. (1970) Soziologische Aufklärung—Aufsätze zur Theorie sozialer Systeme. Opladen: Westdeutscher Verlag.

LÜSCHER, K. [ed.] (1979) Sozialpolitik für das Kind. Stuttgart: Klett.

————(1977) "Sozialpolitik für das Kind." pp. 591–628 in C. von Ferber and F.-X. Kaufmann (eds.), Soziologie und Sozialpolitik. Sonderheft 19 der Kölner Zeitschrift für Soziologie und Sozialpsychologie. Opladen: Westdeutscher Verlag.

MATTHES, J. and F. SCHÜTZE (1973) Introduction: "Alltagswissen, Interaktion und gesellschaftliche Wirklichkeit." pp. 11–53 in Arbeitsgruppe Beilefelder Soziologen (eds.), Alltagswissen, Interaktion und gesellschaftliche Wirklichkeit (vol. 1) Reinbek bei Hamburg: Rowohlt.

OPP, K. D. (1976) Methodologie der Sozialwissenschaften. Reinbek bei Hamburg: Rowohlt.

POPPER, K. R. (1964) "Naturgesetze und theoretische Systeme." pp. 87–103 in H. Albert (ed.), Theorie und Realität. Ausgewählte Aufsätze zur Wissenschaftslehre der Sozialwissenschaften. Tübingen: Mohr.

SCHEUCH, E. K. and D. RÜSCHEMEYER (1965) "Soziologie und Statistik—über den Einfluß der modernen Wissenschaftslehre auf ihr gegenseitiges Verhältnis." pp. 345–363 in E. Topitsch (ed.), Logik der Sozialwissenschaften. Cologne: Kiepenheuer und Witsch.

SCHÜTZE, F. (1976) "Zur Hervorlockung und Analyse thematisch relevanter Geschichten im Rahmen soziologischer Feldforschung—dargestellt an einem Projekt zur Erforschung von kommunalen Machtstrukturen." pp. 159–260 in Arbeitsgruppe Bielefelder Soziologen (eds.), Kommunikative Sozialforschung. Munich: Fink.

SIMON, J. L. (1970) "The concept of causality in economics." Kyklos 23: 226–255.

SMELSER, N. J. (1967) "Sociology and the other social sciences." In P. F. Lazarsfeld, W. H. Sewell, and H. L. Wilensky (eds.), The Uses of Sociology. London: Basic Books.

STEGMÜLLER, W. (1960) "Das Problem der Kausalität." pp. 170–190 in E. Topitsch (ed.), Probleme der Wissenschaftstheorie. Festschrift für Victor Kraft. Vienna: Springer.

STROHMEIER, K. P. and A. HERLTH (1979) "Sozialräumliche Bedingungen familialer Sozialisation." In H. Walter (ed.), Region und Sozialisation (vol. 2). Stuttgart: Fromman-Holzboog.

SUCHMAN, E. A. (1972) "Action for what? A critique of evaluative research." pp. 52–84 in C. H. Weiss (ed.), Evaluating Action Programs. Readings in Social Action and Education. Boston: Allyn & Bacon.

WEBER, M. (1964) Wirtschaft und Gesellschaft. J. Winkelmann, (ed.). Cologne: Kiepenheuer und Witsch.

WEISS, C. H. [ed.] (1972) Evaluating Action Programs. Readings in Social Action and Education. Boston: Allyn & Bacon.

WILSON, T. P. (1973) "Theorien der Interaktion und Modelle soziologischer Erklärung." pp. 54–79 in Arbeitsgruppe Bielefelder Soziologen (eds.), Alltagswissen, Interaktion und gesellschaftliche Wirklichkeit (vol. 1). Reinbek bei Hamburg: Rowohlt.

9

Causal Analysis in Nonexperimental Evaluation Research

Manfred Küchler

*Johann Wolfgang Goethe Universität,
Frankfurt*

INTRODUCTION

The relationship of evaluation research to data-analytic techniques is both complex and opaque: The clarification of this relationship is important not only for "applied" social scientists but for policy makers and program personnel. In this chapter we address these issues through a study of a cancer prevention check-up program in West Germany. The general claims include the following:

(1) Evaluation research usually deals with complex social phenomena. Hence, evaluating the effect of a program or looking for reasons for success or failure also requires complex techniques for data analysis, as Eber (1975) has clearly pointed out.

(2) To identify causes and reasons for program failure or success, sophisticated research designs such as experimental designs, time series analysis, or panel studies are necessary. However, these designs are not feasible in many circumstances.

(3) Meaningful insights are useful for policy decisions and/or program implementation and are possible from simple research designs such as one-time surveys with predominantly categorical data, when new techniques for data analysis (See Goodman, 1978; Küchler, 1979a) are employed in addition to the traditional ones (Cohen, 1975).

(4) Finds have to be formulated in a way meaningful to people outside academia in order to facilitate utilization of results by policy makers and program personnel.

GERMAN CANCER PROGRAM: CASE STUDY

Social security regulations offer a free check-up once a year to each female over 30 and each male over 45. This check-up is restricted to certain types of cancer and certain diagnostic methods. Thus, almost every practicing physician has the capability of offering the benefits of the program. There has been continuing criticism regarding the medical effectiveness of the program.

Participation in the program is a necessary, yet not sufficient, condition for program success. Unfortunately, statistics show male participation at only 15 percent and female participation at 35 percent. Thus, reasons for participation have been subject to research, mainly from the medical perspective. Findings tend to place the responsibility on the patients. People are afraid to hear a diagnosis of cancer; second, they tend to be careless. Not denying the importance of these factors, the research offers little toward actual improvement of the implementation of the program. Additional assistance might guide practical action in reshaping the program.

METHODOLOGY

In 1975, my co-workers and I conducted a survey in the Frankfurt area using a written questionnaire. A random sample of approximately 4000 respondents was selected with a return rate of approximately one-third. We had some support from the local social security agency (AOK Frankfurt), but limitations in funding resulted in a rather weak design. However, the results obtained seem to warrant an extended replication study to further test our findings.

The data are almost exclusively categorical, partially due to the simple research design and the necessity of keeping the questionnaire as short as possible. Our independent variable was participation. It was sometimes difficult to determine from the completed questionnaires whether people had actually participated in the program or just had some medical examination that they thought had something to do with detecting cancer. Also, since participation is low in general, an ordinal indicator for participation (frequency) would not have been helpful. Hence, standard techniques such as multiple regression, path analysis, or analysis of variance, could not be employed (Duncan, 1975). In our original analysis (Fargel et al., 1977), we used a technique proposed by Harder (1975), but later discovered that this technique can be subsumed to the more general and statistically more sophisticated approach of Grizzle, Starmer and Koch (1969). A reanalysis of our data using these more refined techniques has also been published (Küchler, 1978). Given the general interest of this study, we will not present the statistical details, but rather highlight the main ideas from an intuitive perspective. A more detailed, nontechnical introduction into the multivariate ("causal") analysis of nonmetric data can be found in Küchler (1979b); a more rigid treatment, in Küchler (1978, 1979a).

THE GRIZZLE-STARMER-KOCH (GSK) APPROACH

This approach can be described roughly as follows: One tries to find the independent variables that best explain the distribution of the target variable. Here we are looking for the factors best explaining why people do not take part in the program. Naturally, the more factors considered, the better the explanation of the target variable. However, practical reasons call for a model as simple as possible which still adequately reflects the nature of the data. Thus, a compromise has to be achieved between simplicity and precision.

Furthermore, one would like to identify the relative impact of each factor and any interaction effects. The GSK approach allows for measuring the overall fit of the model considered as well as for computing different "effects" to be associated with the single factors respective of special combinations of factors. We will demonstrate this in the discussion of results.

RESULTS

Three factors were most influential on participation:

(1) *Uneasiness* about the medical procedures to be used in the examination;
(2) *Attitude* as to whether regular check-ups provide the best means for prevention; and
(3) *Information* about the program.

The last factor seems to be important for practical program implementation. Our data showed quite clearly that only a minor percentage of those seeing a doctor were directly informed about the program by their physician. Our results strongly suggest the program implementation can be significantly improved if doctors take more time to talk to their patients about the program and encourage their participation.

Table 9.1 presents a multiple classification distribution of the empirical data.

The overall impact of the set of independent variables can be measured by a usual coefficient of association such as Cramer's V; here we obtain $V = .413$. According to conventional rules of thumb, this is a moderately high value, given that we are looking at survey data on individuals. Unfortunately, there is no intuitive meaning to this coefficient; it mainly serves to

TABLE 9.1   Multiple Classification Distribution File: Cancer
Prevention—Frankfurt 1975

UNEASINESS	ATTITUDE	INFORMATION	% PARTICIPATION	SUBGROUP NO.
YES	POS	PHYSICIAN	65,8 (38)	1
YES	POS	OTHER	37,0 (200)	2
YES	NEG	PHYSICIAN	7,7 (13)	3
YES	NEG	OTHER	8,6 (116)	4
NO	POS	PHYSICIAN	75,2 (121)	5
NO	POS	OTHER	59,3 (430)	6
NO	NEG	PHYSICIAN	75,0 (16)	7
NO	NEG	OTHER	26,7 (131)	8

Valid cases: 1065   Missing cases: 294
Cramer's V = .413

compare different sets of factors. Due to limited space we will not discuss
this preliminary step of the analysis.

To determine the relative impact of each factor, "main effects" and "interaction effects" are computed. A main effect measures the impact of a
single factor on the target variable while controlling for the other factors in
the model. This control of the other factors is highly important to guard
against spurious correlations.

Main effects do not show spurious correlations, but measure direct
impact—at least relative to the model under consideration. Nevertheless,
the way they are computed is quite similiar to the computation of well-
known percentage differences in a fourfold table. By looking at three factors
with two categories each, the population can be thought of as divided into
eight subgroups (the rows of Table 9.1). All people within the same subgroup are homogeneous in respect to the independent variables. For each
subgroup rate of participation is next computed, and we expect differing
rates as long as the independent variables chosen have some impact on the
target variable. We then try to relate the differences in rate to the characteristics of the subgroups.

The main effect of *Information* is simply the difference between the
average participation rate of subgroups where people have been personally
informed to the average rate over all subgroups, the "grand mean." In our
data we find that average rate in "informed" subgroups is 11.5 points above
that grand mean (see Table 9.2). The other main effects can be interpreted in
a similiar manner, a minus sign indicating that average rate is below grand
mean.

People familiar with the analysis of variance techniques will have noted a
well-known terminology. In fact, this approach can be viewed as a modified
regression analysis (for the relation to ordinary dummy dependent variable
regression see Küchler, 1980). Interaction effects are computed as in anal-

TABLE 9.2:   Effects for Saturated Model

EFFECTS	VALUE	STAND. VALUE
MEAN	44,4	21,0 +
UNEASINESS (U)	−14,6	− 6,9 +
ATTITUDE (A)	14,9	7,1 +
INFORMATION (I)	11,5	5,5 +
U × A	6,7	3,2 +
U × I	− 4,5	− 2,1
A × I	− ,3	− ,2
U × A × I	7,8	3,7 +

Variance of each effect: 4,46
+ Denotes significance on 5% level in simultaneous test of all effects

ysis of variance, but can also be viewed in a more intuitive way. Note that this analysis is mainly concerned with structural effects. All subgroups are treated equally, disregarding their size. Thus, the grand mean, the mean of subgroup rates, generally will not equal the proportion of participants in the marginal distribution. In our data we arrive at 44.4 percent compared with 47.2 percent in the marginal distribution of *Participation*. Thus, structural analysis might be highly interesting from a theoretical point of view, but people more concerned with practical consequences might feel that subgroup sizes are indeed important for what they are trying to achieve.

Let us consider the following argument against the relevance of our findings. If everyone in our sample who had been informed by a doctor had participated in the program, this would have caused an increase of only 59 in the number of participants and the corresponding rate would have been increased to merely 52.8 percent. On the other hand, the main effect of *Information* in our GSK analysis would have been increased to 33.5, thus grossly exaggerating the impact of this factor. These are two sides to this argument. It is true that GSK effects do not reflect subgroup sizes and that an effect large in value may relate to a small subpopulation which might be wise to neglect from a practical/political point of view. In this case, it is important to ask how many people are seeing a doctor and potentially could be personally informed.

Subgroup size is indeed a factor to consider, even in the analysis. Since computation of effects is based primarily on rates and since some "large sample theory" is involved when testing for the significance of single effects, subgroup sizes should not be too small. Consequently, the number of factors, as well as the number of categories to be distinguished, is limited by sample size. Rules of thumb rather than a precise limit prohibit dividing the population into more than N/40 subgroups and avoiding subgroups smaller than 15 to 20.

Reviewing the concrete data constellation and examining the effects computed (see Table 9.2), we see that all main effects are notably different from zero. The same holds for at least two of the interaction effects. These effects indicate that the main effects do not add up, but that special combinations of values for the independent variables have a more complicated impact on participation rates.

This crude inspection of coefficients can be statistically refined. With weak assumption on the data it can be shown that distribution of the effects is approximately normal. Hence, statistical tests can be applied to determine which of the coefficients may be neglected for substantial interpretation. "Standardized values" can be compared with the standard normal distribution; that is, values above 1.96—disregarding sign—are significant at the 5 percent level. When there is no specific hypothesis stated in advance, the limit of 1.96 should be raised in relation to the total number of effects computed. If k is the number of effects (number of different subgroups), then the 2.5/k-percentile of the normal distribution has been proposed as an adequate limit. Effect with values above that limit have been marked in Table 9.2.

The next step in GSK analysis will be to test whether a reduced or "unsaturated" model including the only significant effects will still fit the data. This is done by a generalized chi-square procedure and utilizing weighted least squares to newly estimate the effects in the reduced model. As pointed out earlier, effects can be interpreted as regression coefficients in a modified regression equation. Because of inherent heteroscedasticity, ordinary least-square regression will not render optimal estimates; that is, estimates with minimal variance. By weighting with the covariance matrix of the subgroup rates viewed as a column vector, optimal estimation is secured.

These last remarks may sound like a foreign language to quite a few people in evaluation research. Simply, this means that coefficients are computed in a way that takes in account that subgroup rates may not be exact values but may include some error. Furthermore, it seems plausible to assume that rates based on many cases may be less error-prone than those based on relatively few cases. Precisely this is achieved by "weighting with the covariance matrix."

A second consideration is that, while main effects can be interpreted satisfactorily in substantive terms, interaction effects—especially those of higher order (equal to number of factors involved)—are hard to grasp. With the GSK approach one can identify interaction by so-called conditional or nested effects. These effects can be interpreted similarly to the main effects. The difference is that they relate only to special kinds of subgroups. In our

TABLE 9.3:   Best Model

A. DESIGN MATRIX

SUBGROUP No.	U	A	I	U<E2<I1
1	1	1	1	0
2	1	1	−1	0
3	1	−1	1	1
4	1	−1	−1	0
5	−1	1	1	0
6	−1	1	−1	0
7	−1	−1	1	−1
8	−1	−1	−1	0

B. EFFECTS

MEAN	43,3	24,5 +
UNEASINESS (U)	−9,6	− 6,6 +
ATTITUDE (A)	15,1	10,4 +
INFORMATION (I)	10,1	5,8 +
U<E2<I1	−23,0	− 3,6 +

C. FIT OF THE MODEL
SUM OF THE SQUARED RESIDUALS = 2,16
DEGREES OF FREEDOM   = 3

COMPARISON TO CHI-SQUARED DISTRIBUTION SHOWS EXCELLENT FIT

data we consider a conditional effect of *Uneasiness* for subgroups of people with negative attitude and personal information (thus constituting the condition). See Table 9.3 for more details on this model and values of effects computed. We consider this our "best model." Best models always will be a compromise between simplicity (in order to stress the main factors) and complexity (in order to fit the empirical data).

INTERPRETATION OF "BEST MODEL"

Among all three-factor models the one with *Uneasiness, Attitude,* and *Information* best explains rate of participation. Relative to average participation rate over all subgroups, average rate is increased for subgroups with people personally informed by a physician by 11 percentage points, for subgroups with people holding a positive attitude toward check-ups by 9 points, and is decreased for subgroups consisting of people who are uneasy about the conduct of the check-up by 7 points. If people with negative attitude have talked to a doctor about the program, then *Uneasiness* leads to a further decrease by 23 points. This last effect is an indication that information dissemination about the program may be very important, for at least a special subgroup of the potential clientele. Practically, it will not suffice to have more doctors talk to their patients about the program, but it is equally important that this information is given in a way to build confidence in the examination.

Introducing *Sex* as an additional variable in the model leads to interesting results. Participation rate among females is higher than among males, which is well documented by official statistics. More important, however, the pattern of impact factors is different for both sexes, in that the conditional effect does not prove significant with females. When refining the analysis in this way, it seems feasible to describe certain "problem groups" that may have specific barriers to overcome before participating in the program.

Though we restricted ourselves to dichotomous data (only two categories per factor), the GSK approach is not limited to that kind of data. Also, the GSK approach offers the option of log-linear modeling, which does have some advantages from a statistical point of view. However, coefficients obtained in this way are hard to interpret in substantial terms. A computer program to carry out the computation, written by Herbert L. Kritzer (1979), can be obtained from him. This program is called NONMET and requires a frequency table as input. For the early stage of analyzing the data, when a number of factor sets have to be "screened," a simpler program working from raw data Küchler's DO has proved helpful. This program considers only saturated models and should be supplemented by the more refined NONMET program for the later stages in the analysis.

CONCLUSION

Since the days of large reform programs seem to be gone, evaluation research will have to be applied more often to ongoing programs. Also, utilization of evaluation research will be enhanced when it offers practical suggestions, thus convincing program personnel as well as policy makers of its value. Small-scale tasks may provide good opportunities to prove the talents of the social science researcher. Gathering data quickly and nevertheless coming up with answers that are solidly grounded in empirical data and that make sense from a practical point of view is possible by using the tools described in this study. However, we do not want to do away with more elaborate research designs altogether. Rather, we see this statement as pragmatic necessity in a phase where evaluation research has yet to unconditionally establish its value for policy-making.

REFERENCES

COHEN, J. (1975) "Multiple regression as a general data-analytic system." In E. L. Struening and M. Guttentag (eds.) Handbook of Evaluation Research, Vol. 1. Beverly Hills, CA: Sage.

DUNCAN, O. D. (1975) Introduction to Structural Equation Models. New York: Academic Press.

EBER, H. W. (1975) "Multivariate methodologies for evaluation research." In E. L. Struening and M. Guttentag (eds.) Handbook of Evaluation Research, Vol. 1. Beverly Hills, CA: Sage.

FARGEL, M., M. KUCHLER, and R. SCHIEBEL (1977) Krebsfrüherkennung—Sozialwissenschaftliche Analyse über das Versichertenverhalten. Deutsches Ärzteblatt 74: 951–957.

GOODMAN, L. A. (1978) Analyzing Qualitative/Categorical Data: Log-Linear Models and Latent Structure Analysis. Cambridge, MA: Abt Books.

GRIZZLE, J. E., C. F. STARMER, and G. G. KOCH (1969) "Analysis of categorical data by linear model." Biometrics 25: 489–584.

HARDER, T. (1975) Daten und Theorie. München: Frank.

KRITZER, H. L. (1979) NONMET II, Version 6.6. Madison: Department of Political Science, University of Wisconsin.

KÜCHLER, M. (1980) "The analysis of nonmetric data: the relation of dummy dependent variable regression using an additive-saturated Grizzle-Starmer-Koch model." Sociological Methods & Research 8: 369–388.

———(1979a) Multivariate Analyseverfahren. Stuttgart: Teubner.

———(1979b) Einführung in die multivariate Analyse nicht-metrischer Daten. (unpublished)

———(1978) "Alternativen in der Kreuztabellenanalyse." Ztschr. f. Soziologie 7: 347–365.

PART IV

TRANSLATING RESEARCH INTO POLICY

No other issue has stimulated discussion more in the recent past than the application of social science and evaluation research to the political and administrative processes. Existing explanatory models have often neglected to shed more light on the linkage of science and policy. Robert Rich reviews the basic questions asked in research utilization studies. He stresses the significance of the nonutilization of science, the need for greater understanding of the role of scientific advice, and the pluralism of forces shaping the policy process. Bernhard Badura explores the difference between the American and European administrative environments and hypothesizes that the receptivity for evaluation research results in Europe is more limited due to the different social and educational backgrounds. Thomas Kiresuk, Nancy Larsen, and Sander Lund explore the roles of social, political, and contextual issues within organizations which are relevant to the employment of evaluation and the subsequent utilization of findings in policy, program, or clinical decision-making.

10

Can Evaluation be Used for Policy Action?

Robert F. Rich

Woodrow Wilson School of
Public and International Affairs,
Princeton University

As Michael Q. Patton points out, the idea of scientifically evaluating government programs is relatively new. In the area of human services, the General Accounting Office developed auditing models for purposes of record-keeping: How many people were being served? How much did a unit of service cost? The auditing models did not even begin to ask questions about the success of programs and the factors that might lead to replicability. As the dollars began to shrink in the early 1970s, difficult questions were asked concerning the viability and effectiveness of programs as opposed to using the standard, Were people happy or is it usual and customary practice?

Even though the idea of formal program evaluation was new to government in the early 1960s, *it is not a new process in human thinking or problem-solving*. Each decision maker or policy maker has an implicit model for assessment (evaluation) that he has developed over time. We are all constantly (on a day-to-day basis) in the position of accepting or rejecting ideas and/or strategies for change that are proposed to us. These "models" are often implicit; yet, they are extremely important because they serve as the basis for decision-making.

Evaluation research was formally introduced to experienced policy makers (experts) who were being asked to replace their "well-learned" assessment or evaluation models with a new mode of inquiry. This formal model of inquiry was steeped in scientific tradition and legitimated by well-known and respected practitioners—a new tool for the policy analyst. Policy makers were uncomfortable with this new tool of research; it was not as reliable (or perhaps not even as valid) as intuition or experience.

Despite these reservations, program evaluation or evaluation research has matured into a discipline with specific training programs, journals, professional societies, and continuing education programs. Evaluation as a discipline has received recognition by the U.S. federal government, particularly the legislative and executive branches, and has been legitimated through legislatively mandated requirements and special offices of departments (for example, the Assistant Secretary for Policy, Planning, and Evaluation), as well as divisions of the Office of Management and Budget (OMB) and the General Accounting Office (GAO).

Evaluation is thought of as a formal component of the problem-solving/policy-making process by academics and practitioners alike. In academic circles, there is a concern for training professional evaluators or, at a minimum, professionals who understand evaluation and can assess the quality and viability of its findings. These professionals are hired in government agencies, large research institutions, and in the expanding number of for-profit consulting firms.

Evaluation has grown and gained legitimacy more rapidly than most traditional disciplines. In strict economic terms, the demand for evaluation continues to exceed the supply of available, well-trained professionals who are capable of meeting the needs of managers in and out of government.

Evaluation research is a form of social science information that policy makers believe can help them in their problem-solving activities. A 1977 General Accounting Office review of the use of social research by national policy makers disclosed high expectations for the utility of information derived from formal evaluation research. More than 70 percent of the respondents, consisting of top management officials in federal agencies, thought that social science should have a substantial or very large effect on the formulation of national policy (Staats, 1979).

In terms of pace, the GAO study showed that 45 percent of the policy makers indicated they were not satisfied with the translation of research results into usable products or into techniques for problem-solving.

There have been a number of explanations put forward to account for the gap between the articulated need for evaluation and the behavior of officials who do not use (or who "underutilize") such information. The most salient explanation seems to be the inherent tensions between the two models of problem-solving that are currently operating within government—that is, the traditional expert model versus the policy analyst model.

As evaluation research continues to grow and mature, several issues will need to be addressed: (1) Are the appropriate methodological tools available and are they being applied? (2) Are evaluation research results effectively being translated into policy/action? (3) What can be done to decrease the abuse and misutilization of evaluation data? (4) What ethical standards should be developed for evaluators, and who will enforce these standards? This list of issues is by no means exhaustive. It does, however, point to a core set of concerns that deserve attention. This essay is devoted to exploring each of these issues, what is at stake, and in what directions the field is developing.

METHODOLOGICAL TOOLS—THE STATE-OF-THE-ART

It is not surprising that one of the ways evaluation research gained relatively rapid legitimacy in academic circles was through the adaption of traditional and proven methodologies to the evaluation process. Students of evaluation learn how to use a set of complex, sophisticated techniques (such as regression analysis, interrupted time-series analysis, log-linear models, and path analysis) as part of their professional training.

To the extent that evaluators unquestioningly apply these tools, the scientific process is being reversed. They have tools that search for a problem rather than clearly defining the problems and then deciding what tools are most appropriate for purposes of research and analysis. The application of models and techniques developed for other problems (and by other disciplines) may produce long-term difficulties.

As Marcia Guttentag pointed out in her testimony before the Senate Committee on Human Resources, experimental designs and classical statistics, where applied to social programs, often either force a set of assumptions on a program or attempt to change the program to be similar to what the research model requires. The literature on the sociology of professions teaches us that this is not atypical to the maturation process of a relatively new professional field.

Evaluation research which is not conducted primarily for scholarly purposes (for example, secondary analysis of data) is seldom in the position of simply being able to develop and apply eloquent statistical models. There are users who need to know whether their programs or projects are "successful." They want to *understand* what is working well and what might be done to improve unsuccessful or problematic program components.

Thus, it seems logical that evaluators should concern themselves with *understanding* the program to be evaluated as well as the *structure* and *environment* in which the program is located. This type of understanding may not be provided by the mechanical application of classical statistical techniques to the day-to-day operations of a program.

The classical statistical model allows for a rather narrow understanding of success as defined in a systematic fashion by performance measures. For example, if one is concerned with the performance of minority students in selective institutions of higher education in the United States, the "classical evaluation model" would stipulate that data be collected on cumulative grade point average, rank in class, postgraduate placement, high school class rank, high school grade point average, and scores on a national aptitude test. These data would then form the core of the variables to be examined. Inputs (such as aptitude test scores and high school grade point averages) would then be correlated with outputs (for example, college cumulative grade point averages) and outputs would be examined in the context of a regression analysis.

Similarly, if one were interested in the impact of a change in the legal drinking age from 21 to 18, one would first define an appropriate output/ performance measure (for example, the rate of deaths in the 18–21 age category due to drunk driving). Data on this criterion variable would be collected over time along with a set of variables that might be correlated with the outcome measure.

There is no doubt that this type of assessment has become sophisticated over time, and one can, as a scholar and practitioner, also learn a good deal from this type of analysis. For example, in his secondary analysis of the Head Start Program data, Thomas Cook had a major insight into the effectiveness of the *Sesame Street* TV program. He found that the gap in rate of learning increased between upper- and lower-class children; this was due to the fact that upper-class children received reinforcement in the home for what they learned from the program. This finding contradicted the original evaluation findings on the success of *Sesame Street* that learning increased significantly among lower-class students. Cook's findings helped encourage those responsible for the program to think about it from a different perspective.

However, it is equally true that this type of evaluation does not provide an understanding of the process that was followed in attaining the outcomes measured. Does one need to understand the operating procedures and processes associated with program operations? The answer to this question is unequivocally "yes." If evaluators are to possess the capacity to suggest or actually prescribe treatments for improving programs, they must understand what the ultimate programmatic goals are in addition to what means are being used to reach those goals.

In his famous article, "Reforms as Experiments," D. T. Campbell contends:

The political stance should be: this is a serious problem. We propose to initiate policy A on an experimental basis. If after five years there has been no

> significant improvement, we will shift to policy B. By making explicit that a given situation is only one of several that the administrator . . . could in good conscience advocate, . . . the administrator can afford honest evaluation of outcomes. Negative results . . . do not jeopardize his job for his job is to keep after the problem until something is found that works [Campbell, 1969].

One does not simply want to move from policy A to policy B in a mechanical fashion ("A has not worked so let us move on to B."). The adoption of policy B should be made with an understanding of the reasons why A failed in contrast to a simple determination that "the performance measures reveal that A was not successful."

In trying to understand structure, environment, and context, evaluation research needs to become even more interdisciplinary than it is at the present time. There is a good deal that can be learned, for instance, from anthropologists and their notion of an "organizational ethnography." Operations research, systems analysis, and management information designers have developed techniques which produce detailed and systematic descriptions of the formal structure of an organization as well as the process that is followed (actors, decision criteria) while engaging in problem-solving activities.

The "decision theoretic" evaluation method, put forward by Guttentag, is an example of a new method which "recognizes the dynamics and multiple levels of decision-making in human service program" (Guttentag, 1978). This method represents a simplified form of multiattribute utility scaling and Bayesian statistics. The goal of this evaluation method is to be sensitive to the expressed goals and alternative options of decision makers.

The evaluation group at the Urban Institute insists that this type of detailed understanding is a prerequisite for engaging in program evaluation. The detailed understanding

> would help determine the degree of correspondence between what the managers and Congressional staff within an agency believe to be a program's functions, and what in fact the program's operations are described to be in the most concrete and mundane reality [Nay et al., 1978].

It seems clear that the successful evaluation teams will avail themselves of the variety of techniques now available and/or in the process of being developed. The more traditional techniques allow one to be confident, in terms of statistical levels of significance, of the findings presented. However, do these "significant findings" speak to the formative problem-solving needs of decision makers? More important, is the evaluator confident that he/she understands the operations of the program being evaluated? In the evaluation area, we may have to face the challenge posed by E. S. Quade: Do social scientists want to be approximately correct or precisely wrong?

ARE EVALUATION RESULTS BEING
EFFECTIVELY TRANSLATED INTO ACTION?

As already alluded to earlier, policy makers are receptive to program evaluation results; they do not feel that the best information is being made available to them, and they do not feel that evaluators are receptive to their needs (Caplan, 1976). On the basis of these empirical results, one can tentatively conclude that there is a need to create effective knowledge transfer mechanisms for translating evaluation information into action/policy.

The research results do not, however, guide us in clarifying who should (and who should not) be engaged in "translating," what types of knowledge transfer mechanisms should be created, and who should be responsible for the "effective application" of these mechanisms. Most of the programs designed to translate knowledge into action have been premised on the belief that if information is timely, relevant, in the proper form, and oriented toward the decision maker's agenda, utilization (that is, action) will automatically follow (Rich, 1979a). Those who subscribe to this belief attempt to change what might be called knowledge—specific characteristics.

Those who adhere to a different perspective on this problem would contend that knowledge-specific characteristics (timeliness, relevance, form) are important; but they are not sufficient for producing utilization. Instead, one should be concentrating on organizational design, bureaucratic structures, and incentive/reward systems (Rich, 1979a, 1979b). There are, however, few examples of projects or programs which have acted out of commitment to this belief. When Thomas Glennan, Jr. was Director of the Evaluation Office of OEO, he tried to create an incentive system that would be responsive to the needs of researchers and decision makers alike.

ABUSE, MISUSE OF EVALUATION RESULTS

At the same time that one is concerned with developing effective measures for the application of evaluation research results, it is worth noting that utilization is not a priori valuable. Presumably, effective knowledge transfer mechanisms are not being developed because it is believed that utilization/application is worthwhile in and of itself.

It is a well-known fact that a use can be found for any study "if it becomes necessary to do so." Thus, one must, as a professional evaluator, be concerned with the quality of utilization. Cook (1978) distinguishes between intentional and unintentional abuse of evaluation research results. He has also introduced the concept of premature use of information.

A good example of premature use of evaluation results is the case of the GE-Westinghouse OEO study. As Williams (1975) has documented, a preliminary draft report which was released exclusively for purposes of OEO internal staff review was disseminated to the White House; the findings were subsequently used in a major policy address delivered by President Nixon. These "preliminary results" were then debated in the public arena. When the final report was released, it did not receive much attention despite the fact that it illuminated some of the very issues raised in the Nixon speech and the ensuing debate.

Unintentional misutilization is pervasive. Evaluations may be misunderstood or selectively cited. It may also be that secondary analysis of data adds dimensions to an overall understanding of a program that was not previously available. It may also be the case that policy makers draw policy conclusions which are not warranted on the basis of the data presented or the levels of statistical significance of the data. These types of activities (overgeneralization) are not under the full control of the evaluator or the staff aide originally responsible for transmitting the data.

Campbell, Philip Hauser, Andrew Gordon, and others have studied the intentional abuse/misutilization of information. This phenomenon has most often been documented in cases where the organizational incentive system encourages such activity. Hauser suggests that statistics are becoming increasingly important for decision-making purposes; thus, they will be particularly open to "the temptation to use statistics for administration, agency or other interests, as distinguished from the public interest."

Jerome Skolnick describes the administrative pressure put on police officers to increase clearance rates (the number of crimes solved over the number of crimes committed) and thus show "what a good job" the police department is doing. In response to this pressure, officers will falsify reports so that they can show that a reduced rate of crime has occurred in the categories their superiors are most concerned with. The same phenomena has been illustrated in the New York City Police Department.

> A Vassar College freshman . . . dashed into the West 100th police station last July 11 to gasp out an account of being robbed of her purse at knife point in Central Park.
>
> To her astonishment, she says, the officer who took her statement told her he was going to record the crime not as felonious assault but as a larceny which is much less serious.
>
> The Officer . . . told her frankly that he was falsifying the report so that the 24th precinct—widely hailed as the city's model precinct—would show a reduction in the rate of violent crime in its areas [Sibley, 1972].

Campbell (1971a) cites two other examples of statistics being used for political ends:

To return to an earlier example, Chicago's reform police superintendent, Orlando Wilson, was wise when he rendered the police records incomparable with previous periods. This may have been necessary as mutinous subordinates might have inflated the records just to embarrass him, easily done when a sizeable portion of crimes have been going unreported. Similarly, in these days many school systems are less vulnerable because their records and summary figures are "color-blind"; they in fact do not know which pupils and which teachers are Negro, nor in which schools Negroes are present. Records of overall achievement and trends over time can be selectively cited by politicians for their political ends.

Alternatively, agencies under pressure may not collect information which could prove to be harmful. Andrew Gordon et al. (1975) studied this phenomenon and reported:

> The Bureau of Labor Statistics abolished the urban poverty survey in the 1972 election year, and the federal administration, embarrassed at the numbers of people defined as poor, has been accused of trying to discontinue the poverty-level index. One wry critic has suggested that to protect themselves fully some agencies would have to conduct business by word of mouth.

This study also suggests that even if the information is collected, the interests of the organization may be better served by storing it in an irretrievable form:

> The data may even be collected in appropriate ways, but only be released after being made useless. For example, the sought information can be coded or presented in ways that render it harmless for investigative purposes. Data are frequently stored and/or presented in irreducible aggregates thus not allowing some questions to be asked of them; for example, police budget data could be available by policy district, but unavailable by precinct or census tract or it could be reducible to only categories like "violence control" rather than to the specific amounts for "juvenile gang control." Unless data are stored in their rawest form, which is quite unusual, some coding decisions must be made. The interests are represented by those who determine the structure of the data files, and thus fundamentally affect what are most likely to be the interests of the top agency personnel. [Gordon et al., 1975].

Clearly, the incentive system—the system of rewards and punishments in bureaucracy—strongly affects the way information is ultimately used.

TECHNOLOGY ASSESSMENT

An important form of evaluation research is represented by a form of "futures research"—technology assessment (TA). Many government officials—especially within the U.S. Congress—have identified TA as a special form of evaluation research. Program evaluation is usually thought of as "assessing" the impact of an ongoing program or one that is about to terminate. In contrast, TA systematically assesses what the impact of the introduction of a new idea (program) is likely to be.

TA has become a popular form of "assessment" in the United States. TA is a form of "systems analysis" which attempts to apply "rational, systematic" approaches to an area of public policy. Specifically, TA represents a class of policy studies which systematically examine the effects on society that may occur when a technology is introduced, extended, or modified, with special emphasis on those consequences that are unintended, indirect, or delayed.

Within the Congress and the executive branch as a whole, TA represents a new form of evaluation research that may allow officials to estimate (forecast) what the consequences of their potential actions are likely to be; as such, TA represents an especially attractive form of *expertise* within a political environment in which decisions are made through bargaining and minimization of risks.

In terms of utilizations, TAs should not be thought of as just another research output or bit of social science knowledge, but instead as *a system of analysis* designed to inform the policy-making process. Systems of analysis can be thought of as both formal and informal. The essential distinction between systems of analysis and more routine knowledge or information is that a system of analysis is associated with a set of general rules, procedures, and processes which guide the production of the end product. In recent history, examples of this kind of system have included the PPB (Program, Planning, and Budgeting System), the Environmental Impact Statement System, and the attempts by some federal agencies to build a routinized survey capacity into their policy-making process.

In committing itself to acquiring and/or using a system of analysis, an organization is making an investment in a particular information resource. It is important to remember that this is a major investment; as such, several implications should be highlighted.

(1) Such an investment cannot be made as part of the discretionary budget of an individual decision maker. It represents a larger investment of resources and requires formal organizational approval (that is, the request for the investment must pass through "regular channels").

(2) A *system* of analysis is costly and represents a much more substantial investment than a single study.

(3) Thus, an investment in a system of analysis represents a formal organizational commitment. One can assume that the system of analysis has been weighed

against other potential organizational investments. Once the decision is made, the organization is monetarily committed to the system of analysis and will not be able to afford another new investment in the short run (see Arrow, 1974).

It follows, therefore, that organizations are not just acquiring new information but are developing the capacity to respond to recurring information needs over time. These needs represent *generic* as opposed to *specific* information needs.

Specifically, TA as a system of analysis is based on a general process that provides a systematic and rational input to societal decision-making and management. These particularized policy studies attempt to account for direct and indirect effects as well as indirect and delayed impacts involved with technological change. To this end, TAs bring together multidisciplinary approaches, recommendations, the perspectives related to a new technological development. Although there is no single methodology common to all TAs, there are a number of common or generic elements involved in the creation of virtually every comprehensive technology assessment. When a decision maker reads a TA, he can expect that each of these elements or perspectives has been taken into account and documented in the TA study.

It is important to distinguish systems of analysis from other, more routine information, whether generated in-house or sent to the organization free of charge, because the process that accompanies the creation of a TA process— which ensures the introduction and reporting of many different perspectives—may be just as important in understanding the ultimate impact of this class of policy studies on decision makers as the substance of the study itself.

IMPACTS OF THE TA MOVEMENT

At this point, it is too early to assess the impacts of TA (as a policy tool) on societal problem-solving. Many OTA studies are still underway, and many NSF-sponsored studies are just being completed. However, from the exploratory interviews with 15 OTA officials and a questionnaire mailed to the principal investigators of 33 NSF-sponsored TA projects, it is possible to report some preliminary findings and present hypotheses which could be tested in future research:

(1) In the case of OTA, some committees are enthusiastic about the results of the studies; but most are reserved and have not made any judgments.

(2) Since OTA studies are dependent upon specific committee requests and report complex data, it is unlikely that it will develop a large, actively supportive constituency within Congress.

(3) OTA-sponsored studies will probably have a greater impact/influence on policy formation and implementation than the NSF-sponsored studies. Similarly, TA-related studies completed within the executive branch are likely to have a greater impact than the NSF-sponsored studies. The issue of control and risk avoidance may be critical in explaining these differences.

(4) The NSF-sponsored studies are geared (in the majority of cases) to a general audience (scientists, engineers, or members of Congress). Final reports are generally disseminated to a large and diverse audience. However, in terms of utilization of study results, one should expect limited and narrow uses from the broad, general audience. In the case of individuals on advisory committees or in the data collection process (that is, as an expert who was consulted) levels of utilization should be considerably higher.

(5) The patterns of utilization which accompany a TA study might well resemble a sampling technique known as snowballing: An individual knows about a study; this person tells someone else who might be interested in it; the second person, in turn, informs another person until a large, informal network of users has been formed. Thus, the process of creating a TA study from the point of agreeing on what categories to collect data to the formation of advisory groups through the completion of the study will have a significant effect on the ultimate impact of the TA. The process of creating the TA may be more important in explaining impact than the format or the substance of the completed study. This emphasis on process would differentiate TA from other forms of policy analysis.

(6) Substantially more utilization may occur during the process of completing the study—as preliminary results become available—than at the time a "final report" is submitted.

ETHICAL STANDARDS FOR EVALUATION

A discussion of abuse and misuse of information as well as an examination of data on how evaluation data are utilized leads one to focus on ethical standards. What ethical standards should be developed, and who (if anyone) should enforce them? It is not surprising that a field which has grown in recognition and legitimacy as quickly as has evaluation research has not devoted much attention to questions of ethical standards and behavior.

As Congress continues to mandate evaluation, as it takes Sunset legislation more seriously, and as budgets of Offices of Policy, Planning, and Evaluation become larger, the issue of ethical standards becomes critical. One dimension of concern is the dependence of agencies on evaluators. Agencies are dependent because legislators demand evaluation and because of the fact that an agency which sponsors evaluations is (from the perspective of government officials) considered to be legitimate. The dependence relationship is, to some extent, also based on the mystique of evaluation research. It is not clear how these professionals produce the sophisticated numbers they do; but it is clear that important policy makers take those numbers into account.

Given this dependence, professional evaluators should consider several issues:

- At what point in the evaluation process do they advise a client that their services are no longer needed?
- Is it "ethical" to advise a client not to fund an evaluation study because of the "current policy environment"?
- Should the evaluator accept the definition of the objectives given to them, or should he/she work with clients to gain a clear consensus on objectives?
- Similarly, who determines what the evaluation criteria should be?
- Is this the sole responsibility of a third party evaluator, or should he/she attempt to gain a consensus among all interested parties?
- If evaluators engage in these consensus-seeking activities, to what extent are they losing their objectivity as outside evaluators?
- Is "objectivity" exclusively a function of "distance" from the process of program/project decision-making? In other words, does the evaluator need (as many would contend) to be an outsider for him to conduct a "truly objective evaluation"?
- What are the limits of an evaluator's responsibilities—at the time a report is submitted or after a decision concerning the effectiveness and/or continuation of the program being assessed?
- If one adheres to the latter position, does this mean that evaluators should assist agency staff in writing summaries for their superiors? Should evaluators be part of agency briefings? Should they make concrete policy recommendations? These are all issues for which there are no clear answers and for which the stakes are high in terms of the recognized objectivity and legitimacy of program evaluation.
- What can the evaluator do to minimize misuse/abuse of research findings? On the basis of the OEO experience, for example, should preliminary results be withheld? If so, how is one to get valuable feedback from agency participants? Does close collaboration with agency staff in translating evaluation findings in recommendations minimize the chances for unintentional misutilization?

Each of these ethical questions helps us to synthesize the rest of the issues raised in this essay.

The ethical issues relate to existing bureaucratic structures and reward systems in the public sector. If evaluation is to impact upon the policy process, then it will be necessary for professional evaluators to address questions having to do with the limits of objectivity, the limits of direct involvement in the policy-making process, and the ability of evaluators to limit abuse and misuse of research findings.

CONCLUSION

When and if we move closer to Campbell's (1971a) notion of an experimenting society, the professional evaluator will take on an increasingly important role basically because evaluation will be a critical instrument for planning and social control.

Even if we never realize the "dream" of an experimenting society, it is clear that evaluation activities are a vital part of the policy-making process at all levels of government and in the private sector as well. Further expansion should not continue without a careful assessment of where we are as a field, where we want to go, and how we might arrive at our objectives in a manner which adheres to agreed-upon professional standards. In other words, the evaluators need to evaluate themselves.

REFERENCES

ARROW, K. J. (1974) The Limits of Organization. New York: W. W. Norton.

CAMPBELL, D. T. (1971a) "Methods for the experimenting society." Presented before the Eastern Psychological Association, April 17.

———— (1971b) "Administrative experiments, institutional records, and non-reactive measures." In W. Evans (ed.) Organizational Experiments. New York: Harper & Row.

———— (1969) "Reforms as experiments." American Psychologist 24: 409–428.

CAPLAN, N. and R. RICH (1976) "Open and closed knowledge inquiry systems: the process and consequences of bureaucratization of information policy at the national level." Presented at the OECD Conference on Dissemination of Economic and Social Development Research Results, Bogota, Colombia, June.

CAPLAN, N. et al. (1976) "The use of program evaluation by federal policy makers at the national level." Presented at an NIMH-sponsored meeting of the Network of Consultants on Knowledge Transfer, New Orleans.

———— (1975) The Use of Social Science Knowledge in Policy Decisions at the National Level. Ann Arbor: Institute for Social Research, University of Michigan.

COOK, T. (1978) "The abuse, misuses and premature utilization of information." Presented at a conference on research utilization, University of Pittsburgh, School of Graduate Business, September 20–22.

EISENSTADT, S. N. (1969) The Political Systems of Empire. New York: Free Press.

GORDON, A. and D. T. CAMPBELL (1970) "Recommended accountability guidelines for the evaluation of improvements in the delivery of state social services." (unpublished)

GORDON, A. et al. (1975) "Public access to information." Northwestern Law Review 68: 285–286.

GUTTENTAG, M. (1978) Testimony before the Senate Committee on Human Resources (quoted in Evaluation and Change, Special Issue, p. 18).

HAUSER, P. M. (1972) "Statistics and politics." Presented at the annual meetings of the American Statistical Association, August 15.

ILLCHMAN, W. and T. UPHOFF (1971) The Political Economy of Change. Berkeley: University of California Press.

KITUSE, J. and A. V. CICOUREL (1969) "A note on the use of official statistics." Social Problems 11: 131–139.

LEVINE, R. A. (1972) Public Planning: Failure and Redirection. New York: Basic Books.

MORSS, E. and R. F. RICH (1979) Government Information Management. Boulder, CO: Westview Press.

NAY, J. et al. (1978) Testimony before the Senate Committee on Human Resources (quoted in Evaluation and Change, Special Issue, pp. 12–13).

RICH, R. F. (1979a) "Editor's introduction." American Behavioral Scientist 22: 327–337.

_____ (1979b) The Use of Social Science Information and Public Policy Making. San Francisco: Jossey-Bass.

_____ (1977) "The use of social science information by federal bureaucrats: knowledge for action versus knowledge for understanding." In C. Weiss (ed.) The Uses of Social Research in Public Policy Making. Lexington, MA: D. C. Heath.

SIBLEY, J. (1972) "Students say a policeman tried to falsify a report of a holdup." New York Times, November 23: 5, 40.

SKOLNICK, J. H. (1975) Justice Without Trial. New York: John Wiley.

STAATS, H. (1979) Address given at a special meeting of the Council of Applied Social Research, Annapolis, Maryland.

WEISS, C. H. (1978) "The use of evaluation research." Presented at a conference on research utilization, University of Pittsburgh, School of Business, September 20–22.

WILLIAMS, W. (1975) Social Policy Research and Analysis. New York: Elsevier.

VON HENTIG, H. (1974) The Criminal and His Victim, New Haven, CT: Yale University Press.

_____ (1941) "Remarks on interaction of perpetrator and victim." Journal of Criminal Law and Criminology 31.

11

The Utilization of
Social Science Knowledge in
the Federal Republic of Germany

Bernhard Badura

Universität Konstanz

THE APPLICATION OF SOCIAL SCIENCE

The utilization of social science knowledge in bureaucracy might actually be a matter of defining "utilization." On one hand, the use of behavioral science knowledge in policy-making seems to be insignificant if "utilization" is defined as the application of a particular piece of knowledge to the successful solution of a certain problem. This might be due to the lack of standardized applicable knowledge in the social sciences, compounded by the complexity of the subject matter.

On the other hand, utilization assumes an entirely different aspect when an alternative definition is employed. In this situation, social science—including research studies, concepts, and theories—influences the perception and definition of societal problems. Weiss terms it "a kind of diffuse undirected seepage of social research into the policy sphere" (1977). This alternative conceptualization suggests a more positive assessment of social science knowledge in policy-making (Caplan et al., 1975). The juxtaposition of these models of utilization was first made, as far as I know, by Janowitz (1972). This conceptual approach, however, is not completely satisfactory. It brings out an important aspect of the production-utilization process. This model emphasizes the differing perspectives and type of knowledge process by the various disciplines—for example, the "hard" knowledge of the natural sciences compared with the "soft" knowledge of the social sciences. It can also explain differences in the relative acceptance of the bureaucracy of certain behavioral sciences, such as economics and psychology, but it does not adequately explain the differences in levels of utilization among various departments or between separate sections of the same government department. My first thesis is that the Janowitz model neglects certain important variables on the demand side, such as the characteristics of the individual policy makers and the user organization.

The "two cultures theory" of James Coleman (1972) explains the under-utilization of social science knowledge. Social scientists and policy makers, according to this theory, live in two different worlds with different time horizons, different languages, and different ways of thinking. The "world of action" is different from the "disciplinary world." It is characterized by conflict of interests and a high degree of redundancy. The theory, however, cannot explain why new findings in medicine, economics, or atomic physics receive more attention in the policy sphere than that of utilization research. It emphasizes interactional problems and rapport between policy makers and scientists but lacks the structural dimension: the power structure of a society, differences in legitimacy of various scientific traditions, and differences in the bargaining position of various social groups and professional associations.

KNOWLEDGE PRODUCTION IN THE FEDERAL REPUBLIC

The "two cultures theory" offers little to explain the lack of political support for some issues in respect to the pleas of German social scientists for an evaluation of medical services. The financial support for various scientific disciplines, as well as their rate of development and the utilization of the knowledge they produce, are essentially based on political decisions. It is, therefore, my second thesis that these factors need an explanation which lie in the role of science policy, in setting national priorities, and in popular beliefs of the usefulness of the various scientific disciplines. Our work on utilization at the University of Konstanz was greatly influenced by Biderman's (1976) discussion of the disparity between a low utilization of behavioral science knowledge and the general acceptance of the natural sciences in the U.S. federal bureaucracy. The demand for various kinds of scientific knowledge by policy makers and the determinants of this demand are, for Biderman, the essential magnitudes of the utilization question. An important factor determining this demand is the degree of "incorporation of social science theories, concepts, and values into the administrative culture." Some segments of the Federal Government possess a social-science-oriented "professional culture," which influences their level of utilization in a positive direction; others have an administrative culture "attached to more traditional bases of status and expertise" (Crawford and Biderman, 1969;

Biderman, 1976). Various factors which are essentially extrascientific and not inherent to the development of a particular discipline, such as the education, recruitment, and occupational socialization of the personnel of a bureaucracy, thus become central variables determining the demand for and the level of utilization of social science knowledge. The concept of "administrative culture" is not, however, operationalized. For this purpose, we employed the framework and instruments developed by social scientists for investigating the diffusion of innovations. Just as in the acceptance of new products and technologies (for example, hybrid corn), investigation on the diffusion of social science knowledge in the policy sphere must concern itself with the factors which facilitate or impede reception of this knowledge. The research on diffusion has demonstrated the role of the attitudes, values, and behavioral patterns of the potential users.

Modern bureaucracies are complex and highly differentiated organizations. Decision-making takes place at many levels and results from a complex process of a long series of consecutive steps. This means that information is selected, distorted, and suppressed according to the needs of the receiving organization. Utilization research must distinguish between the level of receptivity or openness of an organization for various kinds of information on the one hand and the practical relevance of the information in decision-making on the other. As Lazarsfeld and Reitz (1975) note, there is no necessary connection between knowledge and action but rather a leap from knowledge to action. Our study concentrated on investigating the degree of receptivity for social science knowledge in complex organizations in both the private and public sectors. The total sample was slightly over 400 persons. An analysis of a subsample from four departments or ministries at the federal level of the West German government suggest the following:

(1) In comparison to Caplan's positive results from the U.S. federal government, we found a low degree of receptivity of social science knowledge.

(2) There were noteworthy differences in receptivity among the four departments and between sections of the same department. In the midst of what Biderman termed the "traditional culture," we discovered bridgeheads of a social-science-oriented subculture.

(3) The two variables of training in a traditional or social science culture, the educational background of the policy maker and contact with the social sciences at the university, positively influence an individual's receptivity.

(4) "Hard scientists" and engineers are almost unanimous in their negative attitudes toward the social sciences. Law graduates who have been socialized in a social-science culture possess positive attitudes and a high level of receptivity.

The activities of modern government bureaucracies are determined to a large extent by standard operating procedures, which adapt themselves to changing situations in the organization environment very slowly. This is especially true in regard to recruitment policy and information behavior. For this reason, the diffusion of new knowledge and qualifications requires, as a rule, the creation of new organizations within the government. Franklin D. Roosevelt's New Deal is a good model for the creation of new organizations in order to facilitate the acceptance of new ideas.

The later a scientific discipline comes to such an established bureaucracy with its offer of new knowledge, the greater is the resistance of vested interests—of those professions and scientific disciplines already monopolizing the supply of information to the organization. The social sciences, especially sociology and political science, are such *nouveaux arrivées* in the West German policy sphere with tenuous footholds as advisers and gate keepers to the Federal Government. Their power base is not secure, as it depends to a great extent on the specific characteristics and personalities of individual social scientists. The social sciences lack an institutionalized demand for their services on a regular basis; they lack a type of demand based on the needs of established power groups within the traditional bureaucracy. The present small-scale utilization of social science knowledge in West Germany, however, in the long run could allow certain learning processes and a certain amount of personal interaction to take place, so that eventually a "take-off" of the social sciences could occur, similar to that of economics. The demand for and acceptance of new perspectives, such as those of the individual social sciences, can be obstructed when there are both a tradition of government nonintervention and vested professional interests.

A good example of this type of situation and its negative effects on utilization in the German Federal Government is in the area of health policy. In the Anglo-Saxon countries, the contribution of social science concepts, perspectives, and empirical knowledge in the formulation of government health policy is frequently demonstrated. For example, the success of social scientists in the evaluation of competing medical services for a particular health problem is a noteworthy case. In spite of the experience in the United Kingdom and the United States, vested interests in the area of West German health policy resist the application of this sort of social experimentation. The resistance to utilization of knowledge and techniques proven successful in other countries illustrates the importance of political variables in the utilization question.

THE NEED FOR INCREASED UTILIZATION

At present, it seems necessary to reconsider the basic questions and motives of utilization research. The various approaches to the utilization process in the past were concerned with a small number of issues: Who uses what kind of social knowledge? for what purpose? in what situation? with what effect? how often? These questions are important and interesting but somewhat incomplete and one-sided. The perspective must be broadened if it is to be relevant to the current situation in West Germany. Variables from the areas of science policy and the sociology of knowledge ought to be incorporated. The following topics seem to be relevant for consideration and inclusion in the utilization discussion:

(1) In spite of the need for interdisciplinary work, the individual discipline still plays a decisive role as far as one's academic and professional careers are concerned. The individual sciences are also influential in the development, support, and evaluation of academic knowledge, as well as for the reputation of this knowledge among the public, in government, and in the business world.

(2) The knowledge sector in the Federal Republic of Germany, as a whole, has grown with amazing rapidity in recent years. The disparity in the rates of development of the various scientific disciplines, however, must also be emphasized—not only the differences between the natural and social sciences but also among the individual social sciences themselves.

(3) A further important observation is the interaction between producers and users of knowledge, the relation between theory and practice, the amount of feedback from the policy sphere to the academic world in defining the latter's goals and activities. In this area we also find a high degree of disparity in the success of the various scientific disciplines. The profession of medicine, economists, and atomic physicists have proceeded far in this pursuit, while the exchange between policy makers and social scientists remains encumbered with a notable gap persisting between the two.

(4) The reputation, influence, and financial support for sociology in the FRG is, on the whole, relatively small. If one distinguishes between the theoretical contribution of sociology on the one hand and its methodology on the other, it becomes apparent that some types of knowledge are more widely accepted than others. Survey techniques, for example, have found widespread acceptance in marketing and election forecasting; more qualitative methods, such as participant observation, have met with disinterest and skepticism.

(5) The influence of a science in a society certainly depends on the diffusion of its theoretical perspectives and methods. But its influence probably depends to a greater extent on the degree to which these perspectives and theoretical concepts become incorporated in the institutions of society: how the conceptual framework of a particular science influences the perception and definition of a situation, and how new knowledge forces change in established pattern of thinking and behaving. The degree of receptivity for a particular type of knowledge, such as social science knowledge, is the result of the influence of this science on society; but, at the same time, the amount of influence the discipline possesses is determined by the level of its receptivity in the various institutions of society. There is a continuous feedback process between utilization on the one hand and influence on the other. The enlightenment model views the utilization question within a static framework, the influence variable

being held constant, and thus neglects the dynamics of the influence-receptivity dyad. A long-term, macrosociological approach is needed.

Utilization research in the future should emphasize the structural determinants which explain the growth of the various sciences and the degree of receptivity of complex organizations for their products. For this purpose, an investigation of those sciences should be undertaken which may achieve success in respect to the utilization of knowledge—for example, law, medicine, economics, and the natural sciences. The writings of the human relations school, especially the work of Elton Mayo and his collaborators, might shed some light on the question to what extent demand for social science knowledge is determined by the degree of "scientificness" of the knowledge itself or by factors external to the scientific establishment and academy.

REFERENCES

BIDERMAN, A. D. (1976) "Über den Zusammenhang von Einfluß, Förderung und Erklärungskraft in den Socialwissenschaften." pp. 317–325 in B. Badura (ed.) Seminar: Angewandte Sozialforschung, Frankfurt/M.: Suhrkamp.

CAPLAN, N. et al. (1975) The Use of Social Science Knowledge in Policy Decisions at the National Level. Ann Arbor, Institute for Social Research, University of Michigan.

COLEMAN, J. (1972) Policy Research in the Social Sciences. Morristown, NJ: General Learning Press.

CRAWFORD, E. T. and A. D. BIDERMAN [eds.] (1969) Social Scientists and International Affairs. New York: John Wiley.

FRIEDRICH, H. (1970) Staatliche Verwaltung und Wissenschaft. Frankfurt/M.: Europäische Verlagsanstalt.

JANOWITZ, M. (1972) "Professionalization of sociology." American Journal of Sociology 78: 105–135.

LAZARSFELD, F. and C. REITZ (1975) An Introduction to Applied Sociology. New York: Elsevier.

WEISS, C. (1977) "Research for policy's sake: the enlightenment function of social research," Policy Analysis (Fall): 531–545.

12

Management and Evaluation in a Knowledge Transfer Context

Thomas J. Kiresuk
Nancy E. Larsen
Sander H. Lund

*Program Evaluation Resource Center,
Minneapolis, Minnesota*

INTRODUCTION

Although evaluation has been considered by some to be a largely technical enterprise, experience has shown that its success is often contingent upon what have heretofore been considered contextual factors. As distinguished from most forms of scientific inquiry, evaluations are intentionally immersed in complex and frequently turbulent systems of social and political relationships and, indeed, are often intended to create change in such systems. This "special" context of evaluation defines its role and distinguishes it from other varieties of inquiry. What in other forms of social and scientific investigation would be viewed as peripheral considerations, such as the relevance of findings to practical decisions, in evaluation are central in determining its success or failure.

The intention of this chapter is to identify and explore social, political, and other contextual issues germane to the evaluation process, and to illustrate with practical examples how specific techniques from the planned change and knowledge transfer fields can be employed to improve evaluations and enhance the usefulness of evaluation findings in policy, program, or clinical decision-making.

A VIEW ON EVALUATION

Background Issues

Evaluation is distinguished from purely scientific research by a focus on the usefulness of results. The purpose of research is to contribute to the sum of human knowledge, regardless of immediate practicality, while evaluation information is intended for specific use. This disparity of intentions, together with an emphasis on disinterested peer review as the arbiter of the quality of knowledge, is in many respects the source of considerable tension in the evaluation and applied research realm. Having, in effect, no time pressures, those with scientific research orientations are content to wait for the "best" knowledge to rise to the surface, while those concerned with putting information to practical use are often interested in finding means to bridge the gulf between what one author has termed "the two solitudes of research and practice" (Joly, 1967).

A Paradigm for Evaluation

This tension manifests itself in various ways. The first of these regards the basic methodological paradigm appropriate for evaluation. Those who argue for the experiment as the basic model emphasize the need for stringent control of all variables in order to ensure the exactitude of findings. They do not concern themselves as much with encouraging utilization of results, but rather fear that the utilization of imprecise or incomplete knowledge will be destructive. Those who want a different, or at least a broader, paradigm tend to emphasize the need for applicability of findings. The proponents of this second view argue that, given the dynamic nature of operational settings, the experiment is too inflexible, expensive, and cumbersome to be of much use. Additionally, they assert, the results of experiments are only infrequently useful for decision-making.

Many who oppose the strictly experimental paradigm are also those who advocate wider use of such qualitative methods as field observation and in-depth interviewing. As evaluation matures and assumes an independent identity distinct from that of scientific research, there is growing recognition that its special mission will require special tools, including qualitative assessment methods. Support for a broader methodological paradigm for evaluation and applied social research has come from several sources:

> Two major figures, usually identified with the "scientific" approach to evaluation, Campbell (1974) and Cronbach (1975), have recently noted the potential for qualitative methods in evaluation and applied research.

> Suchman (1967) made the distinction between evaluation and evaluative research in recognition of the fact that evaluation encompasses a wider scope of

activities than the mere application of scientific principles to practical problems. In this same regard, Suchman noted that the experimental method can be reserved for critical studies that may be suggested through less rigorous, exploratory, or descriptive inquiry.

Scriven's (1972) well-known distinction between summative and formative evaluation is also relevant. Formative evaluations are generally considered part of the planning and developmental process and may be used for ongoing input into the program. Summative evaluation, on the other hand, tends to be used to make judgments regarding a program or its components. Summative evaluations are often used to determine whether a program should continue. The experiment might be most useful and appropriate when large-scale, summative decisions must be made, but perhaps less useful in formative situations.

In a recent textbook on evaluation, Rossi and his colleagues (1979) explicitly recognize the variable applicability of the experimental paradigm to evaluation questions. In some respects, this is an extension of the work begun by Campbell and Stanley (1966) regarding the use of quasi-experimental designs in contexts where the fully developed experimental approach is not feasible. This permits identification of the potential sources of bias in results.

Given the complex and amorphous nature of many programs, the multiple perspectives that must be served, and the relatively primitive quality of the available techniques and procedures, it is our view that evaluation is best conceived broadly as a heterogeneous family of technologies applicable to different questions, for different reasons, and in different contexts. The fundamental task of the evaluator is to be creative and ingenious in tailoring the evaluation design to the needs and constraints of each new situation.

The Utilization Issue

Acceptance of the notion that the purpose of evaluation is the utilization of knowledge for constructive action has led to the awareness that such utilization apparently occurs rarely. This recognition has led many of those involved in knowledge creation endeavors, including evaluators and researchers, to turn to the knowledge transfer and planned change literature in an attempt to examine and find means to remedy the causes of this phenomenon.

Examples demonstrating the occurrence of time lag between discovery and utilization have come from many fields, including science, industry, education, and social research. Perhaps one of the best documentations of the occurrence of time lag is a study conducted in 1973 under the auspices of the National Science Foundation. This study examined the time needed for 10 well-known products or technologies to become established in the marketplace. The innovations under examination were as varied as the heart pacemaker, hybrid corn, and videotape recorders. This study showed that time lag for these innovations ranged from 6 to 32 years, with an average time lag of nearly 20 years. Persons working in the social science domain soon realized that this latency period might be even more pronounced outside the physical sciences, since, as Weiss (1977) observed, "Social science knowledge is not apt to be so compelling, nor does it readily lend itself to conversion into technologies, either material or social."

One reaction to this "problem of utilization" has been a reexamination of what utilization in the social sciences actually is and how it should be assessed. In a study conducted by Patton (1975) and his colleagues regarding the use of the results of 20 health evaluations, in a majority of cases program administrators and evaluators reported that the findings had "some" impact. Similar results were obtained by Alkin et al. (1974) in surveys of 45 ESEA Title VII programs. In both studies the utilization was often characterized as subtle and indirect. One possible reason for this lack of direct and observable impact may be implied from recent studies of the decision-making process. These studies show that, in most circumstances, the number of influences that must be accommodated by the decision makers are too many and too varied to permit much margin for any single source, even research or evaluation, to have sole impact. As Brandl (1978) asserted, in the political arena evaluators and researchers are viewed as simply another interest group to be accommodated by the decision makers.

In addition, some in the evaluation community have argued that the quality of the existing evaluation technology is insufficient to reasonably expect direct utilization (Mushkin, 1973). Weiss (1976) also pointed out that many decisions are motivated by "non-rational" considerations that are little affected by simple evaluation information.

PLANNED CHANGE AND KNOWLEDGE TRANSFER

To address the problem of nonutilization, a new discipline, sometimes called "knowledge utilization" (Kiresuk and Lund, 1979), is emerging in the social sciences. Drawing upon methods and ideas from fields such as sociology, management science, communications, anthropology, psychology, education, public health, and social work, the purpose of knowledge utilization is to study and facilitate the effective use of knowledge to ameliorate what Rose (1977) has called "undisciplined problems": acknowledged human concerns for which no adequate remedial technology exists. The locus of this enterprise encompasses three related domains: (1) *research and evaluation*—that is, the production of knowledge potentially useful for problem-solving; (2) *knowledge transfer*—establishment of communication links between the producers and the potential users of knowledge; and

(3) *planned change*—development of means to facilitate the use of knowledge for policy, program, and clinical action.

Evaluation relates to knowledge transfer and planned change in at least two ways: first, as a form of change itself and, second, as an impetus for change.

Implementation of Evaluation

In most cases, evaluation itself may be considered a form of change. It can potentially require the acquisition of new knowledge and skills, implementation of new practices, alteration of established administrative structures, reexamination of cherished values, and disruption of interpersonal relationships and routines. For these and other reasons, many evaluations seem to fail literally before they have started, and "resistance," both as a form of specific antipathy toward evaluation and as a manifestation of the generic difficulties that can accompany any organizational change, has been widely discussed in the evaluation literature. Drawing upon the work done in the organizational development and planned social change fields, many evaluations have proposed implementation strategies designed to minimize resistance. A common theme in these strategies has been the systematic involvement of all those concerned with the evaluation and its results in the planning and conduct of the effort, as well as in the interpretation of the results.

Utilization of Evaluation Findings

The belief that "improved decision-making" is the purpose of evaluation implies that "utilization of results" is the criterion of evaluation success; this ultimately leads to the recognition that many evaluations are delinquent in meeting this criterion. The evaluation literature is replete with instances where apparently useful findings did not contribute to relevant decision-making; and although the realization is growing that "utilization" is often subtle and indirect, the cumulative experience of the last two decades clearly suggests that passive reliance on the technical merit of information to stimulate action is the strategy least likely to lead to constructive use. Owing to this realization, substantial attention has been devoted to finding means to facilitate appropriate utilization of the results of evaluative inquiry. Specific inquiry has focused on two topics: knowledge transfer and planned change. Evaluation implementation and evaluation utilization uses related to each of these topics will be discussed in the following sections.

KNOWLEDGE TRANSFER

Both the implementation of evaluation and the utilization of evaluation results require the communication, or transfer, of a body of knowledge from one group of individuals to another. In the case of implementation, this involves assuring that everyone understands the methodology involved; and in the case of utilization, it involves being certain that findings targeted to the information needs of the audiences of the evaluation have reached and been understood by those concerned. Regarding both implementation and utilization, the means often suggested to facilitate knowledge transfer is to systematically involve those concerned with the evaluation in its planning, implementation, and analysis. In this way, we can be relatively confident that both the design and the questions it addresses are germane to its context.

Barriers to Knowledge Transfer

There can be many barriers to the knowledge transfer process. Some of the most common issues raised by the potential knowledge utilizer are (1) that information provided is not useful for decision-making, (2) that information was not provided in a manner which could be understood, (3) that information was not provided at a time when it could be used, (4) that information and the recommendations made were not philosophically consistent with the organization, and (5) that information presented was not convincing.

All of these issues point to the importance of targeting the information to be transferred to the needs of the potential information user—that is, putting the information into a workable context. In the following sections we will discuss some specific strategies that can be used by researchers and evaluators to overcome these barriers and enhance the knowledge transfer process.

The Context of Relevance

A basic task in the evaluation process is determining its "context of relevance" (Lund et al., 1980). This involves identifying the audiences of the evaluation (those who have an interest in the program to be evaluated), determining their information needs, and targeting the evaluation in the indicated direction.

There is a large number of potential audiences for any evaluation, including a program's staff, administrators, governing board, clients and their families, funders, community and special interest groups, policy makers, politicians, other programs, and professional organizations. The information needs of these varied audiences can be, and usually are, quite diverse. For example, program administrators, funders, and governing boards may express the need for information regarding the financial status of the program; or, when a program has several components, they may wish to know which component is the most cost-effective. Service providers may want to know about service outcomes for clients, but may also express a desire to know how well they compare with other staff members in their performance.

Clients and their families will want to know if the treatment works. Politicians, special interest groups, and community groups may want to know what benefits or negative effects might accrue for their constituencies. A professional group might be most interested in the possible impacts the program may have for a profession or discipline as a whole.

While there may be significant overlap in some areas of interest and of information needed, it is important for the evaluator or researcher to target the reports to the appropriate groups or individuals so that they have the correct information needed for the decision-making process.

The Feedback Generator Matrix

One way to help ensure that information gets to the correct audience is to construct a feedback generator matrix. This simple device is constructed by listing the kinds of information that will be provided by the study or the evaluation across the top of a chart, listing the potential audiences along the

	OVERALL PROGRAM EFFECTIVENESS	SERVICE PROVIDER OUTCOMES	COSTS OF PROGRAM OPERATION	COST-EFFECTIVENESS OF PROGRAM COMPONENTS	TREATMENT EFFECTS ON SPECIAL TARGET POPULATIONS	IMPACTS FOR A SPECIFIC PROFESSION	IMPACTS OF THE PROGRAM ON A COMMUNITY	ETC....
SERVICE PROVIDERS	X	X				X		
PROGRAM ADMINISTRATION	X	X	X	X				
CLIENTS & CLIENT FAMILIES	X							
PROGRAM FUNDERS	X		X	X				
GOVERNING BOARD	X		X	X	X			
POLICY-MAKERS	X		X					
PROFESSIONAL GROUPS	X					X		
COMMUNITY GROUPS					X		X	
SPECIAL INTEREST GROUPS					X			
POLITICIANS					X		X	
OTHER ORGANIZATIONS	X			X				

TARGETED REPORTS NEEDED

AUDIENCES FOR EVALUATION

FIGURE 12.1   Example of a Feedback Generator Matrix

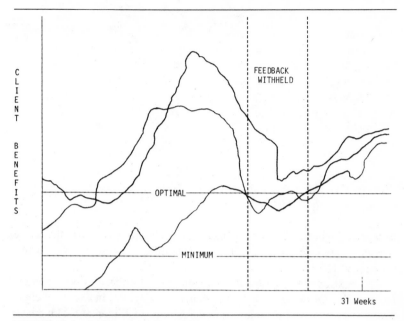

FIGURE 12.2   Differential Effect of Feedback on Three
Treatment Teams

side, and then plotting the information needs by audience. The use of the feedback generator matrix may also be significantly enhanced if the evaluator works with the potential audiences to determine and record the priorities of the information needed and the specific dates on which the information is needed. An example of a feedback generator matrix is shown in Figure 12.1.

The Feedback Effect

The provision of feedback to service providers and clients has been demonstrated to have a positive effect on performance and outcome. The use of feedback for corrective purposes is especially important when a study or evaluation is meant to be used in a formative manner. The feedback effect can be clearly demonstrated in the following two case studies.

In an accountability study conducted by Robert Walker (1972), three teams of service providers were compared on the dimension of client benefits produced before a feedback program was instituted, during provision of feedback, when feedback was discontinued (due to a simulated computer breakdown), and when the feedback program was reinstituted. The feedback to the service providers consisted of monthly reports of the overall agency's achievement for that month along with the individual therapist's distribution of scores within the overall scores. The effects on client benefits are shown

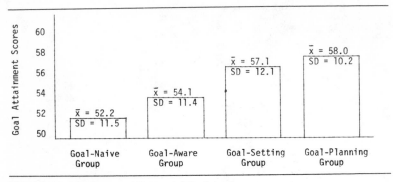

FIGURE 12.3   Means and Ranges of Goal Attainment
                        Scores for Treatment Groups

by team in Figure 12.2. It is both interesting and important to note that as the overall program performance increased, the differences between team performances declined.

The next case example will demonstrate the feedback effect when the feedback is provided directly to the clients of a program. In a study of client goal-setting and goal-planning procedures in a small mental health center (Galano, 1977), 92 adult outpatients were randomly assigned to one of four goal-setting modes. The first mode was the Goal-Naive group. Individualized treatment goals were established for this group by the therapist using the Goal Attainment Scaling method (described later in this chapter); the therapist also independently rated the client's goal attainment level at a later date. For this group, there was no client participation or awareness. The second mode was called the Goal-Aware group. The therapist was again responsible for constructing and rating individualized treatment goals, but in this case the client was allowed to view the completed goal plan. The third mode was the Goal-Setting group. This group differed from the Goal-Aware group in that the client and the therapist worked collaboratively to establish the goals for treatment; but, again, the completed goal plan was viewed only once by the client. The last group participated in both goal-setting and goal-planning and was called the Goal-Planning group. In this group, as well as working collaboratively to set goals, clients were involved in a bimonthly goal-planning; that is, incremental steps were developed by the client and therapist to reach their desired outcomes, along with expected achievement dates for the attainment of these substeps. The mean Goal Attainment scores and standard deviations are displayed for each of the goal-setting modes in Figure 12.3.

As can be seen, as the client groups received incrementally more feedback on the course of treatment, outcomes were substantially increased. This phenomenon has been called "target tropism" (Davis, 1973a), the notion being that if goals are set for and with clients, they will tend to move toward the goal. Similar results have been obtained in related studies as well (Smith, 1976; Jones and Garwick, 1973; Houts and Scott, 1976; Calsyn and LaFerriere, 1976; Still, 1977). Additionally, management studies have also shown that goal-setting and goal-planning can enhance the management process (McClelland and Winter, 1969; Locke, 1968; Latham and Yukl, 1975). These and related research studies have clear implications for evaluators and researchers: their work can have an impact on program and clinical decision-making, but the information must reach its intended audience in a form that can be used.

Using an Evaluation Task Force

An idea recently advanced by Patton (1978) and others is the use of an evaluation task force throughout the course of the evaluation process. Input from this ongoing task force can help to ensure that the information produced by an evaluation will be "utilization-focused." Patton has identified several criteria for the formation of the task force: They should be persons who can use the information to be generated, to whom information makes a difference, who have questions that they want to have answered, and who care about and are willing to share responsibility for the evaluation *and* its utilization. Patton also recommends that provisions be made for continuous, direct contact between the evaluators and the decision makers or information users, that the group be fairly small (approximately 5 to 10 persons is considered the optimal size), and that group members be willing to make a heavy time commitment to the evaluation. Once this task force has been assembled, it is important to involve its members in all phases of the evaluation process. The evaluation task force can assist in constructing the evaluation's feedback generator matrix, act as intermediary between the evaluator and the larger evaluation audiences, help to define the parameters of the evaluation, and facilitate the transfer and utilization of the information produced. The use of such a task force can greatly enhance an evaluation by assisting the evaluator in "keeping his/her finger on the pulse" of the various evaluation audiences and by alerting him/her to any changes that occur in emphasis or timing.

Defining the Parameters of the Evaluation Effort

Defining the parameters of the evaluation to be undertaken serves to provide the evaluator with important information about the program's functioning; it also opens the lines of communication between the evaluator and persons who will figure prominently in the design of the evaluation. Building rapport in this way can be extremely important in determining the ultimate success of the evaluation.

A useful technique in bounding an evaluation is the Evaluability Assessment method (Wholey, 1977), which consolidates the viewpoints of the evaluator and the potential evaluation user. Wholey states, "This task is crucial to evaluation design because it provides the criteria for deciding how much and what types of information to seek in the evaluation." The Evaluability Assessment process allows the evaluator to work with program decision makers and potential information users to clarify the evaluation task. It is important that consensus be reached at this early stage, since the criticism that "the evaluators have not answered the right questions" blocks the utilization of evaluation results. Both Patton and Wholey feel it imperative that evaluators and decision makers work together in the design of the evaluation protocol. As Patton (1978) states,

> The evaluator does not attempt to mold and manipulate decision-makers and information users to accept the evaluator's preconceived notions about what constitutes useful or high quality research, but neither is the evaluator a mere technician who does whatever decision makers want. . . . All participants share responsibility for creatively shaping and rigorously implementing an evaluation that is both useful and of high quality.

The steps for conducting an Evaluability Assessment are described below:

— *Bounding the problem/program:* Determining what national or local activities and what objectives constitute the program—that is, what is the unit to be analyzed?
— *Collection of program information:* Gathering information that defines the program objectives, activities, and underlying assumptions.
— *Modeling:* Development of a model that describes the program and interrelationships of activities and objectives, from the point of view of the intended users of the evaluation.
— *Analysis:* Determining to what extent the program definition, as represented by the model, is sufficiently unambiguous that evaluation is likely to be useful. This step also includes the identification of potential evaluation studies.
— *Presentation to management/intended users:* Feedback of the results of the assessment to representatives of management and intended users and determination of the next steps that should be taken.

Also useful to the evaluator is the examination of possible constraints for the evaluation, conducted concurrently with the evaluability assessment. These constraints may be monetary but may also focus on the level and type of record-keeping procedures that are currently in existence, or the current evaluation skill level held by those who will participate in the evaluation. Once these constraints have been clearly delineated, they should be included in the rationale for the evaluation protocol and in the presentation of the Evaluability Assessment to management and intended evaluation users.

Some Specific Strategies
To Overcome Knowledge Transfer Barriers

The "Correct" Attributes

Factors related to a new idea, and the manner in which it is implemented, can greatly affect the probability of its successful transfer. Glaser (1973) has proposed the acronym CORRECT to summarize seven attributes likely to influence the transfer of knowledge and planned change:

(1) *Credibility*. The degree to which potential users believe an innovation will have beneficial effects hinges on two considerations: first, the strength and scientific merit of the idea and secondly, the prestige and status of the idea's supporters. The value of an advocate of an idea within a program (sometimes called an "internal champion") was found to be a decisive factor in the adoption of new ideas in nine out of ten cases in a study conducted by the National Science Foundation (1973). Additionally, as Zaltman, Duncan, and Holbek (1973) have pointed out, if an idea emanates, or seems to emanate from within an organization, the staff tend to be less resistant to adopting it.

(2) *Observability*. Much initial resistance to an idea may result from confusion or uncertainty regarding its characteristics in actual practice. When potential users can observe an innovation in successful operation, this uncertainty may be alleviated, and the potential utility enhanced.

(3) *Relevance*. Acceptance of an innovation is many times a function of its perceived utility in dealing with persistent or bothersome problems. Innovations should be presented in such a manner that the potential users can easily see the idea's utility to them, as opposed to presentation as a vague or hypothetical model.

(4) *Relative Advantage*. The use or transfer of an idea can be greatly facilitated if the potential users believe that it represents a clear advantage over existing procedures.

(5) *Ease in Understanding*. The feasibility of transferring an innovation to a new setting becomes problematic if the idea to be communicated is complex or unfamiliar. Elaborating on this point, Davis (1973b) has noted that if staff skills are insufficient to implement an innovation, it must be further evaluated for "learnability" and "teachability."

(6) *Compatibility*. A major factor in the success or failure of an innovation is its compatibility with the values, norms, policies, and practices of the potential users. If some aspect of the innovation is inconsistent with a program's underlying philosophy, the probability of its adoption is greatly reduced.

(7) *Trialability, Reversibility, and Divisibility*. Resistance to innovation is mitigated to the degree that a new idea can be safely discarded if it fails to achieve its objectives. "Trialability" is the capacity of an innovation to be imple-

mented on a provisional basis, without irrevocable commitment and risk on the part of the prospective adopter; "reversibility" is the degree to which the effects of an innovation can be erased and the original situation restored; and "divisibility" is the appropriateness of the innovation for implementation in small, self-contained steps. Flexibility in implementation strategy, then, becomes a crucial variable in the adoption of an innovation.

Attention to these correct factors can help the evaluator do a better job of planning a relevant dissemination model. Using this information, the evaluator can then go about choosing a specific plan of action.

Knowledge Transfer Techniques

Several knowledge transfer techniques have already been discussed here, such as the use of a task force, targeting information to the needs of potential users, clarification of the program and the goals of the study to be undertaken, active promotion of use by task force members and the evaluator, and the use of internal championship. Some additional techniques bear discussion at this point.

(1) *Formal Contracting.* During the negotiation phase of setting up a contract between the evaluator/researcher and an agency, a formal segment of the contract might be included which details the way in which the resulting information will be used. The contract should also clearly delineate the roles of program personnel as well as the evaluator in the utilization of the information.

(2) *Interpersonal Communication.* The importance of informal, ongoing interpersonal communication has been exemplified in several studies. It is important, then, to attend to communication that will ensure continual, two-way communication. Vehicles that can be employed by those interested in knowledge transfer include rapport-building sessions, brainstorming meetings, and time spent in mutual planning for the study.

(3) *Written Communication.* Although written communication has been shown to be an inferior technique to transfer ideas, the producers of information can do much to enhance the quality of their written documents. Several guidelines may serve to enhance the applicability of these documents:

Brevity—a short document is much more likely to be read and carefully considered than a long one.

Targeted Communications—documents should be focused on providing the information needed to make particular decisions.

Ordering of Information—the most important points should come at the beginning of the document, where they will have the greatest impact.

Executive Summaries—a one- to two-page summary of the information included in the report can be a highly effective communication strategy.

Language—avoid the use of technical language or jargon—in other words, write the report in a manner that can be understood by the intended audience.

Timing—make sure that the report reaches the hands of the potential information user at a time when that information can be of use. Evaluation timetables can be especially useful for proper timing of reports.

(4) *Demonstrations and Site Visits.* Many times, seeing an idea being successfully implemented can be far more convincing to the potential adopter than any amount of talking or reading ever could. Wherever possible, demonstrations and site visits should be incorporated into the knowledge transfer plan.

(5) *Conferences and Seminars.* This technique can be used when a formal body of knowledge must be communicated to a fairly large body of individuals, and can be most effective when used in conjunction with other communication strategies discussed earlier.

(6) *Multiple Methods.* Probably the most effective strategy is a combination of several methods. In this way, information can be structured in such a way that each experience builds upon and reinforces previous knowledge.

PLANNED CHANGE

Both evaluation implementation and evaluation utilization can be considered as planned change. Some of the most common changes necessitated by the implementation of an evaluation are changes in documentation procedures, adherence to evaluation protocol, and changes in day-to-day procedures. Evaluation utilization may have even broader repercussions within an agency, since evaluation may indicate widespread programmatic revisions. Planned change techniques can be utilized to facilitate the use of evaluation information for clinical program and policy decision-making.

Barriers to Change

One of the most pervasive barriers to change is a generic fear of change in general, the desire to maintain the status quo. Planned change literature has helped to document some of the components of resistance to change, which, in turn, may require a variety of remedial actions. One especially useful tool for evaluators has emerged from the planned change literature: the notion of organizational assessment; that is, the examination of an organization's climate relative to some proposed change before the actual attempt to implement that change. Organizational assessment techniques can help the evaluator isolate the sources of resistance and assist in planning implementation and utilization strategies specifically tailored to each setting.

Planned Change and Evaluation

Our own forays into the field of knowledge transfer and planned change grew out of our attempts to disseminate the Goal Attainment Scaling meth-

ABILITY: AVAILABILITY OR ACCESSIBILITY OF THE MATERIAL, PERSONNEL,
            OR FINANCIAL RESOURCES NECESSARY FOR CHANGE.

            Category 1: Willingness and ability to commit resources
                         to program evaluation.

            Category 2: Present availability and skill level of man-
                         power to plan and implement program evalua-
                         tion. Knowledge level regarding program
                         evaluation of those concerned.

VALUES: THE CONGENIALITY TO INNOVATION OF THE ORGANIZATION'S
            PREVAILING NORMS.

            Category 3: Attitudes and beliefs of those involved to-
                         ward accepting program evaluation.

            Category 4: Organization's history of change and history
                         of support for change.

            Category 5: Characteristics of staff or administrators
                         thought to bear on acceptance of program
                         evaluation (other than skill level).

            Category 6: Work relations; supervisory relations; inter-
                         personal relations.

            Category 7: Employment or personnel policies of the organ-
                         ization (i.e., of the employer).

INFORMATION: QUALITY AND CREDIBILITY OF THE INNOVATION, AND AVAILABILITY
              OF INFORMATION SUFFICIENT TO IMPLEMENT IT.

            Category 8: Availability of information bearing on program's
                         present functioning. Availability and use of
                         procedures and channels for recording and
                         communicating program information.

CIRCUMSTANCES: STABLE ENVIRONMENTAL AND ORGANIZATIONAL ATTRIBUTES INFLU-
                ENCING CHANGE.

            Category 9: Aspects of the program relating to procedures,
                         job duties, job requirements, and job
                         expectations.

            Category 10: Quality of the relationships between the
                          program and those it serves and works with.

TIMING: DYNAMIC ENVIRONMENTAL AND ORGANIZATIONAL FACTORS INFLUENCING
            CHANGE.

            Category 11: Timing of the program evaluation to coincide
                          or coordinate with other program or organi-
                          zational activities.

OBLIGATION: DEGREE OF PRESSURE, OR "FELT NEED," TO IMPLEMENT THE
             INNOVATION.

            Category 12: Felt need to 'do something,' to take action.
                          Pressure to evaluate. Awareness of the
                          present health of the organization.

RESISTANCE: DEGREE OF OPPOSITION TO THE CHANGE; EXISTENCE AND STRENGTH
              OF INHIBITORS.

        Category 13:   Expected or feared negative consequences of
                      program evaluation. Frontstage or backstage
                      fears of loss resulting from adoption of
                      program evaluation.

    YIELD: THE PROBABLE OUTCOME OF THE INNOVATION; THE INTENDED OR
           UNINTENDED BENEFITS AND LOSSES.

        Category 14:   Expected or hoped for positive consequences
                      of evaluation. Payoff or rewards thought
                      to result from program evaluation.

FIGURE 12.4   AVICTORY Change Dimensions and
                 Subscales for the Organizational
                 Assessment of Readiness to Implement
                 Program Evaluation

odology (Kiresuk and Sherman, 1968). Some of our interventions as consultants were extremely successful, while others could be considered disasters. We were anxious to discover why we succeeded in some cases and failed in others.

Organizational Assessment Framework: AVICTORY

Staff of the Program Evaluation Resource Center examined the planned change literature in an attempt to find a working conceptual model to assess organizational readiness to accept program evaluation. The AVICTORY model, developed by Dr. Howard Davis (1973b), seemed to be a viable model. AVICTORY is an acronym for eight determinants of organizational change: A = Ability; V = Values; I = Information; C = Circumstances; T = Timing; O = Obligation; R = Resistances; Y = Yield.

Working from this model, an 85-item questionnaire (Mayer, 1974) was developed to assess readiness for program evaluation. Fourteen subscales were developed and classified according to the AVICTORY paradigm (see Figure 12.4). This breakdown would then allow us to produce scores on each scale which represented the summed value of all relevant items.

AVICTORY Analysis

Although the capacity of the AVICTORY measure to predict adoption of evaluation is as yet undetermined (Studer, 1978), feedback from users suggests that it does provide useful and stimulating descriptive information. The most intriguing use of such data should be to propose remedies for obvious resistance, to develop a positive organizational framework for change, and to identify and use advantages where they exist.

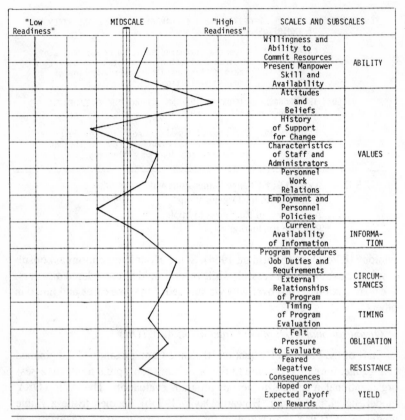

"Low Readiness"	MIDSCALE	"High Readiness"	SCALES AND SUBSCALES	
			Willingness and Ability to Commit Resources	ABILITY
			Present Manpower Skill and Availability	
			Attitudes and Beliefs	
			History of Support for Change	
			Characteristics of Staff and Administrators	VALUES
			Personnel Work Relations	
			Employment and Personnel Policies	
			Current Availability of Information	INFORMATION
			Program Procedures Job Duties and Requirements	CIRCUMSTANCES
			External Relationships of Program	
			Timing of Program Evaluation	TIMING
			Felt Pressure to Evaluate	OBLIGATION
			Feared Negative Consequences	RESISTANCE
			Hoped or Expected Payoff or Rewards	YIELD

FIGURE 12.5   Sample AVICTORY Profile (N = 45)

The results of a sample analysis are presented in Figure 12.5. The overall impression created by the profiles is that generally favorable conditions existed regarding the implementation of GAS. The only exceptions relate to the employment policies and to history of support for innovation. A computerized interpretation (Mayer, 1974) of these data produced the following narrative:

Slack resources exist and the organization is positive about committing them to evaluation. The attitudes and beliefs of the organization are favorable; staff believe program evaluation can be beneficial, is needed and wanted even in the face of resistance. Change has not been handled well in the past; management has not been responsive to staff concerns. The staff feels that they are dedicated, hardworking, caring about the success of the program, and that the administrators are strong enough to accept negative findings. The staff feel they work well together; supervision is adequate; trust level is good. They are consulted in matters affecting them. However, salaries, working conditions and benefits are not competitive or satisfactory. Rewards do not depend on performance. Record-keeping and information flow are adequate. Service user characteristics and program results during and after treatment are known. The organization's reputation is good among clientele, cooperating agencies, sponsors and community. It delivers a valued service. This is probably a good time to begin work on evaluation. Evaluation could be incorporated into the present work flow. There is a felt need to do evaluation in order to improve the program or prevent danger to the program. There is little concern that evaluation will result in job loss, increased workload, or jeopardy to the program. Generally, the organization feels that evaluation could result in good things: lead to greater recognition for those who deserve it, contribute to better services to clients, provide a better way to convince administrators of needed changes and additional funds.

Implementation Strategy

The profiles and interpretation provide useful descriptive information, but the question remains: How can these data be converted into a useful implementation strategy? Here the topic leads into territory new to the traditionally trained mental health professional. For assistance, counsel was sought from Howard Davis, Chief of the Mental Health Services Development Branch of the National Institute of Mental Health. As he reviewed the sample profile, Dr. Davis (Roy and Kiresuk, 1977) made the following observations and recommendations:

1. Work with the source of greatest resistance first; talk it over, allowing for ventilation and clarification. Resistance at this point can be reduced by allowing technical modifications in the innovation.
2. Identify internal zealots who can assist in carrying through the innovation. Capitalize on potential champions of change: these will be younger or older than average, intelligent, not members of organizational elite, and somewhat socially isolated.
3. Try the innovation on a trial basis in a unit where it seems most likely to succeed. Reward success conspicuously.
4. Use peer pressure and reinforcement to support change: get internal opinion leaders to accept the innovation.
5. "Re-invention," changing the innovation so that it seems to be invented at the target program, is often a useful strategy to bring about organizational change.
6. Look at the whole program. Put effort and resources where change is most likely. Leave laggard units until last.
7. Examine obligation-motivation for change. Some individuals and program elements are preconditioned for innovation. Exploit this.
8. If change is unlikely to be successful, don't attempt it. It is better not to try, than to try and fail. Failure can reinforce resistance to change, and make

subsequent attempts at innovation even more problematic. If change is not likely, the change agent should so indicate to the client organization.

9. If GAS is being used to evaluate and monitor the innovation effort, exploit its potential for rewards: attainment of "Better Than Expected" or "Best Anticipated" outcomes should be reinforced lavishly.
10. If there is low perception of need for the innovation, conduct targeted interviews to determine why.
11. Be judicious in using participative decision-making. Staff involvement can often reduce resistance, but in authoritarian organizations can also be interpreted as indecision. Sometimes it is better to just push on through.
12. Segmentalize the groups involved in the innovation, identifying and addressing the unique needs of each segment.

This list of recommendations provides a good overview of planned change strategies. At this point, too, the communication and demonstration strategies discussed earlier in the section on knowledge transfer techniques can be fruitfully employed.

One last strategy that bears mention at this point is the use of the change agent (Havelock and Havelock, 1973). A change agent is a person or group serving as an intermediary between the knowledge producers and the potential users. Depending upon the individual setting, the change agent can serve as a translator of information, a consultant to the adopting agencies, a trainer, leader, innovator or defender of the proposed innovation, all to the end result of facilitating the planned change.

Evaluation: Completing the Cycle

As we mentioned at the outset, we view evaluation, knowledge transfer, and planned change as a cyclical function. At this point evaluation is again brought into play to examine the extent to which the proposed information reached its intended audience and in what form the information reached them. This can then bring about a new cycle of knowledge transfer and planned change.

CONCLUSION

In this chapter we have tried to develop an organic, multisdiciplinary, multiperspective, multimethod concept of evaluation. Evaluation is an activity fully integrated into a learning, knowing, communicating, acting, testing, adjusting program organism. Evaluation is presented as inseparable from its conceptual fraternal twin—knowledge transfer and utilization. Many intra- and extraprogrammatic factors which have been seen as contaminants or distractions to good evaluation are seen here as part of the essential characteristics of a program and its context—factors which determine the relevance of the information of the evaluation system. Without fully integrating these factors—the program, its context, evaluation, knowledge utilization—evaluation systems resemble fantasies of pseudoscience, complex, expensive, and unused by the movers of society and the actors in industry.

REFERENCES

ALKIN, M.C., J. KOSECOFF, C. FITZ-GIBBON, and R. SELIGMAN (1974) "Evaluation and decision making: the Title VII experience." CSE Monograph Series in Evaluation (No. 4).

BRANDL, J. E. (1978) "Evaluation and politics." Evaluation and Change (Special Issue): 6–7.

CALSYN, R.J. and L. LaFERRIERE (1976) "A study of the therapeutic effects of goal attainment scaling." PERC Newsletter: 1–2.

CAMPBELL, D.T. (1974) "Qualitative knowing in action research." Presented at the 1974 Annual Meeting of the American Psychological Association, New Orleans.

———and J.C. STANLEY (1966) Experimental and Quasi-Experimental Designs for Research. Chicago: Rand McNally.

CRONBACH, L.J. (1975) "Beyond the two disciplines of scientific psychology." American Psychologist 30: 116–127.

DAVIS, H.R. (1973a) "Four ways to goal attainment." Evaluation 1: 43–48.

———(1973b) "Change and innovation." In S. Feldman (ed.) Administration and Mental Health. Springfield, IL: Charles C Thomas.

GALANO, J. (1977) "Treatment effectiveness as a function of client involvement in goal-setting and goal-planning." Goal Attainment Review 3: 17–32.

GLASER, E.M. (1973) "Knowledge transfer and institutional change." Professional Psychology 4: 434–444.

HAVELOCK, R.G. and M.C. HAVELOCK (1973) Training for Change Agents. Ann Arbor: Institute for Social Research, University of Michigan.

HOUTS, P.E. and R.A. SCOTT (1976) "Goal planning in mental health rehabilitation: an evaluation of the effectiveness of achievement motivation training for mental patients being rehabilitated to the community." Goal Attainment Review 2: 33–51.

JOLY, J.M. (1967) "Research and innovation: two solitudes?" Canadian Education and Research Digest 2: 184–194.

JONES, S. and G. GARWICK (1973) "Guide to goals study: goal attainment scaling as therapy adjunct?" P.E.P. Newsletter 4(6): 1–3.

KIRESUK, T.J. and S.H. LUND (1979) "Program evaluation and utilization analysis." In R. Perloff (ed.) Evaluator Interventions: Pros and Cons. Beverly Hills, CA: Sage.

KIRESUK, T.J. and R.E. SHERMAN (1968) "Goal attainment scaling: a general method for evaluating comprehensive community mental health programs." Community Mental Health Journal 4: 443–453.

LATHAM, G.P. and G.A. YUKL (1975) "A review of research on the applications of goal-setting in organizations." Academy of Management Journal 18(4): 824–845.

LOCKE, E.A. (1968) "Toward a theory of task performance and incentives." Organizational Behavior and Human Performance 3: 324–329.

LUND, S.H., T.J. KIRESUK and S.K. SCHULTZ (1980) "Individualized goal attainment measurement." In E.J. Posavac (ed.) The Impact of Program Evaluation on Mental Health Care. Boulder, CO: Westview Press.

MAYER, STEVEN E. (1974) "The 'organizational readiness to accept program evaluation questionnaire': scoring and interpretation." PERC Newsletter 6(6).

McCLELLAND, D. C. and D. G. WINTER (1969) Motivating Economic Achievement. New York: Free Press.

MUSHKIN, S. J. (1973) "Evaluations: use with caution." Evaluation 1(2): 30–35.

National Science Foundation (1973) Science, Technology and Innovation (Report on Contract No. NSF-C667). Columbus, OH: Battelle Columbus Laboratories.

PATTON, M. Q. (1978) Utilization-Focused Evaluation. Beverly Hills, CA: Sage.

———(1975) "Alternative evaluation research paradigm." North Dakota Study Group on Evaluation Monograph Series. Grand Forks: University of North Dakota.

ROSE, R. (1977) "Disciplined research and undisciplined problems." In C. Weiss (ed.) Using Social Research in Public Policy Making. Lexington, MA: D. C. Heath.

ROSSI, P H., H. E. FREEMAN, and S. R. WRIGHT (1979) Evaluation—A Systematic Approach. Beverly Hills, CA: Sage.

ROY, C. and T. J. KIRESUK (1977) "Goal attainment scaling: a medical-correctional application." Presented at the VI World Congress of Psychiatry, Honolulu, Hawaii.

SCRIVEN, M. (1972) "The methodology of evaluation." In C. Weiss (ed.) Evaluating Social Action Programs: Readings in Social Action and Education. Boston: Allyn & Bacon.

SMITH, D. (1976) "Goal attainment scaling as an adjunct to counseling." Journal of Counseling Psychology 28(1): 22–27.

STILL, J. D. (1977) "Goal attainment scaling as a method of treatment for offenders placed on probation." Ph.D. dissertation, University of Mississippi.

STUDER, S. L. (1978) "A validity study of a measure of 'readiness for evaluation.'" Ph.D. dissertation, University of Minnesota.

SUCHMAN, E. A. (1967) Evaluative Research. New York: Russell Sage.

WALKER, R. A. (1972) "The ninth panacea: program evaluation." Evaluation 1(1): 45–53.

WEISS C. (1977) "Introduction." In C. Weiss (ed.) Using Social Research in Public Policy Making. Lexington, MA: D.C. Heath.

———(1976) "Analytic typologies for planned change." Presented at meeting of Network of Consultants on Knowledge Transfer, New Orleans.

WHOLEY, J. S. (1977) "Evaluability assessment." In L. Putnam (ed.) Evaluation Research Methods: A Basic Guide. Beverly Hills, CA: Sage.

ZALTMAN, G., R. DUNCAN, and J. HOLBEK (1973) Innovations and Organizations. New York: John Wiley.

PART V

FUTURE NEEDS AND PROSPECTS

The two major issues which are of interest for the outlook of evaluation are the growing professionalization of the field and potential actions to improve the state of evaluation research.

The emergence of evaluation research may be regarded as a response to the increased compartmentalization of the world, the answer to increased specialization and disciplinary professionalization of science. But as evaluation research develops its own professional culture, it may also promote the narrow self-interests of its members. Peter Rossi predicts that the future of evaluation research will reflect the heterogeneity and diversity of evaluation research tasks. The sources of the strength and additional growth of evaluation research are related to the ability of evaluation researchers to draw from the diversified theories and methodology while simultaneously cutting across disciplinary fields to respond to societal and administrative problems. Training to improve evaluation research is therefore a necessary prerequisite for growth and improvement. Winfred Nacken outlines a training process for evaluators, which is organized as an interactive learning process, taking up the perspectives of researchers, users, programmers, and policy makers, as well as those of the target population. This is a "constructive" process which tries to integrate methodological, theoretical, and political developments in science.

13

The Professionalization of Evaluation Research in the United States

Peter H. Rossi

Social and Demographic
Research Institute,
University of Massachusetts

INTRODUCTION

The mission of this chapter is to provide an overview of the current standing of the emerging professional field of evaluation research in the United States. The perspective is that of someone who entered the social sciences as a professional in the early 1950s and who has consistently mixed in his work academic activities and applied work in social science. For more than a fourth of my career I was a full-time administrator of a not-for-profit research institute, the National Opinion Research Center at the University of Chicago. Since then I have engaged in a mixture of teaching and research in social science issues, the latter being largely applied in nature. In short, my perspective has a dual character; I have played the roles of academic teacher and scholar as well as applied social researcher. I dwell on this background partly to establish my credentials as a would-be analyst of the evaluation profession—if such there be—and so the reader may assess my existential bases and the potential biases implied.

As far as I know, there exists no documented account of the history of evaluation research in the United States. Indeed, such an effort would be as pretentious as the autobiography of an eight-year-old, and certainly not as potentially charming. Its emergence in the last decade as a major social science activity is too recent to deserve the scholarly attention of historians of science and certainly too fresh to sustain a detached analysis. However, the consequence for papers such as this is that accounts of evaluation research are more memoirs than they are history. There is always the danger that memoirs undisciplined by scholarship will produce mythical history and heroic accounts. Despite the dangers involved, I will give a short historical account of evaluation activities in the United States as background to an assessment of the emergence of evaluation as a profession.

A portion of this chapter will be devoted to an analysis of the several structural strains that plague evaluation research as a scientific activity. In addition to the strain arising out of the conflicts—intellectual and social-structural—among academic disciplines and their applied counterparts, there are special strains that plague evaluation because of its closeness to the political process. Finally, it is necessary to come to grips with the fact that evaluation has grown large enough to attract the attention of bustling individual entrepreneurs as well as large business firms.

The final section will be devoted to an exercise in futurology. It will be clear from earlier sections that evaluation is trying to emerge as a profession. The issues for the future are whether or not it will succeed and which are its likely forms.

AN INFORMAL HISTORY OF EVALUATION IN THE UNITED STATES

If we define evaluation as the application of social science knowledge and research methods to the assessment of social programs, then it is clear that traces of evaluation activities can be found from the beginnings of empirical social research. The early nineteenth-century epidemiologists assessed the efficacy of public health measures by observing subsequent morbidity and mortality. Nineteenth-century pioneers in corrections and mental hospitals claimed miraculous cures, citing as evidence recidivism rates among their discharged prisoners and patients. Von Humboldt, who dabbled on the side in social reform, has a long account in the published papers of the American Academy of Arts and Sciences on his "experiments" with alternative compensation schemes instituted among the workers of the several textile factories he owned in one of the German provinces. Of course, these early applied social researchers were not social scientists. Indeed, there were very few in that period who called themselves social scientists: those who did social science were amateurs who dabbled in social research as sidelines to their regular activities.

Evaluation as self-conscious social science activity began in the twentieth century with the development of the social sciences as academic disciplines and with the development of specific research techniques. Thus, an evaluation of the so-called Gary plan as a method of instruction in New York City high schools carried out around 1918 by Thorndike and Giddings rested upon the development of quantitative ability and achievement-testing methods. The evaluation of advertising campaigns and of merchandizing strategies beginning in the 1960s was based on the extension of the idea of mental testing to the measurement of consumer preferences and purchasing intentions. Psychology was the major discipline from which these early proto-evaluations grew, especially those psychologists who were closely allied with the mental testing movement.

What was missing in the first half of the twentieth century for the development of a social program as we know it today were three elements: First, there were few American social programs in the first 30 years of this century. A comprehensive social insurance program that involved payments to unemployed workers or to retired workers was not enacted in the United States until 1936. Roosevelt's New Deal started the extensive involvement of the federal government in the provision of transfer benefits to a wide variety of disadvantaged groups as well as providing social services to the same groups. Second those programs enacted in the liberal regime of the New Deal were not regarded as problematic in the same sense as later programs. Third, the technology of social research had yet to grow strong enough to sustain much in the way of research efforts outside of such institutional environments as schools, prisons, and public housing projects. Given these preconditions for the emergence of evaluation as a major activity, it is not surprising that the social programs of the New Deal were not systematically evaluated even though they were controversial. The issues involved were ideological, not technical. Thus, whether the public service employment offered through various New Deal programs was effective was not the issue that concerned political decision makers, but whether such programs were morally justified. In addition, the further extension of mental testing to a variety of human activities and attitude measurement had just begun. Perhaps most important of all, methods for sampling noninstitutionalized human populations and for analyzing large amounts of quantitative data were just being developed.

By the time the second great wave of social programs was started in the 1960s, the stage was set for the emergence of evaluation as a large-scale, applied social science activity. Sampling and measurement methods had been developed to the point of mass application. Electronic computers had become commonplace instruments, and the software for taking multivariate methods out of the textbooks and into large N computations had been developed. Most important, the political conditions existed for a technical orientation to social programs. For example, the issue was no longer whether or not the federal government should provide funds for improving the equality of educational opportunity, but whether the instrumentality chosen to accomplish this end was effective and efficient. It is probably impossible to understand why social legislation that was enacted in the 1960s began to contain provisions that called for evaluation. I believe that much must be attributed to two factors: First, legislators and high-level civil servants who came into office during the Kennedy and Johnson administrations had been exposed to social science in the course of their educational training. Social science had infiltrated the major elite law schools and colored the curricula of the great state university law schools whose graduates man American political positions. Second, this was a period of great skepticism concerning American institutions. There were clearly obvious failures in the public education system, especially its failure with the new urban migrants— Blacks and Hispanics. Unemployment persisted despite prosperity, suggesting a breakdown in the institutions that connected labor markets with a submerged portion of the labor force. Somehow things were not going right with American society. Prosperity, world supremacy, and high standards of living had not solved the problems of crime, poverty, suffering among the aged, and the maldistributions of income, goods, and services. This skepticism was even more enlarged when we engaged in a morally unjustifiable war in Vietnam that we clearly could not even win decisively on the battlefield let alone in the arena of world opinion. When it developed that our president and his major advisors had been corrupt, lied extensively beyond customary limits, and engaged in patently illegal behavior, confidence in the American government sunk even lower.

Social science was also ready to become more involved in the world of politics. American universities had become politicized by the antiwar movement and student radicals' questioning of disciplinary concerns and preoccupations. Many of us began to look for opportunities in which we could show the young that we, too, were concerned with the improvement of our society.

An especially important place in the history of applied social science will undoubtedly be given to the dedicated social scientists who were brought in to man the Office of Economic Opportunity. These "poverty warriors" in their few years of government service did much to establish the fact that social science research methods had much to contribute to our understanding of how social programs could be made more effective through evaluation.

Whatever the scholarly historian of post-World War II social science may come up with as the definitive analysis of this period, it is abundantly clear that within less than 20 years applied social research has grown into a major activity. Evaluation research of one kind or another is at the heart of most applied social research. While current estimates of federal support for applied social research range from a low of $500,000,000 per year to a high of

$1.5 billion (depending on what you count as evaluation), the low side amounts to a fair-sized industry—at least by American standards. If we add to this amount whatever state and local governments spend for applied social research out of their funds, the size of the total activity is truly considerable.

Furthermore, support for evaluation does not appear to be slackening. More and more social legislation contains provisions requiring evaluation of the programs authorized in the legislation. Skepticism regarding social programs does not appear to be lessening. The technical quality of major evaluations appears to be improving, suggesting that our federal agencies and their personnel are becoming better at procuring evaluation services. More interest is being shown in evaluation on the part of academic institutions. Special professional associations and specialized evaluation journals have been started. Evaluation specialists are presently in high demand.

It is clear that evaluation has become firmly established as a valued activity. Federal, state, and local government agencies are willing to pay for evaluations. All of the empirically oriented social science disciplines—education, economics, psychology, sociology, and political science—have evidenced an interest in evaluation. Specialized training programs have been started at both the undergraduate and graduate levels within universities, of which there are currently as many as 10 to 15 either in place or being planned. It should be noted that the interest of the academic disciplines in evaluation research is driven not only by the existence of a growing demand for trained personnel for evaluative activities but also by a lessening of demand for personnel to fill academic positions. In addition, funding for basic social science research in many social science fields has either declined or reached a plateau. In the scramble for funds to support academic departments and for the support of research activities, the existence of a strong demand for evaluation personnel and for evaluation research increasingly appears to universities as a possible avenue to solutions that will maintain the strength of social science academic departments.

The demand for evaluation personnel so far outstrips the supply available that most people currently engaging in evaluation are not trained in evaluation. Indeed, I would venture to say that most are not trained in social science research. A few years ago I was invited to give a seminar at a Federal Civil Service Institute on evaluation research. The purpose of the institute was to provide an orientation to evaluation research for federal civil servants who were assigned either to supervise the conduct of evaluation within their agencies or to manage an extramural evaluation program. Noticing that few of the participants had more than a dim understanding of social science concepts or research methods, I conducted an informal survey of the participants, asking them to indicate the fields in which they had either training and experience. While most were social scientists, they had been trained in parts of their disciplines that were not technically sophisticated: for example, political scientists had been trained in public administration rather than political behavior. The remainder had been trained in a variety of fields not based in social science. Of course, few had any experience with evaluation as a research activity, since they were selected by their agencies to attend the institute for that reason, and were rather puzzled about what research had to do with evaluation. They were familiar with evaluation as clinical judgments and with research as essentially the collation of existing published data, as in the preparation of materials for addresses to business clubs and luncheons.

Perhaps the most spectacular development of the last 10 years has been emergence of a new industry designed to furnish evaluations on a contractual basis to the federal, state, and local governments. This new industry scarcely existed 15 years ago. Some of the organizations which participate in the industry are established firms that have extended their services to include evaluations—the American Institute of Research and the Educational Testing Service were well established in their respective fields of market research and test construction before embarking on evaluation activities. Large business enterprises that had been mainly in fields far removed from social science—established divisions that were supposed to respond to the new demand for evaluation research, such as Westinghouse and General Electric, both basically manufacturers of heavy electrical equipment— established divisions that bid on evaluation contracts, often successfully.

New firms were established: Clark Abt, an MIT Ph.D. in political science, set up a very successful firm in Cambridge. A small number of economists at Princeton founded Mathematica, Inc. Westat was the outgrowth of the retirement from the Census Bureau of a handful of the more technically competent census researchers. Other large firms include the Systems Development Corporation—an offshoot (profit-making) of the not-for-profit Rand Corporation, an organization which also entered the field— and SRI, Inc. (formerly Stanford Research Institute). This handful constitute most of the very large firms that bid for some of the large federal contracts. To provide some calibration on the size of these firms, Abt Associates has an annual gross income of about $50,000,000, employs about 150 social science Ph.D.s, and engages in research in a wide variety of areas, including housing, education, criminal justice, welfare, health services; in addition, it has affiliates and subsidiaries in several other countries, including West Germany. Indeed, the number of professional social scientists employed at Abt exceeds that of almost any but the largest state universities in the United States and the budget exceeds that provided for social science research in any university.

In addition to these large research firms and social research divisions of diversified firms, a large number of smaller firms exist. I doubt if anyone knows the precise number of such firms. Indeed, given the extremely high mortality and fertility rates among them, a census of such firms would become rapidly out of date. Five years ago, Albert Biderman estimated that about 400 separate firms bid on advertized federal evaluation research contracts in one year. This estimate is clearly out of date; current estimates are at least several magnitudes larger. In addition, many firms may not bid for one reason or another during a particular year, and there are many firms which bid only for local and state contracts. Perhaps the best explanation is that there are currently about 2000 firms which furnish contractual services in evaluation research. Of course, most of these firms are very small, with research staffs consisting of one or two persons and with annual gross incomes of perhaps $100,000.

Finally, the universities have not neglected to get into the act. The well-established social science research institutes connected with major research universities—the National Opinion Research Center at the University of Chicago and the Institute for Social Research at the University of Michigan—were quick to enter bids for major federal evaluation contracts. Smaller university-affiliated research institutes are also involved, as are individual social science faculty members and their graduate students. Although in the aggregate, the total amount of evaluation research that takes place within the university is large, it is also clear that university social scientists contribute only a small part of the total funded evaluation research in the United States. However, university social scientists have contributed more than their share to the evaluation research literature: indeed, the leading intellectual spokespersons who establish current state-of-the-art standards are university-based social scientists—Howard Freeman, Donald Campbell, Robert Boruch, Frederick Mosteller, Carol Weiss, and Thomas Cook, to name a few of the most prominent. Apparently, within academia writing about evaluation research competes successfully with doing evaluation research!

Despite the considerable financial support for evaluation research and the large number of professionally trained personnel engaged in such activity, the amount of evaluation research results that could be published in easily accessible media is but a small fraction—perhaps less than one percent—of the total amount of evaluation produced. Most of the evaluation results—including those of the largest and most expensive evaluations—are not published in scholarly or trade books or in professional journals. Results exist mainly in the form of limited numbers of copies of reports delivered to the contracting agency or privately published (usually offset printed) monographs of uncertain shelf life. My own files are filled with such reports that are difficult to archive and even more difficult to retrieve.

It can be argued quite strongly that most evaluation research reports should not be published, since they are of limited interest to any audience outside the agency involved and are of poor quality. Granted, such may be the case for a large proportion of the evaluation studies; yet, given the total volume of evaluation activity in the United States and the fact that perhaps as much as ten percent are of sufficient general interest and technical quality to be worth publishing, it is shocking that the proportion published is so much smaller than that amount.

Several professional societies have been established within the past five years that are concerned exclusively with evaluation research. The largest of these, the Evaluation Research Society, was established through the initiative of the late Marcia Guttentag and now has about 2000 members largely drawn from evaluators associated with psychology as a discipline. The Council on Applied Social Research, begun by Clark Abt of Abt Associates, Inc., has developed as a more elitist organization with a smaller membership (around 300), consisting heavily of the large research firms and academic research centers. It does not appear to have a disciplinary focus. The Evaluation Network, a more informal organization consisting largely of persons engaged in educational evaluation, was founded by Michael Scriven. Sections devoted to evaluation research have been started within the American Educational Research Association, and almost every one of the social science disciplines feature sessions devoted to evaluation problems at their annual meetings.

Professional journals devoted to evaluation research have also appeared within the last few years. *Evaluation Magazine,* heavily subsidized by the National Institute of Mental Health, is distributed to more than 15,000 readers. *Evaluation Quarterly,* edited by Richard Berk and Howard Freeman, now has a subscribership of more than 3000 and appears to be the main outlet for more technical articles.

Finally, publishers gradually have been publishing texts on evaluation research. At present there are probably about ten texts, varying in level of complexity and intended audience, being published by a variety of scholarly publishers.

The historical origins of evaluation research in the United States and the resulting social organization of evaluation research profoundly affect the prospects of evaluation as a professional activity. Its salient historical characteristics have been touched upon in this section: First, its growth over the past two decades has been phenomenal, leading to considerable unevenness in quality. The best of evaluation research lies on the frontiers of our technical skill and theoretical knowledge; but the worst is often simple fraud, with the distribution skewed to the lower end of quality. Second, it has given rise to a new industry, a service industry close to the cottage stage in development, manned by social scientists providing entrepreneurial opportunities on an unprecedented scale (for social scientists). Finally, the credentials held by evaluation researchers that provide legitimacy for their work are diverse and heterogeneous. Anyone with a typewriter and enough funds to print a letterhead can (and often does) set himself/herself up as an evaluation entrepreneur. Persons established as evaluation researchers are trained in a variety of disciplines. There are also signs that evaluation is a serious intellectual field and a socially important activity.

It is from this historical background and assessment of the contemporary scene that we now proceed to consider evaluation as an emerging profession.

EVALUATION AS A PROFESSION

It should have been abundantly clear from the previous section that in the United States activities going on under the name of evaluation are extensive and well supported. At the same time, there also appears to be such diversity and heterogeneity in standards and performance as well as in the skills and training of evaluation personnel that it can scarcely be said that a profession of evaluation exists today. If there exists an evaluation profession, it is primarily in the potentialities of current evaluation activities. It is these potentialities, positive and negative, that we will consider in this section.

The hallmarks of a profession consist of establishing a legal or customary recognition of the existence of a body of theory and corresponding practice that can be imparted. In addition, a profession also has established institutional mechanisms whereby persons can be certified as legitimate, qualified practitioners by virtue of their training and/or experience. The traditional professions—medicine, law, engineering, teaching, and the like—all have their special training institutions, a set of degrees, and licensing procedures, as well as professional associations that act politically to safeguard the "integrity" of the profession. That the professional associations also often act to preserve the value of their profession by enhancing the monopolistic aspects of professionalism and by impeding desirable changes in professional practices is a recognized aspect of professionalization, but not as relevant to this discussion.

The major forces acting to enhance the professionalization of an activity arise both within the activity and from the consumers of the services rendered. Professionalization for practitioners involves guarding against competition from untrained (and hence less expensive) would-be practitioners. It can mean the segmentation of a labor market and a services market such that only certain providers are recognized as having the right to offer such services on the market. From the viewpoint of the consumer, professionalization appears to mean a guarantee of at least minimum quality in services (at the expense, perhaps, of monopolistic prices).

In the case of evaluation research, the drive for professionalization can be expected to come, on the one hand, from among the top levels of evaluators—from the large, successful entrepreneurs and from among the intellectuals who have been attempting to codify and rationalize evaluation as an activity. On the other hand, this drive may come from among the federal legislative bodies and agency executives which are the major consumers of evaluative activities.

There are many forces impeding the development of an evaluation profession, of which we will now consider the more important.

Disciplinary Heterogeneity

Evaluation is a social science activity drawing upon what is common in the way of knowledge and research technology to the several disciplines involved. Each of the disciplines has contributed something to evaluation, and to become a competent evaluator means to become multi-disciplinary, drawing on the fields of education, psychology, sociology, economics, and political science for both substantive knowledge and research techniques. From the field of education, test measurement is perhaps the most important technical contribution. Psychology has contributed the controlled experiment. The sample survey has been the contribution of several social science fields, including sociology, psychology, and statistics.

Contributions of the several social science fields to the substantive knowledge base needed for the evaluation of social programs are somewhat more diffuse. To properly model the presumed effects of a social program means to know enough about the social problem involved to be able to estimate the program's net effects. Although controlled experimental methods often obviate the necessity for precise substantive knowledge, most evaluations are not based on randomized experiments and hence rest heavily on modeling. Thus, an evaluator testing the effectiveness of some mode of treating felons to lower recidivism must have enough knowledge to be able to model recidivism.

One of the consequences of the disciplinary heterogeneity of evaluation is the rise of a customary division of labor among evaluators. Economists have been prominent in the evaluation of income maintenance programs, health insurance proposals, and housing allowances. Psychologists have been engrossed in the evaluation of mental health treatments. Sociologists have been concerned with criminal justice programs and have participated in the income maintenance and manpower training evaluations. Political scientists have dealt with the effects of reorganizations of government agencies. The informal division of labor partly corresponds to substantive concerns of the several individual disciplines involved and is partly a function of the particular histories of the federal agencies involved.

While the separate social science disciplines share a common pool of conceptual knowledge and research techniques, there are enough differences to enable the impartial observer to recognize certain disciplinary styles in the ways each discipline approaches evaluations. There is also considerable borrowing across disciplines and hence some tendency for the various fields to converge. It is difficult, we believe, to discern the difference between, for example, the evaluation Richard Berk and I did of an income maintenance program for released prisoners and that which would have been designed by an economist given the same problem.

Despite the long-run trends toward convergence among social science disciplines, there remain at present, and most likely for some years to come, considerable discipline-related evaluation styles which seriously impede the development of consensus over what is the top state-of-the-art practice in evaluation. One of the consequences of this interdisciplinary variance is that professional societies oriented toward evaluative activities have tended to be dominated by one or another discipline, despite heroic efforts at ecumenism.

In addition, within each of the social science disciplines, applied scholarly work or research is not regarded as the most prestigious disciplinary work. Although there is not much quality difference between the best of basic social science research and the best of applied social science research, highest regard goes to those social scientists whose contributions are mainly in basic social science. The major professional journals tend to spurn applied articles. Publishers prefer general theoretical treatises to applied research monographs, and the best new Ph.D.s are encouraged to take academic positions and hold that they are "too good" for applied social research activities, especially in the private sector. The taint of commercialism is imputed to those of us in academic positions bidding for applied social research contracts. In part, the low prestige given to applied social research tends to perpetuate itself: Low prestige activities tend to attract lesser talents, and the domination of lesser talents in a field tends to validate its low prestige.

The consequence of this lower prestige is that it will be difficult to set up training programs that are directly related to the needs of evaluation as an activity. Training programs will tend to shift toward basic social science concerns and away from contact with practice in order to demonstrate that evaluation training is no different from basic research training. It may also lead to the development of separate institutions, just as business administration is ordinarily taught separately from economics, and sociology and educational schools duplicate the basic social sciences with educational psychology departments and educational sociology departments, a separation that has not been advantageous either to education or to business administration nor to the basic social science disciplines involved.

Evaluative Heterogeneity: The Four Faces of Evaluation

Evaluation as practiced currently displays considerable heterogeneity. The concept of evaluation as applying primarily to the quantitative assessment of net impacts of social programs has hardly diffused to all who use the term nor to those who call themselves evaluators. There are four types of evaluative activities, each tending to have its own way of proceeding and its own types of questions to put to social programs.

The first face of evaluation is as a sort of social engineering, the development of the designs of social programs. This activity, which is known by such names as social policy analysis, social program research, and development, is concerned primarily with the application of social science knowledge to the assessment of existing social programs and to the design of new programs. The assessment is made in terms of whether or not the programs in question are consistent with the existing body of social science knowledge about the social problem and the treatment in question. For example, a social program designed to reduce juvenile delinquency has within it an *implicit* model of the phenomenon of juvenile delinquency and an *explicit* model of how the program treatment operates to prevent or lessen delinquency. Policy analyses of this type may be based on sophisticated computer simulations of microeconomic processes or on less complex demographic data or relatively simple models. Note that social engineering is a priori assessment whose worth is highly dependent on the validity of social science theory and its applicability to the social problem in question.

A second type of social science activity that is often called evaluation consists of providing administrative information on the operation of social programs. Often referred to as "process evaluation" or "monitoring," the purpose of this kind of evaluative activity is to provide administrators of programs or funding authorities with information on how a social program is being administered in practice. Data that is obtained to measure the coverage of a target population, uncovering the quality of services rendered to target populations, developing cost effectiveness measures, and the like are all administrative monitoring research.

A third type of activity is concerned with measuring the effectiveness of a social program. Here the concern is with developing precise estimates of the net effects of programs in the directions desired by program goals. Impact effectiveness studies of this kind rely on research designs that permit unbiased estimates of net effects at the heart of evaluation—at least in my view.

The fourth face of evaluation is what may be called "social accounting," the development of estimates of cost to benefit ratios for social programs based upon estimates of the array of costs and benefits accruing to society, the agency responsible for the program, individual participants, and other parties. Although cost-benefit studies are often made as part of social engineering based on a priori estimates of costs and benefits, the more appropriate use of this approach is ex post facto, when empirically based estimates of actual costs and benefits are available. Clearly, it makes little sense to develop cost-benefit studies of ineffective programs or those which cannot be implemented appropriately.

Note that each of these activities which have been called evaluation of social programs involves different specific parts of social science knowledge and/or research technology; each is more or less associated with different disciplinary skills; and each is designed to answer different questions, often raised at different stages in the design, assessment, and implementation of social programs.

This diversity of evaluative activities, accompanying skills, and associated basic disciplines would not be such an impediment to the development of evaluation as a profession were it not for the fact that evaluators differ in their emphases on one as opposed to another facet of evaluative activities. These internal divisions within the body of evaluators would make it difficult to develop consensus on qualifications for legitimacy and on standards for performance, as well as on appropriate training for evaluative activities.

Problems of Identity:
Is Evaluation Distinctively Different?

Before a particular field can be differentiated clearly from its associated existing activities, it is necessary for it to acquire at least the appearance of being distinctively different. This is clearly not an easy task for evaluation activities since, by definition, it is a social science activity. One way of acquiring distinctiveness is to claim special technology. But there is nothing particularly different about the research methods used by evaluation compared with the basic social sciences. If there is anything unique about evaluation in the way of research technology, it is that evaluation activities tend to be more ecumenical than basic social sciences, employing a variety of research techniques borrowed from the several social sciences involved.

Another common claim to uniqueness may be based on the special substantive knowledge. But even here it would be difficult to claim that there is some special body of knowledge which evaluators have to themselves or which they are currently developing as special and unique. The basic social science disciplines and evaluation share the same knowledge bases. Of course, any evaluation researcher dealing with a particular social problem and its accompanying social program must know more about that area (and previous evaluation efforts) than a generalist from the same social science discipline. But this added depth of knowledge is no more than intradisciplinary specialization is likely to produce.

If there is anything special in the substantive knowledge base of the evaluation researcher it is its interdisciplinary character. Just as in other engineering parts of basic science, the evaluation researcher cannot simply rely on the techniques and substantive knowledge acquired in any single field. Thus, we have observed over the past decade that sociologists who are evaluation researchers have acquired some of the econometricians' bag of tricks, while the economists have had to learn test measurement theory from the educational psychologists and the psychologists have had to learn about population sampling from the statisticians and survey measurement from the sociologists. Interdisciplinary borrowing of theoretical models has also occurred, with sociologists, for example, becoming interested in human capital theory as developed by the neoclassical economists and economists becoming concerned with the testing of deterrence theory as developed by the classical criminologists.

It is this interdisciplinary character of evaluation as an activity that provides some basis for the development of specialized training programs and institutions. Whether that necessity is sufficient basis for such development is largely a judgment call, although it should be observed that some institution-building is currently underway that is premised on that assumption.

Evaluation as Politicized Social Science

Perhaps the most unique feature of evaluation research is its close connection with the political process. Such efforts are instituted usually by a government agency, are purportedly designed to feed into political decision-making, and may often be regarded by the political actors involved in the social program as political acts.

This close connection with the political process constitutes one of the more exciting aspects of evaluation and, at the same time, the source of some of the more aggravating negative facets. On one hand, the prospect of doing something that might be important to the formation and change of social policy can often be exhilarating. It is also a technical challenge, especially when one realizes that there are special reasons to be as careful as possible in the design and analysis of social research. After all, if something is to come of the findings, one must be certain on scientific grounds that statements made are well supported by empirical evidence.

On the other hand, the negative side can be a source of considerable annoyance. With very good reasons, those who commission evaluation research may have strong feelings about its outcomes and unnecessarily harass the evaluator both by overseeing his or her work too closely and by putting unnecessary constraints on his or her efforts. Of course, what is to a researcher an "unnecessary" amount of surveillance and undue pressure to skew findings may be perceived by an administrator as the exercise of necessary caution and prudence as well as a desire to protect a desirable program against irresponsible social science. Whatever the facts in any particular case, it is abundantly clear that evaluation research has special character and force because of its close connection with the political process.

The politicization of social science in evaluation research provides additional incentives for evaluation to become a profession. The latter status may be seen as providing more protection from "undue harassment" than being simply a contractor in the ordinary sense. Part of the prerogatives of a profession is its right to judge its own members, presumably on special technical and professional grounds, of which only other professionals are fully knowledgeable.

The political connections of evaluation also means that political skills are needed in the conduct of evaluation research that are not necessarily important for discipline-oriented research. This may be one of the reasons evaluation research takes place to such a degree outside university research centers. Research firms in the private sector are often sufficiently administered by persons whose political skills are high and whose technical skills may be of indifferent quality.

Marketing Pressures:
Procurement and Selling of Evaluation Services

Evaluation research services are far from uniform goods; they can be procured from a wide variety of sources, from the relatively giant research firms and major universities to untried individual researchers and virtually unknown firms. Quality also varies. Indeed, one of the consequences of this variance in quality is that bids received for advertised evaluation contracts will ordinarily show remarkable heterogeneity. The same heterogeneity in quality characterizes personnel: Some persons who present themselves as evaluation researchers are scarcely more qualified than the average liberal arts college graduate, while the best have more qualifications and skills than the topmost elite layers of the relevant social science disciplines.

Styles of evaluation also vary, partly along disciplinary lines and partly as a function of the diversity in the definition of evaluation as an activity, as discussed earlier. Some evaluators conceive of evaluation as consisting almost entirely of policy analysis; others would define almost every problem as calling for at least an approximate experiment.

The resulting heterogeneity of what is offered on the market as evaluation services must appear confusing to those who have the responsibility to procure evaluation research services. Price does not necessarily reflect quality. Nor does firm size mean very much. The need for ways of evaluating evaluation services is quite strong, especially if one is not simply content to develop a stable of customary suppliers, as have some federal agencies.

The same heterogeneity plagues suppliers. A firm that supplies a product of very high quality is likely to be pitted against one of indifferent respectability in bidding for a contract, with the price asked by the latter often being considerably less than that asked by the former. A naive procurement official presented with widely varying prices might be tempted to choose the services offered at lower costs and consequently find his agency buying services of little or no real value.

Both from the buyer's and from the seller's side of the market, there is clearly a need for some way to separate out suppliers according to reliability, quality, and other desired characteristics. Professionalization, with its accompanying mechanisms for providing credentials, is one of the answers. I am certain that one of the main motivations for both buyers and sellers of evaluation services to join one or more of the evaluation professional associations is both to seek more information (mainly on the part of buyers) and also to gain legitimacy (on the part of sellers).

The Balance of Forces
Concerning Professionalization

The preceding review of the forces favoring and those opposing the possibilities of professionalization must lead to a considerable number of cross-currents, a circumstance that favors a great deal of movement without much direction. Indeed, such appears to be the case to this observer. Given the recent expansion in evaluative activity, its diverse origins in the social science disciplines, the considerable heterogeneity in personnel, style of evaluation, and the lack of an emerging clarity in the definition of what is good evaluation, much less what is the best state-of-the-art practice, it seems highly unlikely that institutions soon will emerge that will make a fully professionalized activity out of evaluation. Entry into the field will likely remain easy. The several competing evaluation styles will most likely continue to rally around their separate and unequal attempts to develop professional societies. The basic social science disciplines will patronize evaluation activities but will resist efforts to recognize evaluation as a prestigious activity.

In short, while the forces favoring professionalization are strong, the fractionalization of the activity will frustrate attempts to fully professionalize the field for some time to come.

THE FUTURE OF EVALUATION ACTIVITY
IN THE UNITED STATES

While it seems unlikely that evaluation will develop into a full profession in the foreseeable future, there are no signs that evaluation as an activity will decline. On the contrary, this is the fastest growth sector in American social science today. Skepticism among political elites about the nature of social programs has increased rather than declined. Indeed, there is a growing conviction that the American governmental bureaucracy is unable to do anything right. This skepticism fuels an increasing support for requiring federal, state, and local agencies to provide evidence that the social programs they administer are providing services that accomplish their professed goals.

At the same time, social science disciplines, despairing that the universities and colleges can provide employment for newly minted degree holders, increasingly will be looking to applied social science fields as outlets for the surplus personnel. While evaluation will likely continue to be regarded as an appropriate spot for the placement of the "second-raters," it is also the case that more recognition will be given the evaluation as a legitimate scientific activity.

Finally, it is likely that the heterogeneity of evaluative activity will lead to the development of specialization and perhaps the rise of subfields, appropriately named, within evaluation. The biggest difference in the field is between research and development activities that are in support of the development and testing of prospective social policies and the monitoring of existing social programs. To the social program R&D activities belong the social experiments and the activities surrounding the application of basic social science theory and knowledge to the treatment of social problems. This subfield will attract the attention of the universities and the larger research firms and those with correspondingly greater talents and technical competence.

Administrative monitoring consisting of the careful measurement of the implementation of existing social programs, the measurement of existing need for social services of all kinds, and the fine-tuning of administrative procedures seems likely to develop as a separate activity. Administrative monitoring is an activity that can be carried out at all government levels and requires less highly developed theoretical and technical skills than R&D, as defined above. This is not to say that the problems of administrative modeling are not as intellectually demanding; rather, they will not demand as much in the way of special social science skill.

If evaluation is ever to develop as a profession, it seems likely that the administrative monitoring wing will be at its core. The R&D wing will most likely remain close to the disciplines and, like the basic disciplines, will resist professionalization in the fullest sense of the term.

14

Evaluation-Training:

A Social Interactive Process

Winfried Nacken

*University of the Armed Forces of the
Federal Republic of Germany*

EVALUATION OF SOCIAL INTERVENTION PROGRAMS

Although there is no generally accepted definition of evaluation research, I want to propose two criteria to facilitate the discussion of training programs for evaluators. Evaluation research can be described as all kinds of research concerning the social-institutional framework, testing and measurement, program implementation, the expected and unexpected processes and effects of social intervention (or innovation) programs. The principle purpose of evaluation research is to contribute to scientific problem-solving in practice.

These criteria of evaluation research imply two theses. The first is that evaluation is not a goal-free activity and not an end in itself. The aims of evaluation research cannot be defined in terms of the interests of the evaluators, a single interest group, or a single social science discipline. The definition of research objectives should be mutually determined by the program participants, organizers, decision makers, and evaluators.

The second thesis is that evaluation becomes *part of a (political) decision-making process* within the framework of social institutions. This implies that the *process* of evaluation studies, especially the social interaction processes among evaluators, program participants, decision makers, and the rest has to be considered *as a part* of the social interaction system which is actually the subject of evaluation research (Sjoberg, 1975; Struening, 1975).

If "social system" is defined as a system of social interactions including mutual interpretations of intentional behavior, it is possible that the validity of the research results also depends on the consensus regarding the mutual interpretations of interests and social interactions among evaluators, program participants, organizers, and others as part of the evaluation research project.

If we agree to these considerations, we can see that some important problems of evaluation research, applied social science, and training programs for evaluators are not to be discussed only with reference to research design techniques or statistical methods. The question "What is a 'good' evaluation study?" cannot be answered without answering two other questions:

(1) What are the methodological norms of applied social science? Is there a generally accepted connection of quantitative research methods and "well"-conducted social research?

This question seems important with respect to the development of alternative methodological norms, especially to some of the recent action theory approaches in West Germany (Kaiser et al., 1977; Kaiser, 1979; Lorenzen and Schwemmer, 1975; Maschewsky and Schneider, 1978; Schwemmer, 1976; Werbik, 1978; Nacken, 1976, 1978a, 1978b; Tippelt, 1979).

(2) What about the methodological relevance of interaction processes among evaluators, program organizers, participants, and decision-makers during the evaluation research process? Do we assign this question to the area of methodologically irrelevant factors, or do we recognize this question as a methodological one?

Both theses imply aspects of social communication and methodology which differ from the problems of conventional applied social research and especially the problems of the behaviorism or the hypothesis-testing methodology (see Figure 14.1).

These aspects are not independent of one another. There are logical, analytical, and empirical dependencies; for example, the solution of problems mentioned in cell 1 implies the solution of problems mentioned in cell 3, and vice versa.

Although these problems illustrate some of the well-known problems of evaluation research, one of the typical difficulties of the methodology is deciding on the ultimate purpose: Is it for the advancement of knowledge or for application in a decision-making process? Will the solution to cells 1 and

Aspects of Social Research	*Characteristics of Evaluation Research* Evaluation is not goal-free activity and not an end in itself (cf. thesis 1)	Evaluation becomes part of a social interaction process (cf. thesis 2)
(A) Aspects of Social Communication	*Problem (1)* Conflicts of goals, and interests among program participants, organizers, and evaluators.	*Problem (3)* Arrangement of rules of social interactions among program participants, organizers, and evaluators with regard to their interaction.
(B) Aspects of Methodology	*Problem (2)* To state the reason for selection of terminology and methods for problem-solving	*Problem (4)* Construction of designs for the systematic control of the cooperation mentioned in cell (2); principles of solving conflicts of interests and of mutual advice procedures

FIGURE 14.1: Social Interaction Perspectives of Evaluation Research

2 determine the selection of the methodology, the theoretical interpretations, and the validity of the results of research?

The answer to this question influences the communication among evaluators, the program's organizers, participants, and also the research objectives. Furthermore, the answer reveals the methodological perspective of an evaluator.

In West Germany at least four distinct methodologies are discussed also in relation to evaluation research procedures: the conventional hypothesis-testing methodology (Friedrichs, 1973; Hofemann, 1977; Musto 1972); several kinds of action research approaches (Bartölke et al., 1979; Cremer et al., 1977; Hameyer and Haft, 1977); theories and research projects on the basis of symbolic interactionism, ethnomethodology, and phenomenology (Gaertner, 1978; Matthes and Schütze, 1976); and theories and research projects on the basis of the constructive logic, ethics, and theory of science (Braun and Wimmer, 1978; Kaiser et al., 1977; Nacken and Wüstendörfer, 1978; Gerum, 1978; Schwemmer, 1976; Tippelt, 1979).

PROBLEMS OF EVALUATION RESEARCH AND TRAINING EVALUATORS

Evaluation research cannot be defined as a special kind of applied social science, since the term "applied social science" does not imply the meaning of the particular tasks of evaluation studies. There are no universally accepted approaches concerning the logical, analytical, and empirical relations between normative-political and methodological tasks of evaluating social intervention programs. Consequently, training programs for evaluators are more difficult than those of most of the other social science programs at universities in West Germany.

Some of the main tasks and problems of evaluation research are similar to those of interdisciplinary social research, understanding the technical terms of the social science disciplines, and finding consensus among scientists concerning the adequacy of various discipline-oriented terminologies with regard to different research aims and goals. The dissimilarity of discipline-oriented technical terms is caused not only by the different theoretical backgrounds but also by incompatible methodological norms.

Some of these problems could be characterized by the story of the five blind men who encountered an elephant but couldn't reach an agreement on what it was. "One, touching the elephant's ear, thought it was a sort of cabbage, another, patting the elephant's sides, thought it was a wall, yet another said it must be a tree because he touched the animal's leg. Each of these men had only 'observed' a specific part of the animal, each had his own hypothesis as to what he had met" (Blaschke, 1978, 1979). If these five blind men are considered as five evaluators emphasizing five different systems of methodological norms, and if they are not analyzing elephants but social intervention programs, we can imagine which kinds of curious findings the five might produce.

There is a very important difference between the normal interdisciplinary social research in the basic social science research and the area of evaluation research projects. While the elephant can't talk about himself, the program participants and decision makers can. They are capable of defining the aims and goals of a program, and thus they can confer with the evaluators about the intentional aspects of the program goals and activities. Consequently, they can contribute to defining the research objectives. If the evaluators, program organizers, and participants do not confer about the mode of describing the program, objectives and design changes to be evaluated could occur without systematic control by the evaluators.

We can draw some general conclusions with regard to the required cognitive orientations of evaluators and to the problems of scientifically training evaluators. First, evaluators should learn to apply empirical methods, theories, and research paradigms for the purpose of scientific advice in practice. The problems should define the methods used, not vice versa (Parlett and Hamilton, 1976). Second, evaluators should learn to discuss the adequacy of theories and methods in relation to the real problems of carrying out social intervention programs. Third, evaluators should be able to transform rather unstructured tasks and problems of social intervention programs into structured tasks of evaluation research. They should also give systematic reasons for the selection of distinct methodological approaches with regard to the effects of the selected methodology on program participants' and organizers' behavior.

These demands refer not only to political-normative decisions of evaluators, but also to the question, How can we talk about the "effects" of social action programs? This question is related to the problem of the selection of a research design, but it is also a more general question of the mode of describing and explaining social interaction processes. Furthermore, this question should be answered with regard to the use of probability hypotheses, which is limited by the condition that we are dealing with probability events. Intentional actions and action strategies, however, should not be defined as probability events if we are capable of systematically reconstructing the rational reasons for intentional actions (Lorenzen and Schwemmer, 1975; Schwemmer, 1976). There are other difficulties faced by training evaluators; these are caused by the system of traditional training courses for social scientists at universities in West Germany.

Fourth, a German study concerning the situation of training courses in psychology, sociology, and education at universities in West Germany and West Berlin (Arbeitsgruppe Methodenlehre, 1977) highlighted several defects of these training programs: for example, the separation of courses in statistics and empirical methods and the separation of theory formation from data collection. As a result, some sociologists and psychologists have profound knowledge of statistics, empirical methods, or theory, but others may lack a combined knowledge of empirical methods, statistics, theory-building, and the various methodological systems (Hamers, 1978).

A fifth difficulty is that many social scientists and evaluators had only minimal contacts with members of administrations or with organizers of innovative programs and their participants during their time at universities. Many young social scientists have only slight knowledge of political processes and politically biased conflicts.

The final problem is the lack of any support programs for the development of approaches to evaluation research. For instance, up to now within the well-financed Special Research Areas (Sonderforschungsbereiche) at West German universities, founded by the German Research Society (Deutsche Forschungsgemeinschaft) 11 years ago to manage problems of interdisciplinary research, there is scarce promotion of evaluation research. Evaluation research is regarded as "applied" social research, and this kind of research is not considered worthy of being promoted within the institutional framework of Special Research Areas. Only specific organizations have been founded to promote research on the methodology of scientific advice and scientific problem-solving in practice—and, in this way, to promote evaluation research procedures (for example, the Society for the Research of Processes of Advice, at Erlangen, founded by members of several universities in 1978).

IMPLICATIONS FOR TRAINING PROGRAMS

Since evaluation research differs from the social disciplines of sociology, psychology, or political science, the training of evaluators must be treated as more than discipline-specific training. Therefore, in my opinion, there are at least two approaches for promoting the development of evaluation research and training evaluators: a change of general university training programs for social scientists, and the development of institutional support for the promotion of evaluation research.

With regard to general training programs for social scientists at universities, we should promote training courses which deal with the complexity of relations among the tasks of applied problem-solving, the application of adequate methodological standards, and the use of empirical social science methods using evaluation research studies as examples. We should also demand that training programs for evaluators include systematic training for specific tasks and the structural components of evaluation research.

The structure of these components is as follows:

(a) the transformation of problems in practice into problems of scientific research *(task of transformation);*

(b) the assessment of adequacy of methodological standards for transforming problems into manageable scientific research problems *(methodological standards);*

(c) the structure and process of scientific research (for example, research design or empirical methods) and the feedback of the results of scientific problem-solving to the program organizers, participants, and others *(scientific problem-solving);*

(d) the possibilities given to program organizers, participants, and decision makers to participate in the conduct of evaluation research *(participation of program organizers, etc.).*

Structure and relations in the process of conducting evaluation research from a (traditional) hypothesis-testing point of view contrast with an alternative view approach based on principles of action theories upon constructive theory of science and advice-oriented research procedures.

There are two basic problems of training programs for evaluators in this regard: isolating areas of activities of program organizers, participants, and evaluators, and isolated methodological standards within the process and structure of evaluation research projects.

In the hypothesis-testing model all important research decisions are made by the evaluator. The transformation of practical problems into problems of scientific research does not influence the selection of methodological standards. The methodological standards are not critical from the practical-normative viewpoint. Within the social sciences there are several methodological systems which can be regarded as more or less compatible with the aims and goals of problem-solving in practice. In an alternative model of evaluation, selection of methodological standards and norms also depends on the results of mutual advice concerning the "task of transformation" and the assessments of the adequacy of methodological norms. In order to apply this model to evaluation training programs, we must develop training programs in methodology without trying to indoctrinate the social scientists interested in evaluation research in a single methodological approach.

There are several obstacles to promoting university training programs for evaluators which are rooted in prejudice against evaluation research from the traditional academic disciplines (Weiss, 1974). Evaluators in West Germany often are in a "no-man's land." They are not representatives of an "original" academic discipline, nor do they represent an "applied" social science. This ambiguous and uncertain academic status of both evaluators and evaluation research might reduce the interests of social scientists in the field over time, especially with few university positions open for evaluation educators.

In order to improve the reputation of evaluation research and increase the promotion of training programs, there should be more interdisciplinary workshops for administrators and university social scientists on evaluation research problems. Research on the structure, methodological standards, and innovations of evaluation research approaches should also be published in traditional journals of sociology, social psychology, and political science more frequently. There must also be more international cross-fertilization and institutional promotion of evaluation research. Journals of evaluation research should be published in different languages. Finally, regular communication among administrators, program organizers, sponsors, and evaluators should be intensified.

REFERENCES

Arbeitsgruppe Methodenlehre (1977) Didaktik sozialwissenschaftlicher Methodenlehre. Weinheim: Verlag/Basel.

BARTÖLKE, R., J. RETTENMEIER, and R.F. WEILFER (1979) "Aktionsforschung in einem Betrieb der holzbearbeitenden Industrie." Arbeitspapiere des Fachbereichs Wirtschaftswissenschaft der Gesamthochschule Wuppertal, Nr. 33, Wuppertal.

BLASCHKE, D. (1979) Organisatorische Bedingungen interdisziplinärer Forschung in den Sozialwissenschaften. (unpublished)

———— (1978) "Management problems of interdisciplinary basic research in the social sciences." Presented at the Academy of Management Annual Meeting, San Francisco, August 9–13.

BRAUN, W. and F. WIMMER (1978) "Überlegungen zur Kritik und Reform des Interessenkonfliktszwischen Kapital, Arbeit und Konsum." pp. 279–299 in B. Biervert, W.F.

Fischer-Winkelmann, and R. Bock (eds.) Verbraucherpolitik in der Marktwirtschaft. Reinbek: Rowohlt.

CREMER, C., H. HAFT, and W. KLEHM (1977) "Entwicklungslinien von Action-Research." pp. 171–198 in U. Hameyer and H. Haft (eds.) Handlungsorientierte Schulforschungsprojekte. Weinheim: Beltz.

FRIEDRICHS, J. (1973) Methoden empirischer Sozialforschung. Reinbek: Rowohlt.

GAERTNER, A. (1978) "Interpretative Sozialforschung: Bemerkungen zur theoretischen und methodologischen Begründung eines Supervisionsforschungsprojektes." pp. 254–285 in C. W. Müller (ed.) Begleitforschung in der Sozialpädagogik. Analysen und Berichte zur Evaluationsforschung in der Bundesrepublik. Weinheim-Basel: Beltz.

GERUM, E. (1978) "Überlegungen zur Rechtfertigung einzelwirtschaftlicher Institutionen." pp. 103–142 in H. Steinmann (ed.) Betriebswirtschaftslehre als normative Handlungswissenschaft. Wiesbaden: Gabler.

HAMEYER, U. and H. HAFT [eds.] (1977) Handlungsorientierte Schulforschungsprojekte. Weinheim: Beltz.

HAMERS, J. (1978) Die Universitätsausbildung von Sozialwissenschaftlern. Frankfurt: Campus.

HOFEMANN, K. (1977) Ziel- und Erfolgsanalyse sozialer Reformprogramme am Beispiel des Bundesausbildungsförderungsgesetzes. Meisenheim a. Glan: Hain.

KAISER, H. J. (1979) Konfliktberatung nach handlungstheoretischen Prinzipien. Bad Honnef: Haag + Herchen.

——, G. KORTHALS-BEYERLEIN, and H. J. SEEL (1977) Überlegungen zum Aufbau einer handlungstheoretisch fundierten Strategie zur Lösung interpersonaler Konflikte, Forschungsbericht 95 des Sonderforschungsbereiches 22. Sozialwissenschaftliches Forschungszentrum der Universität Erlangen-Nürnberg.

KRÜGER, H., J. KLÜVER, and F. HAAG (1975) "Aktionsforschung in der Diskussion." Soziale Welt 26: 1–30.

LORENZEN, P. and O. SCHWEMMER (1975) Konstruktive Logik, Ethik und Wissenschaftstheorie. Mannheim: Wissenschaftsverlag (BI).

MASCHEWSKY, W. and U. SCHNEIDER (1978) "Zusammenfassende Darstellung und Einschätzung des gegenwärtigen Standes der anwendungsorientierten psychologischen Methodendiskussion." pp. 38–62 in C. W. Müller (ed.) Begleitforschung in der Sozialpädagogik, Analysen und Berichte zur Evaluationsforschung in der Bundesrepublik. Weinheim-Basel: Beltz.

MATTHES, J. and F. SCHÜTZE (1976) "Zur Einfuhrüng: Alltagswissen, Interaktion und gesellschaftliche Wirklichkeit." In Arbeitsgruppe Bielefelder Soziologen (eds.) Alltagswissen, Interaktion und gesellschaftliche Wirklichkeit. Reinbek: Rowohlt.

MOSER, H. (1976) "Anspruch und Selbstverständnis der Aktionsforschung." Zeitschrift für Pädagogik 22: 369–376.

MUSTO, S. (1972) Evaluierung sozialer Entwicklungsprojekte. Berlin: Hessling.

NACKEN, W. (1979) "Zur Unterscheidung von 'verhaltens'- und 'handlungs'-theoretischen Strategien der Erforschung sozialen Handelns." pp. 39–80 in W. Nacken (ed.) Terrorismus. Fragen nach den Ursachen und Grenzen einer sozialwissenschaftlichen Erklärung. Hamburg: Hochschule der Bundeswehr Hamburg.

—— (1978a) "Wiedereingliederung von Gastarbeitern. Prozeßberatung und Prozeßevaluation eines Bildungsprogrammes." pp. 169–198 in C. W. Müller (ed.) Begleitforschung in der Sozialpädagogik. Analysen und Berichte zur Evaluationsforschung in der Bundesrepublik. Weinheim: Beltz.

—— (1978b) Die Evaluierung von Curricula zur politischen Weiterbildung im außerschulischen Bereich. Bonn: Gutachten für die Bundeszentrale für Politische Bildung.

———— (1976) Evaluation als Mittel der Politikberatung. Analyse eines Modellprogrammes zur Rückgliederung türkischer Gastarbeiter. Nürnberg: Nürnberger Forschungsvereinigung.

———— and W. WÜSTENDÖRFER (1978) "Verbraucherschutz und Evaluierung. Probleme praxisberatender Untersuchungen zum Verbraucherschutz." In B. Biervert, W. F. Fischer-Winkelmann, and R. Bock (eds.) Verbraucherpolitik in der Marktwirtschaft. Reinbek: Rowohlt.

PARLETT, M. and D. HAMILTON (1976) "Evaluation as illumination: a new approach to the study of innovation programs." pp. 140–157 in Evaluation Studies Review Annual, Vol. 1. Beverly Hills, CA: Sage.

SCHWEMMER, O. (1976) Theorie der rationalen Erklärung. München: Beck.

SJOBERG, G. (1975) "Politics, ethics and evaluation research." pp. 29–51 in M. Guttentag and E. L. Struening (eds.) Handbook of Evaluation Research, Vol. 2. Beverly Hills, CA: Sage.

STRUENING, E. L. (1975) "Social area analysis as a method of evaluation." pp. 519–549 in E. L. Struening and M. Guttentag (eds.) Handbook of Evaluation Research, Vol. 1. Beverly Hills, CA: Sage.

TIPPELT, R. (1979) Projektstudium. Exemplarisches und handlungsorientiertes Lernen an der Hochschule. München: Kösel.

WEISS, C. (1974) Evaluierungsforchang. Opladen: Westdeutcher Verlag.

WERBIK, H. (1978) Handlungstheorien. Stuttgart: Kohlhammer.

Author Index

Subject Index

About the Authors

Bernhard Badura, Professor of Social Science at the "former" Reform University at Konstanz, has numerous publications on social policy and social science. He is currently editor of "Seminar: Angewandte Sozialwissenschaft." He has a close knowledge of the working of the federal institutions (parliament and bureaucracy), having just completed a survey on the use of social science in government.

Georges Ferné graduated in law and political science at the University of Paris (France) in 1965. He has been with the Organisation for Economic Co-operation and Development (OECD) since 1969, and has been involved in a number of projects and studies concerning science and technology policies in the OECD member countries. He is now Acting Head, Science Policy Division, at the OECD Directorate for Science, Technology and Industry.

Stephen J. Fitzsimmons, Vice-president of Abt Associates Forschung and President of Abt Associates in Germany, graduated from Heidelberg University. He has an interest in social indicators research, social impact assessments, and evaluation research. He has been engaged in evaluation research for the federal governments of Germany and the United States.

Howard E. Freeman is Director of the Institute for Social Science Research and Professor of Sociology at the University of California, Los Angeles. He is a consultant to many federal agencies and to the Robert Wood Johnson Foundation. Dr. Freeman is co-editor of *Evaluation Review* and *The Handbook of Medical Sociology.* He has written extensively in the evaluation field, including *Evaluation: A Systematic Approach,* (co-authored by Peter Rossi).

Gerd-Michael Hellstern, workshop co-chairman, graduated from Berlin University. He has been at the Political Science Department and is now with the Center for Social Science Research. He has developed a keen interest in the methodological foundations of evaluation research. His publications include a methodological study on evaluation research for the Department of Building, Housing, and Urban Development.

Franz-Xaver Kaufmann is Professor of sociology in the University of Bielefeld in Basel, Switzerland. He is one of the first proponents of evaluation research in Germany. He has also worked in the areas of socialization, social policy, and the sociology of science.

Thomas J. Kiresuk, a clinical psychologist, is Director of the Program Evaluation Resource Center (PERC), a research and dissemination project funded by the U.S. Department of Health, Education and Welfare's National Institute of Mental Health. He is Chief Editorial Reviewer for *Evaluation and Change*. He received the Myrdal Prize from the Evaluation Research Society in 1979.

Manfred Küchler, a mathematician and sociologist, is Professor of methodology at Frankfurt University. Prior to this position, he held an appointment at the University of Bielefeld. He has been engaged in evaluation studies in the health field, where he often uses log-linear models.

Nancy E. Larsen, a sociologist, is Technical Assistance Coordinator at the Program Evaluation Resource Center. She has conducted numerous workshops and provided organizational consultations on program evaluation and particularly on goal attainment scaling.

Robert A. Levine is an economist whose background includes policy analysis in fields ranging from urban affairs to national security. He received a grant from the German Marshall Fund of the United States to study the use of policy analysis and evaluation in western nations. At the time of the workshop, he was Deputy Director of the Congressional Budget Office. He is now Vice-President and General Manager of the Human Systems at System Development Corporation in Santa Monica, California.

Sander H. Lund, a sociologist, is Associate Director of the Program Evaluation Resource Center and has served as an evaluation consultant to a variety of human service organizations.

Winfried Nacken, currently with the University of the Army, has been engaged in evaluation research at the Center for Research at Erlangen/Nuernberg. He has published evaluations of consumer protection activities and the education and training of guest workers. He presently has a special interest in the development and improvement of social scientific advice to administration.

Martin Rein is a professor at the Massachusetts Institute of Technology and at the Joint Institute of Urban Studies (Harvard University and MIT). His interests include the evaluation of social policy and public programs.

Robert F. Rich currently is at the Woodrow Wilson School of Public and International Affairs, Princeton University. He conducted research on the use of social science in government, working now with Nathan Caplan from Michigan University. He is editor of a new and promising journal on social science use and diffusion, called *Knowledge, Creation, Diffusion, Utilization*.

Peter H. Rossi is the current President of the American Sociological Association. He is Director of the Social and Demographic Research Institute and Professor of

Sociology at the University of Massachusetts. He serves as consultant to numerous federal agencies on evaluation studies. Dr. Rossi is co-author with Howard Freeman of Evaluation: A Systematic Approach. His many interests include the development of quantitative methodology, the study of urban social policies, and the use of experiments in program evaluation.

Marian A. Solomon, currently at System Development Corporation, was in the HEW Office of the Assistant Secretary for Planning and Evaluation at the time of the workshop. At HEW she was responsible for the management and conduct of exploratory evaluations, participated in the development of evaluation policy, and served as advisor on evaluation methodology and health evaluations. She has now moved out of government to SDC where she is Senior Research Manager for Health Evaluation.

Klaus-Peter Strohmeier, currently at the University of Bielefeld, studied sociology in the United States and in Germany. He is a member of one of the earliest research groups on evaluation in Germany. Currently he is engaged in an evaluation study for the Federal Ministry of Youth, Family and Sport.

Joseph S. Wholey is currently Deputy Assistant Secretary for Evaluation of the U.S. Department of Health, Education, and Welfare. He was Director of Program Evaluation Studies at the Urban Institute. He holds a Ph.D. from Harvard University. Dr. Wholey has a long standing interest in shaping and designing federal and local program evaluation. His early publication on program evaluation is still one of the best sources and survey on program evaluation. He is knowledgable regarding problems of inhouse evaluations and their implementation.

Hellmut Wollmann, workshop co-chairman, is currently Professor for Public Administration and a member of the Center for Social Science Research at the Free University of Berlin. Previously he was at Heidelberg University and a Kennedy Fellow at Harvard University. He has written on urban problems and conducted various evaluation research studies commissioned by the Federal Ministry of Housing and Construction. Recently he edited a volume on implementation research.